African Society and Culture

韩红 孙丽华 编著

非洲社会与文化（二）

知识产权出版社
全国百佳图书出版单位
—北京—

图书在版编目（CIP）数据

非洲社会与文化. 二 / 韩红，孙丽华编著. —北京：知识产权出版社，2019.11
ISBN 978-7-5130-6503-0

Ⅰ.①非… Ⅱ.①韩…②孙… Ⅲ.①非洲—概况 Ⅳ.①K94

中国版本图书馆 CIP 数据核字（2019）第 214281 号

责任编辑：国晓健　　　　　　　　　责任校对：谷　洋
封面设计：臧　磊　　　　　　　　　责任印制：孙婷婷

非洲社会与文化（二）

韩　红　孙丽华　编著

出版发行：	知识产权出版社 有限责任公司	网　　址：http://www.ipph.cn
社　　址：	北京市海淀区气象路50号院	邮　　编：100081
责编电话：	010-82000860 转 8385	责编邮箱：anxuchuban@126.com
发行电话：	010-82000860 转 8101/8102	发行传真：010-82000893/82005070/82000270
印　　刷：	北京九州迅驰传媒文化有限公司	经　　销：各大网上书店、新华书店及相关专业书店
开　　本：	720mm×1000mm　1/16	印　　张：14
版　　次：	2019年11月第1版	印　　次：2019年11月第1次印刷
字　　数：	230千字	定　　价：68.00元

ISBN 978-7-5130-6503-0

出版权专有　　侵权必究

如有印装质量问题，本社负责调换。

前 言

多年来，北京物资学院非洲研究团队的老师们深入非洲不同国家和地区进行田野调研，广泛探访非洲社会各阶层民众，积累了大量第一手文字和图片资料，于2012年率先在国内高校开设"非洲社会与文化"素质拓展课。

"非洲社会与文化"丛书共分三册，以社会透视和文化鉴赏为主线，旨在展示一个全面真实而又精彩纷呈的非洲。非洲有54个国家[①]、近13亿人口，是世界上国家最多、人口第二的大陆。

非洲不同国家甚至同一国家不同地区间在宗教、语言、传统习俗和地理环境等方面都存在很大的差异。因篇幅有限，本套丛书只能选取部分有代表性的国家和地区的部分情况加以介绍，难免挂一漏万。此外，由于作者水平有限，不足之处在所难免，敬请读者指正。

韩红　孙丽华
2019年6月18日于北京

[①] 关于非洲国家的具体数目存在不同说法。非洲联盟（African Union）承认的非洲国家一共有55个，包括阿拉伯撒哈拉民主共和国(the Sahrawi Arab Democratic Republic)，但是联合国和世界上大多数国家（包括中国）并不承认。

Contents

Unit VII   African Movies 1

Unit VIII   African Languages..................... 30

Unit IX   African Foods 59

Unit X   African Arts 88

Unit XI   African Literature I 122

Unit XII   African Literature II 144

Key to Questions.................................. 173

Reference 186

Vocabulary List 194

Unit VII   African Movies

　　有关非洲的电影风格迥异，包罗万象，有的绚丽多彩，有的催人泪下，有的令人捧腹大笑。非洲电影主要包括两大部分：非洲人自己拍摄的本土电影，以及外国电影人拍摄的有关非洲的电影。非洲更有"尼莱坞"——尼日利亚的电影制造业。虽然批评之声不绝于耳，但是尼莱坞每年出产的电影数量、提供的就业岗位不容小觑。近些年来，有关非洲题材的电影佳作不断上映，为世人了解非洲社会的方方面面打开了一扇扇窗户。

Two posters outside a cinema in Addis Ababa, Ethiopia
(Photographer: Han Hong)

　　"At first, a lazy eye and mind will have a problem with African cinema. It requires commitment."

　　　　—Dumisani Phakathi, South African director of television, films and commercials

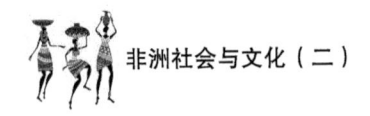

> ◎ **Think and Talk**
>
> ☆ Have you ever seen any movies about Africa? What are they if any?
>
> ☆ Have you ever seen any movies by Africans? What are they if any?
>
> ☆ What are your impressions of movies about Africa and by Africans?

I. HISTORY OF AFRICAN CINEMA

People in Africa have been watching, acting in, and making movies since the early 1900s. Until the 1950s, films were generally controlled by European colonial powers, the colonial governments **oversaw** production and decided which movies could be shown to the public. In the years since African nations gained independence, Africans have developed their own cinema with their own directors and actors. Many of their films have gained worldwide attention for their **passionate** portrayal of social and political issues such as **apartheid**.

1. Cinema during Colonial Times

Soon after its invention in France in 1895, cinema came to Africa. Over the next century, its development was shaped by European colonialism and its postcolonial **aftermath**. By 2005, however, African cinema had **come of age**. In the beginning, only Europeans had cameras, but Africans gradually gained control of the medium and the message. Africans began also to make films about Europeans and Americans, **reversing** a century-old gaze.

The early history of African film was dominated by movies made by and for non-Africans. Imported films were shown in West African colonies as early as 1900, and soon afterward colonists in South Africa were making their own movies. One of the first very successful African pictures was *De Vootrkkers* (*Winning a Continent*), a movie about white South African history made in 1916 by **Afrikaner** and British producers.

Unit VII   African Movies

Many American and British moviemakers came to Africa to film stories of adventure and colonial conquest. These were often enormous productions, with crews and leading actors brought from overseas. The story of Henry Rider Haggard's British Novel *King Soloman's Mines*[1] was filmed in Africa several times. In the first version in 1918, thousands of **Zulu extras** acted in a battle scene. For **Metro-Goldwyn-Mayer**'s 1950 version, the film crew traveled for 12,000 miles and five months through four countries. They gathered truckloads of **footage** of animals and scenery that was used in movies for years afterward. Several foreign actors gained fame for their roles in such films, including African American actors Paul Robeson[2] in the 1930s and 1940s and Sidney Poitier[3] in the 1950s.

Beginning in the 1920s, **feature-length documentaries** about African people, animals, and geography became popular with foreign audiences. In 1928, Americans Martin and Osa Johnson[4] made *Simba: The King of Beasts*, a film about lions; in 1959 **Henri Storck**, a Belgian director, filmed *Les seigneurs de la forêt*(*Masters of the Congo Jungle*). Documentaries about animals were often broadcast on American television.

More numerous than movies of **dramas** and documentaries, however, were the many educational and research films produced in Africa during colonial times. **Anthropologists** and explorers used **film** to record their research on African peoples and cultures. Colonial officials and **missionaries** created educational films to teach black Africans "correct" political and cultural views. The viewpoints expressed in such works are now considered outdated and even racist. However, the films remain valuable historical documents that provide unique images of places and peoples.

Occasionally foreign-made films dealt with issues that troubled the colonial powers in Africa. Such films were usually banned by the colony they criticized. As late as the 1980s, the white South African government prohibited movies that criticized apartheid.

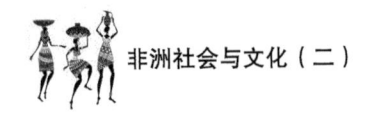

2. The Rise of African Cinema

Africans have also used movies to explore social themes and present them to wide audiences. **Senegalese** director Ousmane Sembène[5] is considered by some to be the founder of African film making. He produced African-language films dealing with such topics as colonialism, poverty, corruption, and the role of women. Between 1972 and 1982, **Ola Balogun** of Nigeria made ten **feature films**, some of which are based on traditional plays of the **Yoruba** people.

During the 1970s and 1980s, many African filmmakers explored political subjects. Pictures such as ***Sambizanga*** (1972) portrayed Angola's revolutionary struggle. Ethiopian Haile Gerima[6] studied film in California before making *Harvest: 3,000 Years* in his country in 1974. He also produced *Sankofa*, a 1993 movie about slavery in Ghana. His 1995 picture *Waati* (*Time*) is a vision of the African continent as discovered by a young girl. As people throughout the world gain greater appreciation for different cultures, the distinctly African cinema of these artists may reach movie and television audiences everywhere.

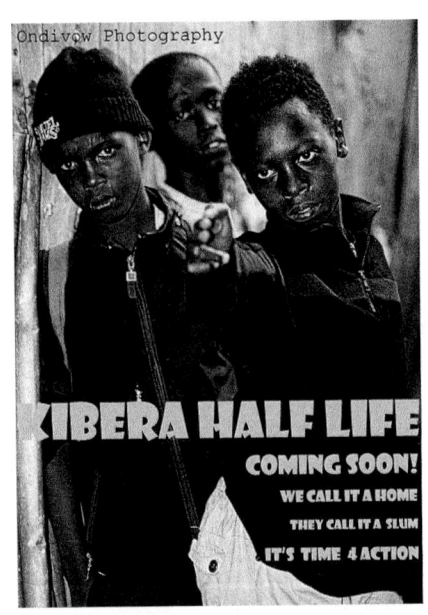

A poster of Kibera Half Life, by Ondivow
(Photographer: Du Fengyan)

II. ORIGIN OF AFRICAN CINEMA

Some film historians assume that African cinema didn't exist before independence, which came to many colonies in the 1960s, but clearly it did–in Egypt, and even in apartheid South Africa. The principal colonial powers, Britain

Unit VII   African Movies

and France, created two distinct film cultures in the areas under their control. In the British colonies of east and west Africa, a **pragmatic** and businesslike attitude toward the film medium came in with the colonizers. In the French colonies, the local **elites** were educated in French philosophy, literature, and art, and filmmakers took on a sense of film as art and an attitude of **opposition** to **Hollywood**.

Independent Kenya built up its communications infrastructure in the 1970s, and **Nairobi** became a center of television production and of satellite **distribution**. Blessed with wild animals and scenery, in addition to film crews, Kenya became a favored location for Hollywood. *Out of Africa* (1985) was filmed at **Isak Dinesen**'s **meticulously** restored coffee **plantation** in the highlands, with the Kenyan novelist Meja Mwangi serving as **assistant director** to **Sidney Pollack**.

Ghana's first president, **Kwame Nkrumah**, understood the importance of film for cultural and political ends. But state-funded production **trailed off** as equipment aged and was not replaced. Ghanaian **entrepreneurs took up the slack**, and the first truly free cinema in Africa was born. The Hollywood-trained **playwright** and musician Kwah Ansah set up his own companies to produce **commercials** and feature films. *Love **brewed** in an African Pot* (1980) was a **critique** of **arranged marriage**, and *Heritage Africa* (1987) was the **poignant** tale of Quincy Arthur Bosomfield, a former **martinet** in the colonial administration, who received a **talking-to** by his **ancestral** spirit and went back to being Kwesi Atta Bosomefi, to his family's relief.[7] In the 1990s, theaters disappeared from most African cities as video distribution replaced film. A **vibrant** Ghanaian video industry sprang up and was soon producing dozens of features a year.

Nigeria, with its population of 125,000,000, is the largest market in Africa, and the Nigerian **diaspora** is important as well. The **preeminent Hausa**-language filmmaker was Adamu Alhaji Alilu, who made a film about Shehu Omar in 1977, the Hausa religious leader, and another in 1979 about Kanta of Kebbi, a **medieval** hero of the **Songhai** wars. In the south of the country, Ola Balogun was for many years the most **prolific** Yoruba-language filmmaker; for about a decade he **churned out** a film a year, alternating hits and misses.[8] In the 1990s, **Nollywood** was born in **Lagos**.

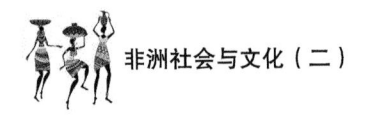

The wide range of cultures and classes depicted in Nigerian films is striking: they range from the working-class dad in Tade Ogidan's *Owo-Blow* (1997), to desperate housewives in Lancelot Imasuen's *Emotional Crack* (2003), and **posh** London businessmen in Zina Saro-Wiwa's *Hello Nigeria!* (2004). Distributed on inexpensive DVDs, Nigerian films **outsell** Hollywood in Nigeria, and reach the remotest parts of Africa and beyond.

III. FILM AND CINEMA

The history of African cinema is composed of three **strands**. The first and best known is the commercial cinema: feature films made in Africa for the entertainment market. The second are the documentary films made in Africa by scientists, educators, political **activists**, and the like. Finally, since independence, a **self-conscious** African cinema has come into being, created by African directors and shown primarily at film festivals, but also available on DVD. **Overwhelmingly**, however, the films that reach African viewers are American ones. **Bollywood musicals** from India and kung fu films from Hong Kong of China are also very popular.

The Gods Must Be Crazy I and II DVDs,
(Photographer: Han Hong)

African cinema has always posed the question of **authenticity**, and none more **starkly** than the best-known South African film, *The Gods Must Be Crazy*.[9] Its director, **Jamie Uys** (1921–1996), had been a successful producer of **Afrikaans-**

language films. *The Gods Must Be Crazy* began with a Coke bottle dropped from an airplane, and featured elephants, children, an Afrikaner scientist, a British school teacher, Angolan **guerrillas**, a **Land Rover**, and a **Bushman**, most of whom did gently funny things. Because of the cultural blockage against South Africa, the film was released in **Botswana** in 1980. World audiences, particularly in Sweden and Japan, were **enchanted** by a lighthearted **fable**, whereas political activists sharply criticized the film's **racism** and **fakery**. But there was nothing inauthentic about its foreign exchange earnings, which surpassed $84 million.[10]

South African independence in 1994 cleared the way for a more open cinema, with commercial and cultural links to other countries. A production **consortium** from South Africa, Britain, Cameroon, Ghana, Kenya, and Nigeria produced the first **pan-African** action thriller, *Critical Assignment* (2003), starring **Guinness** advertising **icon** Michael Power as a kinder and gentler African James Bond.[11] The Industrial Development Corporation of South Africa produced *Hotel Rwanda* (2004) and *Tsotsi* (2005). Production in all formats and **genres** flourished, from TV dramas and children's films to exceedingly frank documentaries. In this atmosphere of freedom, the young **Dumisani Phakathi** developed in a distinctive personal style. His *Christmas with Granny* (2000) and *Waiting for Valdez* (2002) brilliantly showed children's lives in **Soweto**, where he grew up. Phakathi told an interviewer: "At first, a lazy eye and mind will have a problem with African cinema. It requires commitment."[12]

IV. NOLLYWOOD

Nollywood is the nickname for Nigeria's flourishing film industry, which has emerged in the past few years. Although most of the movies are filmed in Lagos and are made by Yoruba filmmakers, they can be found all over Nigeria in numerous languages. The industry generates an estimated 2,000 low-budget films per year, with two-thirds of them in English, which exceeds India's Bollywood.

The origin of this distinct variety of films is unclear. One theory is that it started accidentally in 1992 when a Nigerian trader based in **Onitsha** was trying to sell a large stock of blank **videocassettes** he had bought from Taiwan. He decided they would sell better if something was recorded on them, so he shot a short film called *Living in Bondage*, which sold more than 750,000 copies. Today, each film costs between $15,000 and $100,000, without bank loans. The financial **constraints** and cultural **infusion** have created a unique Nollywood style. Many of the movies tackle social and cultural problems—corruption, drugs, love triangles—and rely heavily on **melodrama**. In general, these **melodramatic** films are long, with simple dialogue and low-quality production. They show clear symbols of wealth, modernity, and tradition. They typically deal with the themes of **witchcraft**, romance and deceit. These films tend not to focus on the military, politics, or **ethnic** conflict, and often **steer away** from sexual content. Attached to this **burgeoning** film industry is advertising using famous actors and video rentals. A successful film may sell as many as 50,000 copies. Some viewers are concerned that these films present Nigeria poorly to the rest of the world, and critics claim that they lack artistic content and encourage ethnic and religious **stereotypes**. Nonetheless, they remain popular. The documentary *This is Nollywood* (2007) provides a glimpse into the production of this **up-and-coming** genre.

A video rental store in Nairobi, Kenya
(Photographer: Qi Lin)

Unit VII African Movies

With an average of 2,000 films produced every year, Nollywood, which developed out of the digital **boom** of the 1990s, is one of the biggest cinema industries in the world. That puts it in the same **bracket** as movie-mad India, although revenues–thought to be about $590 million a year–are considerably less. In 2013, the United Nations estimated that Nollywood, which releases about 50 films a week, employed some one million people and could create one million more jobs if properly run.

Most are sold as DVDs at the roadside, either at market **stalls**, from **wheelbarrows** or by **hawkers** at traffic lights. Online distribution has started through Internet platforms such as **iROKOtv** and via cable and satellite television, expanding their audience and **appeal** across Africa.

1. New Nollywood

"New Nollywood" is a phrase used to describe a recent strategy by some Nigerian filmmakers to make films with higher budgets, to **screen** them in cinemas both in Nigeria and abroad, and to enter them in international film festivals. This is a major structural shift in the Nollywood model of film production and distribution. Kunle Afolayan **exemplifies** this trend: his restless experimentation as a director and producer reveals the current structure of opportunities, and his situation as a filmmaker informs his films culturally and **thematically**. There are practical limits to the current possibilities of New Nollywood, but New Nollywood is likely to prove to be an invaluable preparation for coming transformations in the Nigerian film industry as Internet **streaming** and the construction of movie theaters in Nigeria take the place of the sale of films on discs as the central mode of Nollywood distribution.

2. Nigeria's Nollywood Seeks a Worldwide Audience

Kunle Afolyan, Nigerian film producer and director of the movie *The CEO* hopes the movie could drive changes in Nigeria's hugely popular and prolific movie industry, Nollywood. The 41-year-old told **AFP** "*The CEO* represents Africa as a continent. By virtue of the kind of story, the actors, the team and every element of the film to a large extent embrace who we are as Africans".

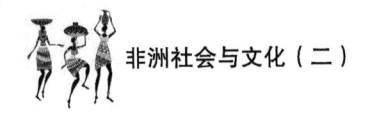

The film's plot is about a **telecoms** firm looking to replace its boss. Five members of the company's management are **dispatched** across Africa to find the best candidate.

Afolayan has secured financial backing from **Air France**, which is banking on his reputation to drive up its brand in Nigeria. The company has provided tickets for shooting to take place in Kenya, South Africa and even at Paris' main airport, **Charles De Gaulle**. With a budget of more than $1 million and corporate sponsorship, *The CEO* is **a far cry from** the **shoestring** productions that characterize the bulk of Nollywood's output. Some cost as little as $25,000 to make–a **fraction** of the $250 million average in Hollywood—and can be turned around within a month from filming to sale. The financial backing of the airline allowed the filmmakers to shoot on location in Kenya, South Africa and also in France while the **cast** reflects its appeal to all Africans, including a fairly great mix, with Benin's **Grammy** award-winning singer **Angelique Kidjo**, as well as actors from South Africa, Kenya, Côte d'Ivoire and Morocco.

Nollywood is the world's second-biggest movie industry in terms of production, churning out on average a thousand films a year. Only the Indian film industry, including **Hindi**-language Bollywood, makes more.

Better financing, it is hoped, will change Nollywood's image of poorly made films with **wobbly** cameras, poor sound and often **rudimentary** editing.

His ambition fits into a wider context of a greater role for Nollywood in Nigeria's economy and recognition of its value for the country. In April 2014, Nollywood was included in Nigeria's economic data for the first time—a sign of its growing power and influence. The film industry was estimated to be worth $4.3 billion or 1.2 percent of GDP. Nigeria's President **Muhammadu Buhari** earlier in 2015 ordered a **crackdown** on **bootleg** copies, to regularize sales and give actors and producers a fairer deal of revenues.

For Afolayan, better quality films, as producers and directors **hone their skills**, and with actors from across Africa, will boost interest on the continent and beyond. The filmmaker has already shown his films at a Nollywood festival in Paris, which has become an annual **fixture** since 2013. "Some people are very comfortable in making low-quality products because for them it is only a means of **livelihood**, for them they only make money," he said. "For me film is not about earning a living, film is life for me. I breathe film, I sleep film."

3. Nollywood Looks to the Future

In the early 1990s, the **resourceful** Nigerian entrepreneur Ken Nnebue sponsored the production of *Living in Bondage,* a video movie in **Igbo**, a major Nigerian language–with English **subtitles**. That movie, shot with rudimentary equipment, turned out to be **phenomenally** popular in Nigeria. Thus was born Nollywood, the Nigerian video movie industry which describes itself as the third most vibrant film industry in the world, after California's Hollywood and India's Bollywood.

Living in Bondage was a **morality** tale about evil people **scheming** to deny the son of a **polygamous** chief his inheritance by means which included resort to "**black magic**". At the end of the day, evil is defeated and the forces of good **triumph**. Before *Living in Bondage,* a number of Nigerian television **comedies** and soap operas had enjoyed a lot of popularity. But *Living in Bondage* broke all previous records.

The television dramas that **preceded** *Living in Bondage* had mostly been rather polite, rather middle class. Where such dramas treated sexual relations or supernatural forces, they did so **coyly**. In contrast, *Living in Bondage* was bold, even **lurid**, especially in the portrayal of the practices of "**witchdoctors**" and the desperation of their clients. The suggestion in the movie that a lot of the wealth of Nigeria's new rich came from **diabolical** practices **resonated** widely in a society of incredible inequality.

The successful formula of *Living in Bondage*—bold storytelling, a good dose of "black magic", and quick and easy distribution by video—has given birth to thousands of Nigerian video movies. The industry has produced its **seasoned** directors and star actors and actresses, complete with **cult** following. And Nollywood's films have spread far beyond Nigeria and **spawned** similar industries across Africa.

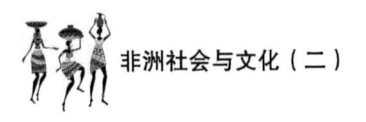

Several thousand movies later, Nollywood is now asking itself: what next? This soul-searching is prompted in part by the criticisms the industry has attracted. One of the most common charges is that its focus on "black magic" is **detrimental** to the image of Nigeria. The argument goes that at a time when we are striving to attract foreign investment, movies which depict Nigerians as attached to supernatural forces will give foreigners the idea that we are a backward people. This argument, which you encounter mostly among middle class Nigerians, **smacks** of **hypocrisy** (never mind whether our first priority should be to attract foreign investment or to encourage local creativity, which our movie industry shows is quite abundant). The **reverence** for diverse supernatural forces is widespread in Nigeria as it is all over Africa, in spite of centuries of Islamic and Christian penetration. That is why the "black magic" movies have proved so popular. To try to hide the hold such beliefs have on the imagination of our people is silly.

A **weightier** charge is that in emphasizing the **allegedly** diabolical aspects of our traditional religious practices, some home movies **distort** these practices and their underlying philosophies. The goddess of the river or of the forest in many a home movie is a **fearsome** agency of death for **adulterers** or people who have acquired ill-gotten wealth and so on. But the investing of rivers, forests, the natural elements and so on with religious significance arose from an appreciation by many African communities of how essential certain objects and phenomena are to the very survival of humankind. Our ancestors made goddesses out of rivers from a deep connection to and reverence for nature, and not to kill adulterers—as some of our video movies appear to suggest.

Nollywood has also been criticized for **shoddy** production and **disjointed** storylines. The typical video movie is shot in a week or two from a hurriedly written **script**, usually a **rehash** of the last successful movie. Because movie producers are in too much of a hurry to hit the market, there is hardly any effort to seek and develop new talent. Instead, the demand for our handful of popular actors and actresses is so heavy

Unit VII   African Movies

that they virtually walk from movie set to movie set all year round—which is reflected in the uneven quality of their work.

Tawdry sex scenes have been a favorite selling point. For a few weeks recently, a poster for a new movie showing a plump woman with enormous breasts wearing only a net **top** was pasted on nearly every **billboard** in Lagos. And there is a constant battle over movie **ratings** between the **censor**, a civil servant in the Federal Ministry of Culture, and movie makers, who are always seeking new ways to stay ahead of the competition.

Nollywood acknowledges its problems, but points out that it is learning all the time. Its products have included not only the "black magic" films, but also many thoughtful stories about love, loss and tragedy, and several films which fully reflect the Nigerian gift for laughter. Its most amazing contribution might be the films in Nigeria's **indigenous** languages which do justice to the depth and **dynamism** of those languages and reach the millions of Nigerians who do not understand English. Some of its producers and directors like Tunde Kelani, Charles Novia, Ebereonwu and Tade Ogidan have displayed sensitivity and/or ambition and some of its actors like Ramsey Noah and Omotola Ekeinde have more than earned their great fame. For Nollywood, the future looks very bright indeed.

V. FIVE REPRESENTATIVE MOVIES

1. *Out of Africa* (1985)

Out of Africa is a 1985 American **epic** romantic drama film directed and produced by Sydney Pollack and **starring** Robert Redford and Meryl Streep. The film is based loosely on the **autobiographical** book *Out of Africa* written by Isak Dinesen (the **pseudonym** of **Danish** author **Karen Blixen**), which was published in 1937, with additional material from Dinesen's book *Shadows on the Grass* and other sources. This film received 28 film awards, including seven **Academy Awards**.

Out of Africa is drawn from the life and writings of Danish author Isak Dinesen, who during the time when the film's events occurred was known by her married name, Karen Blixen-Flecke. For convenience's sake, Karen has married **Baron** Bor Blixen-Flecke (Klaus Maria Brandauer). In 1914, the Baron moves himself and his wife to a plantation in Nairobi, then leaves Karen to her own devices as he returns to his **womanizing** and drinking. Soon, Karen has fallen in love with a charming white hunter Denys Finch Hatton (Robert Redford), who prefers a **no-strings** relationship. A woman who prides herself on her independence, Blixen finds herself unhappily **in thrall to** an **aloof** man—and doubly unhappy for living out such a **cliché** situation. Although Redford received **a lion's share** of criticism for his too-American performance, Streep has rarely been better, and the film's perfectly measured pace is **complemented** by David Watkin's stunning location photography. The movie was **nominated** for 11 Academy Awards and won 7, including Best Picture, Best Director for Sydney Pollack, Best Adapted Screenplay for Kurt Luedtke, and Best **Cinematography** for Watkin.[13]

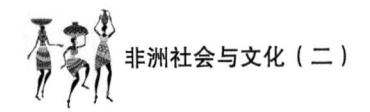

Karen Blixen Museum in Nairobi, Kenya
(Photographer: Han Hong)

2. *Moolaadé* (2004)

In an African village, this is the day when six 4-9-year-old girls are to be cut (the act of **female genital mutilation**). All children know that the operation is horrible torture and sometimes **lethal**, and all adults know that some cut women can only give birth by **caesarean section**. Two of the girls have drowned themselves in the **well** to escape the operation. The four other girls seek "magical protection" (moolaadé) by a woman (Colle) who seven years ago refused to have her daughter **circumcised**. Moolaadé is indicated by a colored rope. No one would dare step over and fetch the children. Moolaadé can only be **revoked** by Colle herself. Her husband's relatives persuade him to whip her in public into revoking. Opposite groups of women shout to her to revoke or to be **steadfast**, but no woman interferes. When Colle is at the edge of fainting, the merchant takes action and stops the maltreatment. Therefore he is hunted out of the village and, when out of sight, murdered.

A snapshot from the movie Moolaadé
(Photographer: Han Hong)

Ousmane Sembène is a **colossus** among African filmmakers. He is what **Akira Kurosawa** and **Satyajit Ray** are to Asia. At 82, this man is making films on women's problems, on colonialism, on human rights without losing sight of African culture.[14]

Moolaadé deals with rebellion by African women against female circumcision, a tradition upheld by elders, Muslims and **animists**, in a **swathe** of countries across Saharan and Sub-Saharan Africa. Interestingly, the film is an **uprising** within the social traditions that allow the husband full powers over his wives and acceptance of other social codes to whip his wife in public into **submission**. How many women (and **feminist**) directors who preach about female **emancipation** would have dared to make a film on this subject in Africa? The subject could cause riots in countries such as Egypt. Sembène is more feminist than women and is admired for this and other films he has made. He graphically shows how women are deprived of sexual pleasures through this practice and how thousands die during the crude operation.

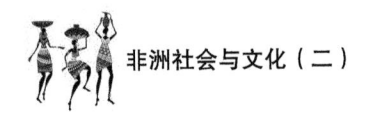

Moolaadé deals with other aspects of Africa as well. It comments on the adherence to traditional values that are good–six women get protection through a code word and a piece of cloth tied in front of the entrance to the house. It comments on **materialism** that **pervades pristine** African villages (as shown by the return of a native from Europe and the increasing dependence on radios for entertainment and information).

Sembène is concerned not with making great cinema for art's sake but using it creatively to improve the human condition of a slice of humanity the world (and the media) prefers to ignore.[15] His cinema is not **stylish**—its style stems from its simplicity and its **humane** values. Sembène's films allow non-Africans to get inside the world of the real Africa far removed from the world of constant hunger and the **epidemic** of AIDS that the media underlines as Africa today.[16] Sembène's film is not history, it is Africa today. The performances are as close to reality as you could get.

3. *Hotel Rwanda* (2004)

Hotel Rwanda was a 2004 American historical drama film directed by **Irish** filmmaker Terry George, who co-wrote the script with Keir Pearson.

Twenty years ago, some of the worst **atrocities** in human history took place in Rwanda–and in an era of high-speed communication and round-the-clock news, the events went almost unnoticed by the rest of the world. In only 3 months, one million people were brutally murdered. In the face of these unspeakable actions, inspired by his love for his family, an ordinary man Paul Rusesabagina summons extraordinary courage to save the lives of over 1,000 helpless refugees, by granting them shelter in the hotel he manages.

Hotel Rwanda tackles one of the most **horrifically** ugly events in recent history, when the **Hutu extremists** of Rwanda initiated a terrifying campaign of

Unit VII African Movies

genocide, **massacring** hundreds of thousands of minority **Tutsis** (who had been given power by the departed Belgian colonists), while the rest of the world looked on and did nothing. Don Cheadlestars as Paul Rusesabagina, the hotel manager at the fancy **Hotel Des Milles Collines** in **Kigali**. Paul is a Hutu, and a very successful businessman who smoothly **greases the wheels**, making powerful connections in all **strata** of Rwandan life. His wife, Tatiana (Sophie Okonedoof Aeon Flux), is a Tutsi. She urges Paul to use his influence to help local Tutsis, who are being **harassed** and beaten with increasing frequency, but Paul will only use the political capital he's built up to help his own family, if and when they need it. Soon enough, the violence **escalates**, and the Hutus begin their genocide of the Tutsis. European guests and staff at the hotel are flown out of the country, and Paul is left in charge. He finds that his **conscience** won't allow him to watch as the innocent are **slaughtered**, and before long, the hotel has become a **well-appointed** refugee camp. Paul is seen as a **traitor** by some, putting his life in danger, and the **predicament** of his "guests" grows more **precarious** every day, but despite good intentions on the part of a journalist (Joaquin Phoenix) and a UN peacekeeping **colonel** (Nick Nolte), the rest of the world is not eager to intervene and stop the massacre. While most of the world took no action to stop the killing, Rusesabagina sheltered more than 1,000 people inside his hotel. He gave them water from the pool so they wouldn't die from **dehydration**, **smuggled** in food so they wouldn't starve, and held off the **militia** who came to the hotel by bribing them with alcohol and cigars.

4. *Tsotsi* (2005)

Tsotsi is directed by Gavin Hood and produced by Peter Fudakowski. The film won the 2006 Academy Award for Best Foreign Language Film and was nominated for the **Golden Globe** for Best Foreign Language Film in 2006.

Set in an Alexandra **slum**[17], in Johannesburg, South Africa, the film tells the story of Tsotsi, a young street **thug** who steals a car only to discover a baby in the back seat.

A snapshot from the movie Tsotsi
(Photographer: Han Hong)

Because his mother is dying of a terminal disease, David (Benny Moshe) runs away from an **abusive** father and lives with other homeless children in a series of large concrete construction pipes. A few years later, David, who now goes by the name Tsotsi (Presley Chweneyagae), is the leader of a **gang** which includes his friends Butcher (Zenzo Ngqobe), Aap (Kenneth Nkosi) and Boston (Mothusi Magano). After getting involved in a murder committed by Butcher during a **mugging**, Tsotsi and Boston get into a fight which leaves Boston badly injured. Tsotsi later shoots Pumla (Nambitha Mpumlwana), a young woman, while stealing her car, only to discover a three-month-old baby boy in the back seat. Tsotsi hastily strips the car of its valuables and takes the baby back to his **shack**. Pumla survives the attack and works with a police artist to create a **composite sketch** of Tsotsi's face, which is then run in the newspapers.

Realizing that he cannot properly care for the baby on his own, Tsotsi spots Miriam (Terry Pheto), with a young child **strapped** to her back, collecting water from a public tap. He follows her to her shack and forces her at gunpoint to feed the kidnapped child. Meanwhile, rich gang leader Fela (Zola) begins attempting to **recruit** Aap, Boston and Butcher to work for him. When Tsotsi takes the child to Miriam a second time, she asks him to leave the boy with her so that she can care for him on Tsotsi's behalf, and Tsotsi agrees.

Unit VII African Movies

Tsotsi decides to take care of injured Boston, and has Aap and Butcher take Boston to his shack. Boston, who is called "Teacher Boy" by his friends, explains that he never took the teachers' examination. Tsotsi tells him that the gang will raise money so that Boston can take the exam, which means they will have to commit another robbery.

Tsotsi and Aap go to Pumla's house. When Pumla's husband John (Rapulana Seiphemo) returns from the hospital, they follow him into the house and tie him up. Aap is assigned to watch John while Butcher **ransacks** the bedroom and Tsotsi collects items from the baby's room. When Aap goes to raid the fridge, John **activates** the alarm. In panic, Butcher attempts to kill John with John's pistol that he found, but Tsotsi shoots and kills Butcher with his pistol and he and Aap escape in John's car moments before the security company arrives.

Traumatized by Tsotsi's killing of Butcher and fearing that Tsotsi will one day harm him too, Aap decides to leave the gang and quit as Tsotsi's friend. When Tsotsi goes back to Miriam's house, she reveals that she knows where he got the baby, and begs him to return the child to his parents. Tsotsi sets off to return the baby. He reaches John's house, tells John over the **intercom** that he will leave the child outside the gate. Meanwhile, an officer stationed at the house alerts Captain Smit (Ian Roberts), who rushes to the scene, arriving just as Tsotsi is about to walk away.

The police point their guns at Tsotsi, ordering him to return the baby. However, John urges them to lower their weapons so that he can **retrieve** the baby himself. As Tsotsi holds the baby in his arms, John convinces him to give up the baby. Tsotsi emotionally hands the baby to John, then is told to put up his hands and turns himself in as the film ends.

A month before *Tsotsi* received the Oscar for Best Foreign Language Film, thousands glimpsed the forthcoming moment of glory when they screened the South African film in a nearby African American **enclave** in the city. *Tsotsi*, based on South African playwright **Athol Fugard**'s 1950s novel, is a dark drama about a young, **alienated** Johannesburg **shantytown** thug's attempt to **exorcise** personal **demons** and find **redemption**. It was both the centerpiece and Best Feature winner of 2006's

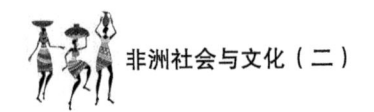

Pan African Film & Arts Festival, held in February at the Magic Johnson Theaters, in the Baldwin Hills-Crenshaw Plaza. *Tsotsi* (a **Sotho** word for "gangster") is a poignant **peek** at the **grimy**, urban **underbelly** of South Africa's multiracial democracy. The dialogue of *Tsotsi* is a **stew** of youth slang from several different indigenous and foreign languages and is fueled by a potent, **streetwise** music called **kwaito**, similar to **hardcore hip-hop**.

5. *Virunga* (2014)

Nominated for an Oscar in the Best Feature-length Documentary category 2015, *Virunga* is a story that takes the viewer into the **chaos** of the war-torn eastern Congo and **Virunga National Park** in the Democratic Republic of the Congo, where dedicated park **rangers** struggle to protect the last of the **mountain gorillas** and preserve the park and its residents.

Poachers endanger the gorillas. Park rangers discover a massacre of gorillas by people trying to **exterminate** them for the land. Militia groups, including the **rebel group M23**, make war against the Congo government, adding another layer of fear. International corporate entities interested in the rich natural mineral resources of the area, including **drilling** for oil in Virunga National Park, create a situation where park rangers and officials are **at odds with** SOCO International PLC,[18] the oil exploration corporation. While the humans fight for their piece of the pie, Virunga National Park, a **UNESCO** World Heritage site, and its inhabitants, animals of all types, become vulnerable. For some interests, the gorillas, and all the other animals are **expendable**.

One of the themes in the documentary involves three young **orphaned** gorillas rescued by the park rangers and now in their care. As the war **encroaches** on the park, the care of the young gorillas becomes increasingly difficult. Seeing these young gorillas and their affection for the rangers is heart-warming.

It seems that the animals and humans in and around Virunga face similar problems as the war **engulfs** their constant struggle for survival. This documentary does an excellent job of telling the story by being there in the park. The filmmakers are with the rangers, the oil company (SOCO) security, the indigenous people living in the area, government soldiers and rebels as events progress. The documentary shows the refugee camps on the southern border of Virunga Park where thousands of people are living **displaced** by the rebels and war. Interviews and conversations with certain characters seem to be done without the **interviewees** knowing it. This is a pretty risky **tactic** for the filmmakers if they are caught since there is little concern for people's life.

Virunga combines nature documentary and journalistic reporting from a war zone. The filmmakers face many life-threatening situations as they go with park rangers through the park to check on the gorillas and other animals. The rangers must deal with poachers and rebel militias. Virunga is a story that demonstrates the cruelty and greed of humans and the **humanity** shown by a few people in times when all around them is made hostile. It is a documentary that brings into focus the realities of this area of Africa and perhaps sheds light on some of the problems facing many of the former European colonies in Africa. The indigenous people have no history of self-rule. Even with independence, they are still **fair game** for exploitation by international corporate entities that can buy their way into these countries.[19]

Orlando von Einsiedel, a director and producer, and a former professional **snowboarder**, began making short documentaries in 2010 skating through the streets of **Kabul**, Afghanistan. He then continued working in Africa directing several **shorts** across the continent, and that is when a photograph of a group of rangers at Virunga National Park caught his attention. The story was far too **compelling** for a short, so he decided to direct his first feature documentary centering on the current situation in the Congo. The park rangers are completely committed to protecting the wildlife where the world's remaining mountain gorillas live, but as in most parts of the African continent, the unstable government situation has made their survival difficult. With rebel groups trying to fund their armies, the rich minerals present in the park are their means to it. But these dangerous rebel groups aren't the only enemy that the rangers face. SOCO, a British gas company, was given permission by the

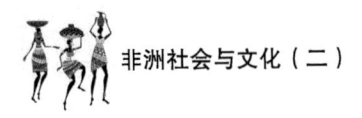

Congolese government to explore the territory for **oil reserves**. The **contradiction** is that Virunga is a protected park due to the endangered species living there. Through a series of interesting investigative work, a reporter named Melanie Gouby manages to befriend SOCO employees and discovers a link between them and the rebel groups. She also exposes the corruption behind some of the officials. What results is a fascinating documentary that gets more and more exciting as the story develops.

As to why he made the documentary, Orlando von Einsiedel said: "The thrust of the project was to try to tell the story of the rebirth of the eastern Congo because there had been a period of stability for a few years, and I came across the story of the park's brave rangers. And I thought their story was a sort of metaphor for the wider rebirth of the region. Within a few weeks this new civil war started, and I found out about the oil discovery. So I ended up making a very different film."

Unit VII   African Movies

Explanations

［1］***King Soloman's Mines***:《所罗门王的宝藏》是英国作家亨利·莱德·哈格德（Henry Rider Haggard, 1856—1925）的成名之作。1885年，这部探险小说一经面世就受到广大读者，特别是青年人的热烈欢迎。这本书被译成多种文字，至今仍在世界各地流传。作者根据有关南非的真实历史资料，结合南非的实际地理环境，用扣人心弦的故事情节完成了这部杰作。故事的梗概是：英国爵士亨利·柯蒂斯和约翰·古德上校结伴去南非，在从开普敦到纳塔尔省的船上遇到猎手艾伦·夸特梅因，柯蒂斯请夸特梅因帮忙寻找失踪的弟弟乔治。三人在土著昂伯帕的帮助下进入马塔比尔国。虽然动机各不相同，但四个人在探险过程中共同经历了重重困难，逐渐产生了友谊。在这片陌生而又危险的土地上，他们战胜了所有的艰难困苦，不仅找到了神奇的宝物，还通过一场场胜利体验到自己的力量。

［2］**Paul Robeson:** 美国黑人演员保罗·罗宾逊（1898—1976）多才多艺，既是演员，又是职业运动员、作家和民权斗士。

［3］**Sidney Poitier:** 西德尼·波蒂埃生于1927年，是美国最伟大的黑人演员。他出生在美国佛罗里达州迈阿密。1958年以反种族影片《挣脱锁链》（*The Defiant Ones*）赢得了英国电影学院奖"最佳男主角奖"以及柏林电影节影帝头衔，因而迅速成为好莱坞头号黑人演员。1964年再以《田野里的百合花》（*Lilies of the Field*）勇夺奥斯卡"最佳男主角奖"，成为美国历史上第一位黑人影帝。此外，波蒂埃还是一位导演、作家和民权斗士。他的成功为后来的黑人演员开辟了一条通往好莱坞的光明之路。2002年，为表彰其卓越贡献，美国电影艺术与科学学院（the American Academy of Motion Picture Arts and Sciences）为他颁发了奥斯卡终身荣誉奖（Academy Honorary Award）。

［4］**Martin and Osa Johnson**：马丁·埃尔默·约翰逊（Martin Elmer Johnson, 1884—1937）和妻子奥萨·海伦·约翰逊（Osa Helen Johnson,1894—1953）是美国冒险家，纪录片制片人。1924—1927年，夫妻俩在肯尼亚

23

北部以当地动物和居民为对象拍摄了大量素材。1928年,他们用这些素材剪接出了电影《狮子:百兽之王》(*Simba: King of the Beasts*)。

[5] **Ousmane Sembène:** 塞内加尔作家兼导演乌斯曼·塞姆班(1923—2007)用法语和沃洛夫语进行创作,被称为"非洲电影之父"。在2004年戛纳电影节上,他凭借电影《割礼龙凤斗》(*Moolaadé*)一片获得"天主教人道精神奖"(Prize of the Ecumenical Jury)。

[6] **Haile Gerima:** 海尔·格里玛是埃塞俄比亚最富盛名的电影导演,曾多次荣获国际大奖。1946年,格里玛在埃塞俄比亚贡德尔出生,1968年在美国加州大学洛杉矶分校学习。格里玛既是一名优秀的黑人导演,又是一位哲学家、艺术家和电影制片人。他坚持不懈地努力,希望通过电影来纠正世人对黑人历史的错误看法,因此赢得了广泛尊重。

[7] **The Hollywood-trained playwright and musician Kwah Ansah set up his own companies to produce commercials and feature films.** *Love brewed in an African Pot* **(1980) was a critique of arranged marriage, and** *Heritage Africa* **(1987) was the poignant tale of Quincy Arthur Bosomfield, a former martinet in the colonial administration, who received a talking-to by his ancestral spirit and went back to being Kwesi Atta Bosomefi, to his family's relief:** 曾经在好莱坞学习的加纳剧作家、音乐家克瓦·安塞创建了自己的公司,从事商业公告和故事片的拍摄。1980年,他在电影《非洲罐中酝酿的爱情》中,对包办婚姻提出批判。1987年,他的电影《遗产非洲》讲述了一个深刻的故事:Kwesi Atta Bosomefi 为殖民政府工作,一向严格遵守纪律。出于对本部族传统文化的蔑视,他擅自改名为Quincy Arthur Bosomfield,但是在被祖先灵魂"训斥"以后,他重拾旧名,家人这才如释重负。

[8] **In the south of the country, Ola Balogun was for many years the most prolific Yoruba-language filmmaker; for about a decade he churned out a film a year, alternating hits and misses:** 多年以来,奥拉·巴洛贡是尼日利亚南部地区用约鲁巴语进行创作的最多产的导演。大约十年之间,他每年拍一部电影,但是作品的表现参差不齐:一部大获成功,下一部则惨遭票房失败,再下一部又好评如潮。

Unit VII　African Movies

[9] **African cinema has always posed the question of authenticity, and none more starkly than the best-known South African film, *The Gods Must Be Crazy*:** 非洲电影的"真实性"也是一个大问题。最典型的例子就是最著名的南非影片《上帝也疯狂》。

[10] **Because of the cultural blockage against South Africa, the film was released in Botswana in 1980. World audiences, particularly in Sweden and Japan, were enchanted by a lighthearted fable, whereas political activists sharply criticized the film's racism and fakery. But there was nothing inauthentic about its foreign exchange earnings, which surpassed US$84 million:** 由于南非受到文化封锁，1980年这部电影在博茨瓦纳公映。全世界的观众，尤其是瑞典人和日本人对这部轻松的世外桃源剧非常着迷。但是政治活动家们对于电影反映出的种族主义和与现实不符之处提出了尖锐批评。可是无论如何，没人能够质疑《上帝也疯狂》在海外市场取得的巨大票房成功，累计票房收入超过了8 400万美元。

[11] **A production consortium from South Africa, Britain, Cameroon, Ghana, Kenya, and Nigeria produced the first pan-African action thriller, *Critical Assignment* (2003), starring Guinness advertising icon Michael Power as a kinder and gentler African James Bond:** 2003年，来自南非、英国、喀麦隆、加纳、肯尼亚和尼日利亚的一个跨国团队合作拍摄了电影《危急时刻》，这是第一部具有泛非意义的惊险动作片。为健力士黑啤酒代言的迈克尔·鲍尔出演的男一号演绎了非洲版"詹姆斯·邦德"，而且更友好、更温柔。

[12] **At first, a lazy eye and mind will have a problem with African cinema. It requires commitment:** 乍一接触非洲电影，懒得思考的人不会喜欢，要付出努力才能看得懂非洲电影。

[13] **Although Redford received a lion's share of criticism for his too-American performance, Streep has rarely been better, and the film's perfectly measured pace is complemented by David Watkin's stunning location photography. The movie was nominated for 11 Academy Awards and won 7, including Best Picture, Best Director for Sydney Pollack, Best Adapted Screenplay**

25

for Kurt Luedtke, and Best Cinematography for Watkin: 在电影《走出非洲》中，尽管罗伯特·雷德福过于美国化的表演饱受诟病，梅丽尔·斯特里普的表演却算得上炉火纯青，影片节奏无懈可击，此外，大卫·沃特金拍摄的外景也如诗如画。影片一共获得11项奥斯卡提名，最终斩获7项大奖，其中包括"最佳影片奖"、西德尼·波拉克的"最佳导演奖"、科特·路德特克的"最佳改编剧本奖"以及大卫·沃特金的"最佳摄影奖"。

[14] **Ousmane Sembène is a colossus among African filmmakers. He is what Akira Kurosawa and Satyajit Ray are to Asia. At 82, this man is making films on women's problems, on colonialism, on human rights without losing sight of African culture:** 对于非洲电影界而言，塞内加尔导演乌斯曼·塞姆班拥有至高无上的地位，他相当于日本的电影大师黑泽明，或者印度的萨蒂亚吉特·雷伊。在82岁高龄的时候，他依然在拍摄涉及妇女问题、殖民主义以及人权等主题的电影，他的作品深深植根于非洲文化当中。

[15] **Sembène is concerned not with making great cinema for art's sake but using it creatively to improve the human condition of a slice of humanity the world (and the media) prefers to ignore:** 塞姆班从来没有为了艺术而拍摄伟大的电影，他关心的是在国际社会（以及媒体）不愿提及的非洲大陆上，如何创造性地利用电影来改善人民的生存状况。

[16] **His cinema is not stylish—its style stems from its simplicity and its humane values. Sembène's films allow non-Africans to get inside the world of the real Africa far removed from the world of constant hunger and the epidemic of AIDS that the media underlines as Africa today:** 塞姆班不追求时尚，他的电影朴实无华，闪烁着人文主义光芒，有助于世界其他地方的人了解真实的非洲，而非媒体笔下的非洲——饥荒遍地，艾滋病发病率居高不下。

[17] **Set in an Alexandra slum...:** 故事发生在亚历桑德拉贫民窟……

[18] **SOCO International PLC**：SOCO是一家总部设在伦敦的跨国公司，该公司在越南、刚果共和国和安哥拉三国从事石油和天然气的勘测和生产，是一家伦敦股票交易所的上市公司。

[19] **Even with independence, they are still fair game for exploitation by international corporate entities that can buy their way into these countries:** 即便独立以后，一些非洲国家依然在遭受跨国公司的剥削，后者凭借自己的经济实力将魔爪伸向昔日的殖民地。

Exercises

I. Read the following statements and decide whether they are true (T) or false (F):

_____ 1. During colonial times in Africa, more educational and research films were produced than movies of dramas and documentaries.

_____ 2. Nigerian director Ousmane Sembène is considered by some to be the founder of African film making.

_____ 3. South Africa, with its population of 125,000,000, is the largest market in Africa, and the South African diaspora is important as well.

_____ 4. However, the films that reach African viewers are British. Bollywood musicals from India and kung fu films from Hong Kong are also very popular.

_____ 5. "New Nollywood" is a phrase used to describe a recent strategy by some Nigerian filmmakers to make films with even lower budgets.

_____ 6. Nollywood is the world's second-biggest movie industry in terms of production, second only to Hollywood.

_____ 7. *Out of Africa* was nominated for 11 Academy Awards and won 7.

_____ 8. *Moolaadé* deals with rebellion by African women against female circumcision, a tradition upheld by elders, Muslims and animists.

_____ 9. *Virunga* was nominated for a Golden Globe Award in the Best Feature-length Documentary category in 2015.

_____ 10. Virunga National Park is situated in Rwanda, where dedicated park rangers struggle to protect the last of the mountain gorillas and preserve the park and its residents.

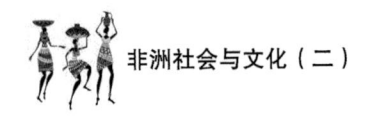

II. Fill in the following blanks with words that best complete the sentences.

1. Many American and British moviemakers came to Africa to film stories of _____ and _____.
2. The viewpoints expressed in works by colonial officials and missionaries are now considered _____ and even _____.
3. Blessed with _____ and _____, in addition to film crews, Kenya became a favored location for Hollywood.
4. The history of African cinema is composed of three strands. First and best known is the _____ cinema: feature films made in Africa for the entertainment market. Second are the _____ films made in Africa by scientists, educators, political activists, and the like. Finally, since independence, a self-consciously African cinema has come into being, created by African directors and shown primarily at film _____, but also available on DVD.
5. Nollywood generates an estimated _____ films per year, with _____ of them in English, which exceeds India's Bollywood.
6. Some viewers are concerned that these films present Nigeria poorly to the rest of the world, and critics claim that they lack _____ content and encourage ethnic and religious _____.
7. Nigeria's President Muhammadu Buhari earlier in 2015 ordered a _____ on bootleg copies, to _____ sales and give actors and producers a fairer deal of revenues.
8. In the early 1990s, the resourceful Nigerian entrepreneur Ken Nnebue sponsored the production of *Living in Bondage*, a _____ movie in Igbo, a major Nigerian language with English _____.
9. *Moolaadé* comments on the _____ to traditional values that are good and _____ that pervades pristine African villages.
10. The filmmakers face many _____ situations as they go with park rangers through the park to check on the _____ and other animals.

Unit VII   African Movies

Review and Reflect

✧ What are your impressions of movies by Africans?

✧ What do you think of the future of Nollywood? Why?

✧ Who can produce better movies about African countries or people, Africans or foreigners?

Unit VIII　African Languages

　　非洲语言种类繁多，约占世界语言总数的三分之一。非洲语言历史悠久，有丰富的语汇和表达方式。出于殖民统治和传播基督教的需要，欧洲人从19世纪初就开始将一些非洲语言拉丁化。很多重要的非洲语言，例如斯瓦希里语和豪萨语原来都是用阿拉伯字母拼写的，19世纪它们先后被拉丁化了。民族独立以后，很多非洲国家将前宗主国的语言作为官方语言，其中包括英语、法语和葡萄牙语。随着种族同化和文化融合过程的不断加深，不少非洲语言正逐步走向消亡。另一方面，不断高涨的民族主义使一些主要的非洲语言不断发展壮大。

Greetings from Zanzibar, Tanzania ("jambo" means "hello" in Swahili)
(Photographer: Lan Fengyun)

　　"If you speak in a language they understand, you speak to their head. If you speak in their own language, you speak to their heart."

—Nelson Mandela, 1993 Nobel Peace Prize laureate

◎ Think and Talk

☆ How many languages are there in Africa?

☆ Do you know some English words that originated from African languages?

☆ Do you know the meaning of "Hakuna Matata"?

Unit VIII   African Languages

I. OVERVIEW

With more than 1 500 different languages, Africa **boasts** greater **linguistic** variety than any other continent. The tremendous range includes major languages such as **Swahili** and **Hausa**, spoken by millions of people, and minor languages such as **Hazda**, which have fewer than a thousand speakers. The linguistic situation is constantly changing. While many of the continent's major languages are rapidly expanding, smaller languages are disappearing.

The choice of language is shaped by a variety of factors. As a result of European colonization, many Africans speak English, French, or **Portuguese** in addition to their **indigenous** languages. Centuries of Arab influence in North Africa have led to the widespread use of **Arabic** or one or more European languages as their official languages.

II. CLASSIFICATION OF AFRICAN LANGUAGES

Most scholars today adopted a system of **classification** of African languages that was established in the mid-1900s. Under this **scheme** African languages are divided into 4 major groups: **Afroasiatic, Niger-Congo, Nilo-Sarahan**, and **Khoisan**. In addition to these four groups, the continent contains a variety of **creole** and **pidgin** languages that have developed from the interactions between African and European languages.

1. Afroasiatic Languages

The Afroasiatic languages consist of about 230 modern and a dozen dead (no longer spoken) languages, which originated in northern and eastern Africa and in western Asia. They are divided into five major language families: Ancient Egyptian (a dead language), **Berber, Semitic, Chadic**, and **Cushitic**. Some **linguists** include a sixth family, **Omotic**, in the Afroasiatic group. The number of people who speak a particular language within these five linguistic families ranges from a few hundreds to millions.[1]

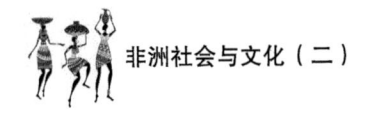

The Semitic language group, which includes Arabic, boasts the greatest number of speakers. Modern Arabic alone is used by more than 160 million people in North Africa, northeastern Africa, parts of northwestern Africa, and southwest Asia. The Chadic family, named after its place of origin near Lake Chad, contains about 150 languages. Hausa, with about 40 million speakers throughout western Africa, is the most widespread language in the group. The Cushitic language family of eastern Africa can be found from Sudan in the north to Tanzania in the south.[2]

North Africa is home to the Berber language. Berber, an Arabic word, came from the Greek *barbaros*, which originally referred to someone speaking a language other than ancient Greek. This is also the root of the English word *barbarian*.

2. Niger-Congo Languages

Most branches of Niger-Congo languages are found in western Africa, considered the homeland of this major language group. However, **Kordofanian**, one of these language branches, exists only in Sudan. Some scholars believe that Kordofanian speakers migrated to that region from western Africa. Others, however, consider Niger-Congo language to be part of the Nilo-Saharan group. If that is true, then Sudan may be the homeland of Kordofanian, and other Niger-Congo languages may have migrated to west Africa from there. The **Mande** and **Ubangi** languages of this group are each spoken by at least 3 million people. **Fulani**, the language ranging over the widest area, is found throughout western, central, and eastern Africa.

Bantu, a special subgroup of Niger-Congo languages, has been long considered a separate language family. The Bantu languages are the most widespread of any linguistic group in Africa. Bantu speakers—more than 200 million—can be found throughout Africa south of an **imaginary** line that runs roughly from Cameroon in the west to Kenya in the east. The large number of Bantu speakers is matched by the number of Bantu languages: estimates vary from more than 300 to nearly 700. Scholars disagree as to whether these are all distinct languages or whether many are simply **dialects** of major Bantu tongues. Swahili has the largest number of speakers of any single Bantu language, but **Gikuyu**, **Zulu**, and **Xhosa** also claim millions of speakers.

Most scholars trace the origin of Bantu, some 2000 or 3000 years ago, to an area around present-day Nigeria and Cameroon.[3] From there, Bantu-speakers migrated east and south. A second migration, along the western coast of Africa, took place later. As a result of these various migrations, some Bantu languages have many similarities, while others are quite different from each other.

Most countries where Bantu is spoken contain dozens of different Bantu languages and dialects. This has made it difficult for government officials, educators, and others to choose a common language to conduct business and other activities. East African countries use Swahili for such purposes. However, in most places where Bantu languages dominate, the language of the former European colonial power serves as the official means of communication. Meanwhile, the local Bantu tongues are used in private conversation, in markets, in local primary schools, and sometimes in secondary schools.

3. Nilo-Saharan Languages

The Nilo-Saharan languages are found mostly in central and eastern Africa, from the Lake Chad area into southern Sudan and Kenya. A western branch of this group, **Songhai**, is spoken along **the Niger River** in southern Mali. However, recent studies have shown that Songhai shares features of Niger-Congo and Afroasiatic languages and may actually be a creole language. Although some 150 Nilo-Saharan languages exist, only 3 of them—**Kanuri**, **Luo**, and **Dinka**—are widely spoken. Linguists still debate whether Nilo-Saharan should be a separate group or whether these languages are properly included under the Niger-Congo and Afroasiatic groups.

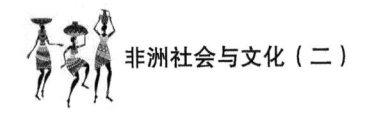

4. Khoisan Languages

Khoisan languages are restricted to southern Africa, particular in present-day Namibia and Botswana. Notable for the use of **click** sounds, they are sometimes called click languages. The three main Khoisan language groups are the Zhu (northern), Khoi (central), and Qwi (southern). Each group is distinct, and speakers of one group cannot readily understand speakers of another group. Khoisan languages have had a significant impact on the sounds and vocabulary of Bantu languages in southern Africa, and they have themselves been strongly influenced by Bantu and European cultures. The dominance of Bantu languages, English, and **Afrikaans** (a language developed from Dutch in the 1600s) in southern Africa has led to the decline of the Khoisan languages, and few of them claim more than a few thousand speakers today.

5. Creole and Pidgin Languages

When two languages come into contact, one typically becomes **dominant** because more people speak it or because its speakers enjoy a higher social status. This interaction often leads to the development of creole, a mixture of the two languages. Creole languages are usually based on the vocabulary and grammar of the dominant language, but they include many features of the **subordinate** language.

In Africa, most creole languages developed as a result of contact between indigenous languages and nonstandard versions of European languages spoken by colonial settlers. In some cases, however, creole languages appeared where speakers of a dominant African language, such as Swahili, came into contact with speakers of less widespread African languages. This often occurred near colonial trading posts or factories, where Africans who spoke many different languages came together and needed a common tongue to communicate.

The term pidgin was first used in the early 1800s to describe the form of English adopted by Chinese merchants in the city of **Canton** who conducted businesses with Europeans. Pidgin languages differ from creoles in that they generally have no native speakers, are used for limited purposes such as trade, and have less complex grammatical structures. Some scholars claim that creoles originally developed from pidgin languages adopted by children who used them as a form of everyday speech. However, historical facts surrounding the development of some creole languages tend to **contradict** this view.

III. LANGUAGE CONTACT AND USE

When the same speakers use two or more languages, those languages are said to be in contact. This occurs frequently in Africa because of the many different languages spoken on the continent. Throughout the long **multilingual** history of the African continent, African languages have **been subject to** phenomena like language contact, language expansion, language shift, and language death. Language contact often leads to the replacement of one language by other, or to one language emerging as the dominant form of communication. A case in point is the Bantu expansion, in which Bantu-speaking peoples expanded over most of Sub-Saharan Africa, thereby **displacing** Khoisan speaking peoples in much of east Africa. Another example is the Islamic expansion in the 7th century A.D., which led to the extension of Arabic to much of North Africa.

1. Language Contact

By examining language contact, linguists can determine how languages have influenced each other. Studies of sounds, grammar, and use of words often show the impact that one language has had on another. Borrowed words may indicate the type of situations in which contact between different groups was most important. For example, Swahili religious and legal **terminology** contains many words borrowed from Arabic, indicating that contact in these two areas was more intense than others.

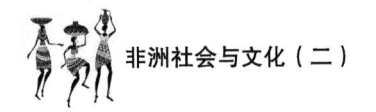

The intensity of language contact often relates to social and economic factors. When language contact occurs, the language with higher social and economic status tends to become a second language for speakers of subordinate tongues. Moreover, languages with lower status tend to borrow more from a dominant language, rather than the other way around.[4] In the long run, speakers of a subordinate language may abandon their original language in favor of the dominant tongue. This generally takes place in stages over a period of time. One part of the group or community may abandon the language first, followed by others until the language dies out completely. Such a change from one language to another is called language shift. An example of language shift occurred in east Africa in the late 1800s and early 1900s, when Aasáx speakers adopted the **Maasai** language, and their own language became **extinct**.

Language contact does not always lead to the abandonment of one language for another, especially when many more people speak the subordinate language. For example, when the Fulani took over the Hausa kingdoms of western Africa in the early 1800s, they did not impose their own language but instead adopted Hausa as an official language. This not only made the change in leadership less noticeable, but also allowed the Fulani to use their own language as a secret form of communication. English colonists sometimes followed a similar course. When they found that African languages such as Swahili or Hausa were widely spoken in an area, they often learned those languages and used them to communicate with local people. In fact, before leaving Europe for Africa, English colonial officials were encouraged to learn the most important local languages in the areas to which they were assigned.

2. Language Policies

Language is not only a form of communication, it also serves as a way to **transmit** local and cultural values. When a country adopts a particular tongue as its official language, it gives an advantage to the people who speak the language. Those who do not speak it have a **hardship**.

The European powers that colonized Africa established their own languages as the official ones for government business and legal matters. This policy gave European languages a much higher status than indigenous tongues and provided a reason for local people to learn them.

The French and Portuguese conducted all businesses and even basic education in their own languages. Children in **missionary** schools or government-run schools learned French and Portuguese from the earliest age. Local languages were considered acceptable only for personal communication. In the French colonies, the need to master the French language led to the development of a rather **sizable** group of African upper classes who spoke French. However, a much smaller percentage of the indigenous population was **literate** than in British colonies.

The first missionary schools in British colonies used local African languages for instruction. This was motivated largely by the desire of missionaries to train Africans to **preach** to local people, as well as to spread Christian ideas by producing Bible translations in indigenous languages. When British government took over colonial education, they continued the policy of using African languages in schools. Though English was the official language, African languages were widely used for many purposes, even by colonial officials. For this reason, British colonies had people who learned to read in a local language, but only a small group of Africans who mastered English.

After independence most African nations adopted the language of the former colonial power as their official language. Although only a small percentage of the population spoke that language, it provided a universal means of communication for official purposes. Thus, many African countries have made English, French, or Portuguese their official language.

Some countries use African language for government business. In Kenya and Tanzania, Swahili has become the official language because it is widely spoken. It is not, however, the primary language of most people in either country. A number of African countries have two or more official languages, which may include a European language and widely spoken African ones.

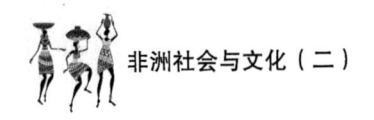

3. Language Choice in Writing

Since the colonial period, European languages have also dominated African literature. Two reasons are mainly responsible for this. First, many African languages had no written form before colonization, so most Africans learned to write in the language of colonial power. Second, because African languages are virtually unknown outside Africa, the easiest way for African writers to reach a large audience is by using a major world language such as English and French.

Many African writers have accepted the dominance of European languages in literature, and some have even suggested that African languages are inadequate for literary expression. In recent years, however, a number of noted African authors, including **Chinua Achebe**, have begun to reconsider this idea. These authors are now using more African vocabulary or grammar in their works, and some are even writing in local languages. Nevertheless, European languages will probably remain the main ones for African literature in the near future.

IV. OFFICIAL LANGUAGES

The high linguistic diversity of many African countries (Nigeria alone has 250 languages, one of the greatest concentrations of linguistic diversity in the world) has made language policy a vital issue in the post-colonial era. In recent years, African countries have become increasingly aware of the value of their linguistic **inheritance**. Language policies being developed nowadays are mostly aimed at **multilingualism**. 2006 was declared by the African Union as the "Year of African Languages". However, although many mid-sized languages are used on the radio, in newspapers, and in primary school education, and some of the larger ones are considered national languages, only a few are official at the national level.

Unit VIII African Languages

1. Demographics

In the 1.186 billion Africans (as of 2015, from the UN website), about 17% speak an Arabic dialect. About 10% speak Swahili, the **lingua franca** of southeastern Africa, about 5% speak a Berber dialect, and about 5% speak Hausa, a western African lingua franca. Other important western African languages are **Yoruba**, **Igbo** and Fulani. Major northeast African languages are **Oromo** and Somali. Important southern African languages are Zulu and Afrikaans (related to Dutch). English, French and Portuguese are important languages: 130, 115 and 20 million speak them as secondary in general.

2. Official Languages

In many African countries, there are several official languages. Besides the former colonial languages of English, French, Portuguese, and Spanish, only a few languages are official at the national level. These are:

- Arabic, in Algeria, **Comoros**, **Chad**, **Djibouti**, Egypt, **Eritrea**, **Libya**, **Mauritania**, Morocco, **Somalia**, Sudan, and Tunisia
- Swahili in Tanzania, Kenya, Uganda, Burundi, and Rwanda
- **Chichewa** in **Malawi**
- **Amharic** in Ethiopia
- Somali in Somalia
- **Tigrinya** in Eritrea (technically a working language)
- **Kinyarwanda** in Rwanda and the closely related **Kirundi** in Burundi

Ethiopian alphabet
(Photographer: Han Hong)

- **Sango** in the Central African Republic
- **Swazi** in **Swaziland** and South Africa
- **Malagasy** in Madagascar
- **Seychellois** creole in the Seychelles
- **Shona** in Zimbabwe
- Afrikaans, **Ndebele**, (isi)Xhosa, (isi)Zulu, **(se)Pedi**, **(se)Sotho**, **(se)Tswana**, (si)Swazi, **(Tshi)Venda**, and **(xi)Tsonga** in South Africa, the only multilingual country with widespread official status for its indigenous languages, in addition to English.

A signpost in both Amharic and English in Addis Ababa University (Photographer: Han Hong)

V. WRITING SYSTEMS

Although there are thousands of African languages, most of the systems used to record them originated outside the continent. A number of factors determined the writing system chosen for each language, including which system seemed to fit the language best and various social and political reasons.

1. Types of Writing Systems

There are two basic types of writing systems: **logographic** and **phonetic**. The symbols in logographic systems represent whole words or **morphemes**, units of language that cannot be broken down into smaller meaningful parts. An example would be "most", such as the words "mostly" or "almost". Phonetic systems are either **syllables**, in which symbols represent whole syllables, or alphabets, in which each symbol represents a single **vowel** or **consonant**. Most African languages use phonetic writing systems.

Roman **script**, the writing system used by English and many other European languages, is the most common script in Africa. It was spread throughout the continent by missionaries and colonial rule. European missionaries prepared the first written forms of many African languages. Later, European nations established colonies all over Africa and held power there for many years. In most places where the Roman script was introduced, it eventually replaced any previous writing systems. In most cases, administrators, educators, and publishers all preferred Roman script, which in turn influenced the general public. Roman script tends to have fewer and less complex symbols than other scripts, which gives it a real advantage over the competition.

In areas of Africa influenced by Arab culture, Arabic script is often used for writing. The Swahili language, the official language of Tanzania, developed after 700 A.D., when Arab traders mixed with east African populations. Many Swahili-speakers use an Arabic script for writing.

Very few indigenous African writing systems remain in use today. Among the most widely known are alphabets for Somali, **Wolof**, **Kpelle**, **Mende**, and **Bamum**. Most of them developed in the late 1800s and early 1900s. According to their inventors, both the **Vai** and Bamum are unrelated to either Roman or Arabic scripts. Wolof uses characters similar to Arabic, but some of the pronunciations are different.

2. Adapting Foreign Systems to African Needs

When Africans embraced foreign writing systems, they adapted the scripts to fit the specific needs of each different language. They had to make numerous adjustments. Many African languages are **tonal**, meaning that the words must be pronounced at specific **pitches** to make sense. However, very few writing systems indicate tone. In addition, a foreign script may contain symbols that represent sounds not used by the African languages, or it may lack symbols for certain sounds in the African language.

3. Writing Numbers

While Roman script is most often used for words, the **Indo-Arabic system**, adopted by Western cultures, is most commonly employed for numbers. It uses only ten symbols (0 through 9) to represent all numbers, which makes it very adaptable and convenient for calculation. Other systems exist, however. The Arabic system has two sets of numbers as well as letters from the Arabic alphabet. The Ethiopian system is based on modified Greek symbols. Both have special symbols for 10, 20, 100, 200, 1000, and so on.

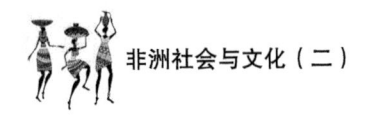

VI. GE'EZ (GI'IZ, GHEEZ)

Ge'ez was the Semitic language of the **Axumite Empire**. In the first century A.D., immigrants from south Arabic settled along the Ethiopian coastline and in the highlands, bringing with them the **Sabaean** language and script. This language eventually evolved into Ge'ez. The process by which Ge'ez became a different language no longer **intelligible** to traders from the Red Sea's east coast was gradual. Several important phonetic and **morphological** changes took place in the language during this transformation. The Ge'ez dictionary **resembles** that of **South Arabian** but many words received new and special meaning. Ge'ez is written from left to right. In the 8th century, the decline of the Axumite Empire began and was followed a century or two later by **eclipse** of Ge'ez as a spoken language, Ge'ez continued to **thrive**, however, as Ethiopia's literary and **ecclesiastical** language. In fact, the classical period of Ge'ez literature was between the 13th and 17th centuries, hundreds of years after Ge'ez had ceased being the common spoken language of highland Ethiopians.

From the end of the first **millennium** until recently, Ge'ez functioned in Ethiopia in a manner similar to that of Latin during the Middle Ages.[5] It was considered the only worthy language for literary work. The use of Ge'ez in churches and **monasteries** led to a fairly high rate of literacy in Ethiopia. Under **Zara Yakob**, for example, there was a flowering of Ge'ez literature. The language also is important to scholars because the Axumites used Ge'ez to keep the royal **chronicles** and other official and religious records. Indeed, the large number of Ge'ez **manuscripts** forms the basis of the world's understanding of Ethiopia's early history. Today, the use of Ge'ez is confined to the **Ethiopian Orthodox Church**.

VII. SWAHILI LANGUAGE

Swahili belongs to Bantu language and is one of the most widely spoken African languages. It is the official language of Tanzania and Kenya and is spoken as a lingua franca throughout most of east Africa, as well as parts of central Africa. The language is heavily influenced by Arabia—a result of the long-standing trading relationships in the region—while many **contemporary** words are adapted from English. The main dialects of Swahili, or Kiswahili, as it is also called, are Kiunguja, Kimvita, and Kiamu.

Swahili has a long tradition of literary production, and poetry has been written in Swahili since at least the middle of the 17th century. It draws on Arabic, **Persian**, and **Urdu** literary sources. Though Swahili was originally only written in Arabic script, **Latin** script became more popular in the mid-19th century and has since become standard.[6] The oldest surviving Swahili **epic** is the Hamziya, which was written by

Swahili books in a bookstore in Dar es Salaam, Tanzania
(Photographer: Sun Lihua)

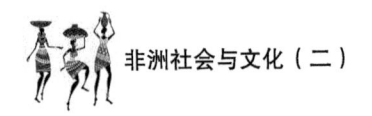

Sayyid Aidarusi in Arabic script in the old Kingozi dialect in 1749. Bwana Muku Ⅱ, the ruler of the **Island of Pate**, off the coast of present-day Kenya, **commissioned** the poem. Mwana Kupona binti Msham was a well-known poet of the 19th century, who wrote tenzi, **didactic** poems that were traditionally concerned with Islamic religious subjects and public **commentary**. This form is still used by contemporary poets such as Abdilatif Abdalla. Perhaps the most famous contemporary Swahili author is **Shaaban Robert**, a Tanzanian known for his poetry, children's literature, essays and novels. Many works of Western authors have been translated into Swahili, such as the well-known **renderings** of William Shakespeare's plays by **Julius Nyerere**.

VIII. LANGUAGE POLICY IN SOUTH AFRICA

South Africa's **sociolinguistic** landscape, as we know it today, is the result of different groups of people speaking different languages at different stages, **propelled** by **sociohistorical** forces that, to a large extent, determined the ways in which those who came later related to those who had arrived earlier. Before colonial conquest, the different peoples who at different times inhabited the present territory of the Republic of South Africa interacted with one another in both cooperative and **conflictual** ways. Their languages influenced one another, as is most evident in the clicks that characterize both the indigenous Khoisan and **Nguni** languages.

The Bantu languages **encompass** most of the languages spoken in Africa south of the Sahara. They have been spoken in the southern African region since the dawn of the modern era. With **episodic** exceptions, the languages of **Khoikhoi** and the **San** are no longer spoken in South Africa, although highly endangered varieties of these are still **extant** in Namibia, Angola, and Botswana. The **dispossession**, **bondage** or **extermination** of the speakers of these languages **inexorably** led to many of the survivors being integrated into the evolving colony and, **incidentally**, becoming **integral** to the evolution of the Afrikaans language, or being forced into the **arid** northern parts of what eventually became South Africa.

The two **Germanic** languages, Afrikaans and (South African) English, are directly traceable to the country's colonial conquest and occupation during the 17th and 19th centuries, respectively. Afrikaans, despite the often passionate debates about its real–that is, European or non-European—origins, is essentially a Dutch-based creole.[7] Other languages spoken in South Africa are **vestiges** of the mother tongues of earlier (Asian and European) or recent (most African) immigrant groups, many of whom arrived in South Africa in search of work or of a better life. Most, however, were the result of forced migrations **emanating** from economic or political pressures in their homelands. Of these, the most prominent are the **indentured** laborers who were transported to **Natal** from India between 1860 and 1913. As with the people of Indonesian, Malaysian, Indian, and east African origin, who constituted the **bulk** of the slaves that were brought to **the Cape Colony** by the **Dutch East India Company** in the 17th and 18th centuries, the linguistic result was that the **progeny** of the slaves adopted a variety of their masters' languages: Dutch (Afrikaans) at the Cape and English in Natal. Three-hundred-and-fifty years after the colonization of South Africa by Holland and Britain, the sociolinguistic map of the country has become relatively stable.

1. Language Policy Before 1910

Colonial language policy under both Dutch and British **overlords** was based on the **imperial** principle: "The natives should learn our language rather than we learn theirs." The Dutch East India Company more or less ignored the indigenous peoples' languages. Under British rule, however, especially beginning with **Lord Charles Somerset**'s governorship, a century of **Anglicization ensued**, which was specifically aimed at the Dutch/Afrikaans-speaking population. In spite of **sporadic**, but increasingly violent, resistance on the latter's part to the English—only policy, it was extremely successful.[8]

For the one-and-a-half centuries between the British occupation of the Cape in 1806 and the **Afrikaner**-led **National Party**'s victory at the (white South African) **polls** in 1948, which **inaugurated** the **Apartheid** Era, the development and use of the indigenous peoples' languages in those domains that were relevant to the colonial system—especially education and religion—were viewed as the responsibility of the Christian missionaries. Until 1910, the colonial state at the Cape and in Natal, **insofar as** it concerned itself directly with language matters, was intent on ensuring that English was the language of power and high status in all the key social domains. Resistance to British **imperialist** strategy in southern Africa was initiated from the independent **Boer** Republics[9] of the **Transvaal** and **the Orange Free State** as the direct result of the discovery of diamond and gold in the territories of those republics. Britain's policy of **annexing** the republics in order to gain control of the regions' mineral wealth **engendered antagonistic contradictions** that resulted in the Anglo-Boer War (1899–1902)[10]. From the point of view of language policy, the significance of this struggle (against Lord Alfred Milner[11]'s policy of forced Anglicization) is that it firmly **entrenched** the notions of mother tongue education among Afrikaans-speaking white South Africans. This **fixation** was to have a decisive influence on language policy and practice in the 20th century.

The missionaries, just as they did elsewhere on the African continent, reduced the indigenous languages to writing in the course of translating the Bible and the Christian **hymnal**, among other **proselytizing** texts.[12] Not only did their literacy activities open the possibilities of these languages becoming the languages of teaching and learning in modern educational institutions such as the school and the church, they also constituted an important part of the political platform on which the subsequent African groupings, and thus some of the most taken-for-granted ethnic entities of modern times, were based. Besides church and school-related texts in the African languages, the first creative works appeared in languages such as isiZulu, isiXhosa, seSotho, and seTswana from about the middle of the 19th century.

2. Union of South Africa: 1910—1948

After **the Treaty of Vereeniging** in 1902, which marked the British military victory of the Anglo-Boer War, all social policy in the British colonies, which now included the Cape Colony, Natal, and the two former Afrikaner republics of the Orange Free State and Transvaal, was geared toward the **reconciliation** of both the Boers and the British. In the domain of language policy, therefore, in spite of the immediately preceding hated policy of Lord Milner, the British **high commissioner** in the period from 1901 to 1905, both Dutch and English were **elevated** to the position of the **Union of South Africa**'s official languages. In 1925, under General James Hertzog[13]'s administration, Afrikaans became a third official language by means of an expanded definition of Dutch and gradually displaced Dutch altogether as the second official language.

This period of **segregation**, roughly between 1910 and 1945, saw the rapid advancement of Afrikaans as a public language, fueled by a combination of government and civil society **initiatives** as well as the flowering of an ethnic white Afrikaner literature.[14] In the public service, although Afrikaans gradually became more **pervasive**, most transactions and communication continued to be conducted in English. In the private sector, with the exception of the **militant** Afrikaner-empowerment **enclaves**, all activities were conducted and documented in English.[15] The indigenous African languages were mostly ignored or, at best, neglected, even though **liberal** and **philanthropic** groups, especially those motivated by their

Cape of Good Hope sign in both English and Afrikaans
(Photographer: Sun Lihua)

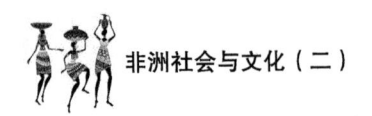

religious or educational missions, assisted individual efforts at publishing sporadic works. Virtually all non-textbook works in local African languages saw the light of day through the financial and editorial **mediation** of a mission-related enterprise.[16] One of the most **prolific** and enduring of these publishers was the **Lovedale Press**.

These publications and related developments were important for the future of the African languages, but the "mission elite", including many of the founding members of the African National Congress (**ANC**), as well as other formally educated black South Africans became almost completely oriented toward English as the language of **aspiration**.[17] It came to be viewed as the language of political unity and later of liberation.

3. The Apartheid Era

In the domain of language policy, as in most other domains, apartheid amounted to the formal legal **institutionalization** of the racial order and the intensification of the social practices of the segregation era. This had the **paradoxical** consequence that much more attention was given to African languages **given** apartheid's emphasis on defining South Africa's population along racial and ethnic lines. At the same time, Africans were deprived of the necessary material and skilled human resources, through inferior black education and the **relegation** of Africans to low-paying, unskilled work and professions, that would have made it possible for at least some of them to **emulate** "the miracle of Afrikaans" that was transformed into a dominant language by virtue of the **prevalence** of wealthy, educated Afrikaners in top business and government positions. In language terms, the National Party's victory in the elections of 1948 marked the final acknowledgment of Afrikaans as a public language of high status. This party's entire history up to 1990 can be read in terms of a strategy to Afrikanerize South African society by, among other things, making Afrikaans equal to English as the preferred official language in the public sector.[18] By the mid-1960s, there were five **fully-fledged** Afrikaans-medium universities. There were also vibrant if mostly racist and **reactionary** radio and print media along with many giant

Unit VIII African Languages

private and **parastatal** corporations with a decidedly Afrikaans orientation.

With regard to the African languages, the situation was very different and much more complex. They were deliberately developed as Ausbau languages–that is, even where it was possible in either linguistic or political terms to allow the varieties of a particular language **cluster** or subgroup, such as the Nguni group, to **converge** into a more embracing standard written form, these languages were systematically kept separate through **lexical** and other **corpus**-planning **maneuvers**. This was an integral aspect of the more general policy of using linguistic diversity to divide and rule people who were being driven into unity by the apartheid state's **oppressive** racist policies. For the same reason, the universally valid and generally applied **pedagogical** principle of mother tongue education was not only abused in this way but came to be associated in the minds of native speakers of the indigenous languages with the **inculcation** of an inferior, racist, and divisive **curriculum**. Bantu education was the most devastating **blight** to affect South African life in the second half of the 20th century. The African languages were deliberately starved of essential material and human resources so that they could not in any sense become languages of real power. There were very few teachers of African languages and very few texts translated into African languages. Social and political policies ensured that they remained languages of low status throughout the era of high apartheid.

Widespread and continuous resistance to Bantu education by all the forces active in the national liberation struggle **culminated** in the Soweto Student **Uprising**[19] of 1976, which was triggered by the National Party's policy of insisting that both English and Afrikaans not only had to be learned as subjects by African language-speaking pupils but also had to be used as languages of teaching (media of instruction) in the higher primary and junior secondary schools. The waves of revolutionary, antiapartheid **mobilization** that followed the uprising **heralded** the end of the policy of Afrikaans and English as the media of instruction and, in the early 1980s, gave rise to **grassroots** educational movements that were inspired and mostly organized by Black Consciousness Movement[20] activists. One **manifestation** of this movement was a strategic move in 1983 to systematically address the language question in South Africa. The **ephemeral** Education Coordinating Council of South Africa was created, and one of its initiatives, the National Language Project, came to play a significant **catalytic** role in language policy debates and democratic language policy formulation in the years leading up to and immediately after the negotiations that gave birth to the new South Africa in 1994.

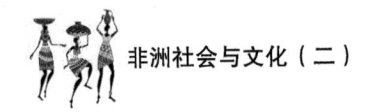

By the time the negotiations between the African National Congress and the Afrikaner **nationalists** began, waiting in the wings were two sets of language policy and planning specialists. On the Afrikaner side were men and women who in practice and in some cases with deep theoretical understandings had been planning language and formulating policy in the apartheid **regime**'s interest. On the side of the liberation movement were those who, because of the consequences of Bantu education, had to learn about language planning as an instrument of liberation.

Without Afrikaner insistence on the maintenance of equality between English and Afrikaans, it is unlikely that postapartheid South Africa would have ended up with the democratic language **provisions** that **adorn** its **Constitution**. These are reflected in legislation such as the Pan South African Language Board Act of 1995 (amended in 1999), the Language in Education Policy of the National Education Policy Act (1996), and the National Language Policy Framework (2002). Like most other postcolonial African elites, the representatives of the African majority at the negotiations, with some exceptions but including the ANC, would probably have chosen the path of one official language, that is, English, rather than the apparently **impracticable** final decision to have 11 official languages.

4. Language Policy in Postapartheid South Africa

As the result of Afrikaner **intransigence** on the language question, the new South Africa not only has 11 official languages but one of the most **progressive** sets of constitutional provisions on language. In terms of Section 6 of the Constitution (Act 108 of 1996), the official languages are: Afrikaans (13.3%), English (8.2%), isiNdebele (1.6%), isiXhosa (17.6%), isiZulu (23.8%), sePedi (9.4%), seSotho

(7.9%), wseTswana (8.2%), siSwati (2.7%), tshiVenda (2.3%), and xiTsonga (4.4%). Other significant sections of the Constitution protect and promote the right of the individual or the relevant "linguistic community" to use their mother tongue or another official language of their choice in all interactions among themselves as well as between themselves and the state.

Because of the **hegemonic pro-English** attitudes that prevail among most of the middle-class elites and other formally educated South Africans, with the significant exception of a majority of Afrikaans-speaking citizens in these categories, the translation of these provisions into daily practice has been **beset** with serious problems. The shaping of a genuinely democratic multilingual language policy and practice reflecting the values and the aspirations of the Constitution will require decades, perhaps even generations, of **see-saw** progress.

Since democratization, the beginnings of the **requisite** language infrastructure have been put in place:

The Pan South African Language Board (PANSALB), representatives of all the official languages as well as the South African **sign language**, responsible for advising government on language policy;

Nine Provincial Language Committees, whose main task is to represent PANSALB and to **oversee** the implementation of official language policy at the provincial level;

Thirteen National Language Bodies, whose main task is to promote the corpus development of their respective languages; and Eleven **Lexicographic** Units, each of which ultimately creates and maintains a comprehensive **monolingual** explanatory dictionary for the respective language.

Except for the South African Broadcasting Corporation, which has an improving record as far as the use of indigenous languages, most media, the public sector, and the vital **tertiary** education sector have tended to join the slide toward a **unilingual** public policy delivery, in spite of the fact that this **disposition** favors the English-speaking elite and thus deepens the **asymmetry** of power relations in South Africa. Because each province has its own official language, the Provincial

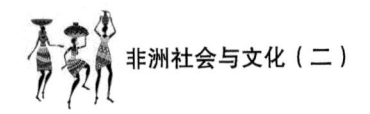

Language Committees play a potentially decisive role with respect to developments on the ground. In practice, however, few of them have the necessary skills and resources at present, and the **de facto** language policy in most provinces is a **laissez-faire** English mainly policy.

The key challenges that have to be addressed at the beginning of the 21st century are the increasing **hegemony** of English; the need to raise literacy levels by means of, among other things, the successful implementation of appropriate language-medium policies in both the schools and the universities; and the need to demonstrate the positive relationship between functional multilingualism and economic efficiency and productivity. The inculcation and **nurturing** of a culture of reading in African Languages is the key to all of these issues.

Unit VIII　African Languages

Explanations

［1］**The number of people who speak a particular language within these five linguistic families ranges from a few hundreds to millions:** 这五个语系各自包含很多不同种类的语言，各种语言的使用者数量不等，少则数百，多达数百万。

［2］**The Cushitic language family of eastern Africa can be found from Sudan in the north to Tanzania in the south:** 在东非地区，在北起苏丹南至坦桑尼亚的广阔土地上都有人使用库希特语族的语言。

［3］**Most scholars trace the origin of Bantu, some 2000 or 3000 years ago, to an area around present-day Nigeria and Cameroon:** 大多数学者认为：班图语支2000—3000年前来自当今尼日利亚和喀麦隆附近的某个区域。

［4］**Moreover, languages with lower status tend to borrow more from a dominant language, rather than the other way around:** 此外，两种语言会互相渗透，主要趋势是次要语言向占支配地位的语言学习借鉴。

［5］**From the end of the first millennium until recently, Ge'ez functioned in Ethiopia in a manner similar to that of Latin during the Middle Ages:** 从10世纪末开始，吉兹语成为埃塞俄比亚东正教会使用的语言，就好像拉丁语在中世纪基督教会中所起的作用。

［6］**Though Swahili was originally only written in Arabic script, Latin script became more popular in the mid-19th century and has since become standard**：起初，人们用阿拉伯字母书写斯瓦希里语。到了19世纪中期，拉丁字母开始流行起来，从此成为斯语的标准书写形式。

［7］**Afrikaans, despite the often passionate debates about its real–that is, European or non-European–origins, is essentially a Dutch-based creole:** 尽管关于阿非利堪斯语是否来源于欧洲存在着激烈的争论，阿语基本上是一种以荷兰语为基础的克里奥语。

［8］**In spite of sporadic, but increasingly violent, resistance on the latter's part to the English-only policy, it was extremely successful:** 英国殖民政

府在南非推行的英语化政策仅仅遭到来自阿非利卡人的反抗，反抗时断时续，但是逐步升级。该政策总体而言非常成功。

[9] **Boer Republics:** 布尔共和国是由来自南非开普省，说荷兰语的人及其后代建立的自治共和国。它们分布在今天南非的中部、北部、东北部和东部地区。其中最著名的两个就是德兰士瓦共和国（Transvaal）和奥兰治自由邦（Orange Free State）。

[10] **Anglo-Boer War (1899—1902):** （第二次）"英布战争"又称"布尔战争"或"南非战争"，是指1899年10月11日至1902年5月31日之间，英国殖民者和布尔人为了争夺对钻石矿和金矿的垄断权、争夺南非地区霸权而进行的一场战争。战争一共持续了两年零7个月，以布尔人的失败而告终，但是交战双方都付出了惨重代价。经过这次战争，布尔人之间的民族凝聚力进一步加强，经历了长期演化和认同过程之后终于形成了阿非利卡族。在"英布战争"之后，英国在南部非洲的殖民地连成一片，控制了通向非洲大湖区的通道。好望角地区以广袤的南非腹地为依托，成为大英帝国（the British Empire）最重要的前哨基地之一。来自南非的黄金使得伦敦迅速成为全球金融业和黄金交易的中心。但是，这场战争也标志着英国海外扩张的终结。战争的高昂代价迫使英国放弃孤立政策，在全球范围内开始战略收缩。

[11] **Alfred Milner:** 阿尔弗雷德·米尔纳勋爵（1854—1925）是英国政治家、殖民地统治者。在19世纪90年代中期到20世纪20年代初期，他参与制定了英国许多重要的国内外政策。在很大程度上，正是他的错误外交政策才引发了第二次"英布战争"。

[12] **The missionaries, just as they did elsewhere on the African continent, reduced the indigenous languages to writing in the course of translating the Bible and the Christian hymnal, among other proselytizing texts:** 传教士们在非洲大陆各地的所作所为如出一辙——对于他们而言，本土非洲语言的唯一价值就是便于传播基督教，因此他们致力于将《圣经》、赞美诗集和其他基督教文献翻译成所在地区的非洲语言。

[13] **James Hertzog:** 詹姆斯·赫洛（1866—1942）是南非政治家、军人。在第二次"英布战争"期间，他担任布尔人的将军。1924—1939年期

间，他担任南非联邦（the Union of South Africa）首相。他一生都致力于推动阿非利堪斯文化的传播和发展，保护阿非利卡人不受英国人的影响。

[14] **This period of segregation, roughly between 1910 and 1945, saw the rapid advancement of Afrikaans as a public language, fueled by a combination of government and civil society initiatives as well as the flowering of an ethnic white Afrikaner literature:** 大约在1910—1945年，由于南非政府推行种族隔离政策，阿非利堪斯语的地位迅速上升，成为一门公共语言。政府和公民社会的新政策，以及欣欣向荣的阿非利堪斯语文学也提升了阿语的地位。

[15] **In the private sector, with the exception of the militant Afrikaner-empowerment enclaves, all activities were conducted and documented in English:** 在私人领域，阿非利堪斯语除了在激进的阿非利卡人赋权领域使用以外，所有活动的开展和记录都离不开英语。

[16] **Virtually all non-textbook works in local African languages saw the light of day through the financial and editorial mediation of a mission-related enterprise:** 由于一个有基督教背景的企业在财务和编辑两方面所做的努力，用非洲语言出版非课本著作终于有了希望。

[17] **…including many of the founding members of the African National Congress (ANC), as well as other formally educated black South Africans became almost completely oriented toward English as the language of aspiration:** 许多非国大创始人，以及其他接受过正规教育的南非黑人都倾向于通过英语来实现自己的人生梦想。

[18] **This party's entire history up to 1990 can be read in terms of a strategy to Afrikanerize South African society by, among other things, making Afrikaans equal to English as the preferred official language in the public sector:** 从创建之日起到1990年，南非国民党的整部历史都可以归结为一点"将南非社会阿非利堪斯语化"。手段之一就是使阿非利堪斯语成为和英语同等重要的官方语言。

[19] **Soweto Student Uprising:** "索韦托学生起义"——1976年6月16日，

南非索韦托镇近两万名黑人中小学生举行大规模示威游行，抗议白人当局"在黑人学校使用阿非利堪斯语作为教学语言"的规定。南非白人当局的血腥镇压激起了广大黑人的愤怒情绪，斗争迅速扩展到南非大部分地区。当局出动上千名军警进行血腥镇压，先后造成176人死亡，上千人受伤。这是自1910年南非联邦成立以来，黑人群众与警察之间最严重的暴力冲突事件。索韦托学生起义成为南非人民反抗种族隔离制度的象征和转折点，扭转了整个南非的命运。该事件引起了国际社会的广泛关注——联合国安理会举行紧急会议，谴责南非当局镇压黑人学生的暴行；国际社会也纷纷予以谴责，并对南非实施各种制裁。此后，南非人民要求释放政治犯、解除对政治团体的禁令、成立南非民主政权的呼声日益高涨，直到种族隔离制度被彻底废除。

[20] **Black Consciousness Movement**："南非黑人觉醒运动"兴起于20世纪60年代末，开始时只是一种影响有限的思潮，在轰轰烈烈的反种族隔离、反种族歧视的群众性抗暴斗争中得到传播。70年代初、中期出现了数十个以黑人觉醒思想为指南的黑人群众组织，统称为"黑人觉醒运动"，其中坚力量是黑人学生。黑人觉醒运动的兴起和发展起了动员、教育和组织群众的作用，把沉寂了将近10年的南非被压迫民族争取民族解放的斗争推向新高潮。

Exercises

I. Read the following statements and decide whether they are true (T) or false (F).

_____ 1. With more than 2,000 different languages, Africa boasts greater linguistic variety than any other continent.

_____ 2. The Semitic language group, which includes Arabic, boasts the greatest number of speakers.

_____ 3. Hausa, with about 40 million speakers throughout eastern Africa, is the most widespread language in the Semitic language group.

_____ 4. Fulani, the language ranging over the widest area, is found throughout Africa.

_____ 5. The Bantu languages are the most widespread of any linguistic group in Africa.

_____ 6. A much smaller percentage of the indigenous population in French colonies was illiterate than in British colonies.

_____ 7. Although there are thousands of African languages, most of the systems used to record them originated outside the continent.

_____ 8. Swahili is the official language of Tanzania and Kenya and is spoken as a lingua franca throughout most of west Africa.

_____ 9. A century of Anglicization in South Africa was specifically aimed at black population in general.

_____ 10. The Treaty of Vereeniging in 1902 marked the Boer Republics' military victory of the Anglo-Boer War.

II. Fill in the following blanks with words that best complete the sentences.

1. The tremendous linguistic range in Africa includes major languages such as _____ and _____, spoken by millions of people, and minor languages such as Hazda, which have fewer than a thousand speakers.

2. The Afroasiatic languages consist of about 230 modern and a dozen dead (no longer spoken) languages that originated in northern and eastern _____ and in western _____.

3. Khoisan languages are restricted to southern Africa, particular in present-day _____ and _____.

4. Creole languages are usually based on the vocabulary and grammar of the _____ language, but they include many features of the _____ language.

5. Pidgin languages differ from creoles in that they generally have no _____ speakers, are used for _____ purposes such as trade, and have less complex grammatical structures.

6. Some countries use African language for government business. In _____ and

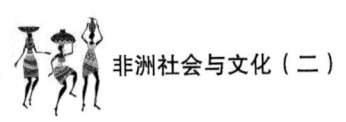

_____, Swahili has become the official language because it is widely spoken.

7. The 11 official languages of South Africa are: _____, Ndebele, (isi)Xhosa, (isi)Zulu, (se)Pedi, (se)Sotho, (se)Tswana, (si)Swazi, (Tshi)Venda, and (xi)Tsonga in addition to _____.

8. Many African languages are _____, meaning that the words must be pronounced at specific _____ to make sense.

9. The _____ languages encompass most of the languages spoken in Africa _____ of the Sahara.

10. Resistance to British imperialist strategy in southern Africa was initiated from the independent Boer Republics of the Transvaal and the Orange Free State as the direct result of the discovery of _____ and _____ in the territories of those republics.

Review and Reflect

- What a role does a language play in its culture?
- What do you think of the future of African languages?
- Do you think it necessary to have some knowledge of an African language? Why or why not?

Unit IX African Foods

　　非洲饮食丰富多彩。这里的食品多为天然有机食品，营养丰富，具有很强的地域多样性和民族独特性，同时大量吸收了来自亚洲（尤其是阿拉伯国家、东南亚、南亚）、欧洲（英国、法国、意大利、葡萄牙、荷兰等）和美洲的异域饮食元素。东非风格的"煎饼"英吉拉松软可口，南非的什锦香锅鲜香酣畅，西非风情的花生糊醇厚诱人，还有历史悠久、全民共享的埃塞俄比亚"咖啡道"……读完本章"舌尖上的非洲"，你必不会与这些美味佳肴擦肩而过！

A variety of beans in buckets and round wash bowls in a market in Malawi
(Photographer: Du Fengyan)

"The image of Africa is focused too much on hunger. People also eat, and they eat well."

—Tierno Monenembo, Guinean writer

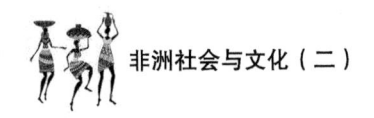

> **Think and Talk**
> ☆ Have you ever heard of or tried any African food?
> ☆ Where did coffee originate according to your knowledge?
> ☆ African foods have taken in many foreign elements. Which countries do you think have exerted their influence on African foods? Why?

I. OVERVIEW

From the soft injera[1] of Ethiopia and Eritrea to the dried **caterpillar** of the Congo, African foods and eating habits vary according to the local resources available. Religion and custom also play a crucial role in determining **dietary** patterns. Throughout Africa, the way people live influences what they eat. The diets of a **nomadic herder**, a farmer, and a city **dweller** are likely to be significantly different.

There are many misconceptions about African food. Africa is frequently viewed as a place with nothing to offer but starvation, **misery** and **strife**. Nothing could be further from the truth.[2] With more than 50 countries and hundreds of **ethnic groups** on this vast land, Africa boasts plentiful and varied food traditions. African food is natural, healthy and full of nutrients.

African food culture is dynamic, which has constantly **incorporated** new foods into the farming system and diet through the ages. In many areas, traders and **colonists** from other continents introduced new foods and ways of producing them. Tomato, for example, was brought from **the New World** by the Portuguese in the 16th century, and is now cultivated and consumed throughout much of Africa. In coastal East Africa, **spices** from Asia and the Middle East **flavor** the **sauces** served on rice and fish. Nowadays, eating habits are changing as more people begin to live in cities, and imported and fast foods become more widely available.

Unit IX   African Foods

A variety of spices in a market in Harar, Ethiopia
(Photographer: Han Hong)

II. WHAT DO AFRICANS EAT AND DRINK?

African **cuisine** is basically a rural one, derived from a rural way of life. Much of Africa's large agricultural population is still growing, preparing, and consuming foods in traditional ways. Although traditional foods vary from region to region, certain **staples** can be found throughout most of Africa. Common African foods tend to be organically grown and without artificial **additives**.

The foods and **beverages** vary by geographic regions. Most African diets are based on **cereals** (or grains) or **tubers**. Because rainfall determines where crops and plants can be grown, climate affects what kind of foods the people of a region consume. Grain is more common in drier zones, while tubers are the staple foods in humid and forest areas. Meat, **dairy products**, vegetables, and fruits add variety and **supplement** the nutritional value. Milk and dairy products are absent in the humid **tropics**, because the climate is **unfavorable** for cattle, while they are part of the cattle-owning **nomads** and farmers of the **Sahel** and East African highlands.[3] The main cooking oils are peanut oil, **palm** oil, **sesame** oil, and butter made from **shea nuts**.

1. Grains

The core of most meals in **Sub-Saharan Africa** is **starchy porridge** made from cereals or tubers, accompanied by a soup or **stew** of cooked vegetables or crushed pea-

Seswaa from Botswana
(Photographer: Sun Lihua)

nuts. If a household can afford meat or fish, the soup or stew may contain pieces of these protein sources as well. The **recipe** itself varies depending on the region. Along the coastline, people mix fish into the soup or stew; while in the middle of the continent, they use meat. The soups or stews are also flavored with different spices that are regional in nature. Soups or stews tend to be cooked for a long time until meat falls apart and vegetables become thick sauce.

Common grains include **maize** (or corn), **millet**, **sorghum**, **barley**, and wheat, which are usually ground into flour. In Ethiopia, a kind of staple **pancake**-like bread called "injera" is made from a kind of grain with limited production called "**teff**". Maize, or corn, is now cultivated in most parts of Africa. It was brought to Africa from America in the 1500s, as were tomato, **chili pepper**, and cassava[4]. A root vegetable with starchy flesh that can be easily **pounded** into **edible paste** after it is boiled, cassava has spread widely through Africa and is becoming an essential staple. **Plantains**, which are similar to bananas, but firmer and less sweet, can also be easily processed into flour, which is often boiled or fried.

2. Meat and Dairy Products

Meat is rare in some regions of Africa and very common in others. Common meat involves chicken, beef, mutton and lamb. Cattle cannot survive in rain forest areas because of disease carried by flies, but milk and dairy products are part of the diet of cattle-herding people in other regions. In many areas, people do not routinely kill domestic animals just for cooking other than **fowls**. Instead, the animals are offered as **sacrifices** to gods or ancestors, whose meats are eaten as part of the **ritual**.

Unit IX   African Foods

Raw beef is a delicacy on Tigray weddings, Ethiopia
(Photographer: Sun Lihua)

In Ethiopia, beef is very common and is often present at celebratory gatherings. Fresh beef is sometimes served raw with **condiments**. In South Africa, a spicy dried **jerky** is commonly eaten alone or used in cooking. Many people in West Africa combine meat and fish to create **savory** stews.

In some areas, people hunt **games** for food items, such as **bushpigs**, **antelopes**, monkeys and snails (especially in the rain forest), etc. People who live near the ocean or along inland waterways eat various types of seafood frequently, including fish, **calamaris**, **crabs**, **shrimps**, **lobsters**, **prawns**, **mussels** and **oysters**.

3. Vegetables and Fruits

African vegetables and fruits are eaten fresh or used as an **ingredient** in cooking. African salads don't necessarily involve a lot of green vegetables, but instead feature plantains, **bell peppers**, onions, **avocados** and cucumbers, etc.

Common vegetables include **okras**, **peppers**, onions, **pumpkins**, beans, **eggplants**, **yams**, cassava, cucumbers, and **sweet potatoes**, etc.

A mango tree bearing lots of fruits in Meru County, Kenya
(Photographer: Han Hong)

An amazing variety of fruits grow in Africa: apples, pears, bananas, plantains, mangoes, pineapples, grapes, melons, peaches, **lychees**, **sugar canes**, **figs**, **papayas**, coconuts, avocado, **apricots**, oranges, **grapefruits** and **tangerines**, etc. They are eaten raw or cooked, or made into jams. Coconut milk is used in a variety of African recipes. Most favored by women and children, fruits are especially important in remote rural areas and during times of famine.

A fruit and vegetable market
(Photographer: Sun Lihua)

4. Wild Foods

Only a few Africans still depend entirely on hunting and gathering for food. Many rural people may add wild foods to diets, including game meat, wild insects, wild fruits and edible wild herbs. Wild insects–the valuable sources of protein and vitamins, including caterpillars tasting like shrimp (in Central Africa **savanna** particularly), flying ants and locusts, are considered to be appealing **delicacy**. In woodland areas, women and children will gather many varieties of wild mushrooms, and then sell them at roadside **stands**.

5. Spices and Seasonings

African dishes often rely on strong and **flavorful** seasoning. Salt and red pepper are used widely as **seasonings**. Pepper is very common across the continent, including green peppers, chilies or **black pepper**. Common savory spices include **cinnamon, clove, ginger, nutmeg, curry, cumin,** and **coriander**. In Africa, onions or **parsley** can also be used as seasoning.

6. Beverages

Africans prepare and consume a variety of beverages ranging from coffee and tea to beer and fruit juice.

Sub-Saharan Africa has an age-old beer tradition, making it from **fermented** sorghum, millet, corn, or banana, which explains the presence of flourishing modern **breweries** producing bottled and **draft beer** in most African countries. Although large-scale commercial breweries exist, family **brewing** continues. Apart from being a pleasant beverage, beer plays an **indispensable** role in ceremonies and certain social gatherings. When neighbors lend a hand in harvesting someone's crops, they usually receive beer as a gift for their efforts.

In the forest zones the typical alcoholic beverage is palm wine, made from the fermented **sap** of palm trees. Ethiopia is well known for its mead[5], a wine fermented from honey.

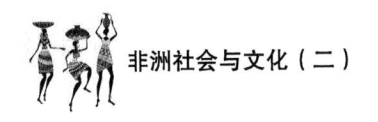

African traditional alcoholic beverages are **perishable** and have to be consumed soon after being made, which shapes its drinking customs. While many Europeans drink a small amount of alcohol on a regular basis, Africans tend to drink larger amount at one time. When a household invites neighbors and friends to share a newly made beer or wine, the guests would be expected to stay until everything is consumed.

European traders and colonists introduced **distilled liquors** such as **rum**, **gin**, brandy, and whiskey. Some cultures began using imported liquors in their rituals and social events. Beginning in the mid-1800s, however, anti-alcohol movements led colonial governments to enact strict regulations on the production, sale, and consumption of alcohol. The popularity of bottled beer has increased since 1960s. Today, breweries are among the most profitable industries in Africa, and liquor taxes form an important part of national income in many countries.

As to non-alcoholic drinks, coffee, tea, milk and **soft drink** are popular. In Ethiopia, **coffee ceremony** forms a typical part of culture. Tea with sweetened **condensed milk** and sugar was introduced by the British at the end of the 19th century, and has become a preferred drink in the Anglophone countries[6]. In the Francophone countries[7], coffee with milk, often combined with a piece of bread, is quite popular. South Africans enjoy mango and pineapple juice.

III. FOODS AROUND AFRICA

The continent of Africa is the second largest landmass on the earth, and is home to hundreds of different ethnic groups. This diversity is exactly reflected in the many local distinctive cuisines in terms of choice of ingredients, style of preparation and cooking techniques.

Traditionally, various cuisines of Africa use a combination of locally available grains, meat, vegetables, fruits, and dairy products. Depending on the regions, there are also quite significant differences in eating and drinking customs: east Africa,

Unit IX African Foods

west Africa, southern Africa and central Africa, with their own distinctive dishes, preparation techniques, and consumption customs.

1. East Africa

The cuisine of East Africa varies from area to area. In the inland savanna, the traditional cuisine of cattle-keeping people is distinctive in that meat is generally absent. Cattle, sheep and goats are regarded as a form of **currency** and a store of wealth, and are thus not generally consumed as foods. In some areas, people may consume the milk and blood of cattle, but rarely the meat. Elsewhere, other peoples are farmers who grow a variety of grains and vegetables. In **Uganda**, **steamed** green bananas are consumed as staple food.

Around 1 000 years ago, Arabs settled in the coastal areas of east Africa, whose influence is especially reflected in coastal cuisine—steamed rice with **pomegranate** juice and spices in **Persian** style: **saffron**, cloves, cinnamon, etc.

Several centuries later, Portuguese came and introduced techniques of **roasting**, **marinating**, and the use of spices turning the **bland** diet into **aromatic** dishes. Portuguese also brought from their Asian colonies fruits like oranges, lemons, and **limes**. From their colonies in the New World, Portuguese brought exotic items like chilies, peppers, maize, tomatoes, pineapples, bananas, and domestic pigs, all of which have become common elements in African foods. Later the British and Indians came, both bringing their foods, like Indian curries, **lentil** soups, and a variety of **pickles**.

The main traditional dish in Ethiopia and Eritrea is injera. Eritrean and Ethiopian cuisines (especially in the northern half of Ethiopia) are very similar, given the shared history of the two neighboring countries. Traditional Ethiopian cuisine employs no pork or **shellfish**, as they are forbidden in Islamic, Jewish, and **Ethiopian Orthodox Christian** faiths.

Somali cuisine consists of an exotic mixture of diverse **culinary** influences, which is the product of Somali's rich tradition of trade and commerce. Despite the variety, there remains one thing that unites various regional cuisines: all food is served halal[8]. There are therefore no pork dishes, alcohol, and blood. Varieties of rice usually serve as the main dish, and spices like cumin, **cardamom**, cloves, cinnamon and **sage** are used to **aromatize**. Somalis serve dinner as late as 9 pm. During Ramadan[9], dinner is often served after prayers–sometimes even as late as 11 pm.

"**Halva**" is a popular **confection** served during special occasions such as **Eid** celebrations or wedding receptions. It is made from sugar, corn **starch**, cardamom powder, nutmeg powder, and **ghee**, and peanuts are also sometimes added to enhance its **texture** and flavor.

Ugali[10]

"Ugali" is the East African version of West Africa's "**fufu**". It is a dish of maize or corn flour cooked with water into a kind of firm **dough**. The traditional method of eating it is to roll a piece of it into a ball with the right hand, and then **dip** the ball into a stew or sauce. "Ugali" is relatively inexpensive and is easy to make. It is the most common staple starch featured in the local cuisines of East Africa and Southern Africa, whose name varies with specific regions.

Ugali is being made of yellow corn powder
(Photographer: Han Hong)

Injera

Injera is a famous and typical Ethiopian and Eritrean dish, which is a large flat pancake with **spongy** texture and uniquely sour taste. This national dish is eaten daily in virtually every household in these 2 countries, whose preparing process requires considerable time and resources.

The most valued grain used to make injera is the tiny and **iron-rich** "teff".

However, its production is limited to **Ethiopian Highlands** with adequate rainfall, so it is relatively expensive for the average household. As a result, corn, wheat, barley, sorghum, or rice flour are sometimes used to replace the valuable teff.

Making

In making injera, teff flour is mixed with water and then fermented for 3 or 4 days, producing a mildly sour taste. Then it is poured onto the baking surface, either on a special electric stove or, more commonly, on a large clay plate placed over a fire. The bottom part, which touches the heating surface, will have a relatively smooth texture; while the top will become **porous**, making it easy to **scoop up** and absorb meat, vegetables, and sauces.

Ingera and a variety of wat served in Habeshe Restaurant, Ethiopia
(Photographer: Han Hong)

Eating

When eating, diners generally share food from a very large tray placed in the centre of a low dining table. Numerous thin injera pancakes are neatly layered on this tray and topped with various meat, vegetables and sauces. People do not eat with **utensils**, but instead use their right hands. Diners break into the pancakes in front of them, tear them off into small pieces and then use the pieces to grasp the meat, vegetables, and sauces for eating. Injera is thus **simultaneously** food, eating utensil, and plate. When the entire "tablecloth" of injera is gone, the meal is over.

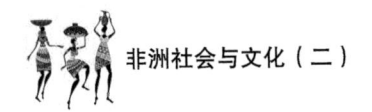

It's similar **variants** are eaten in Somalia, **Djibouti**, Yemen, Sudan and other African countries, whose names vary with specific areas. Outside East Africa, injera may be found in **grocery stores** and restaurants specializing in Eritrean, Ethiopian, or Somali foods.

Coffee ceremony in Ethiopia

A coffee ceremony is a traditional and ritualized form of making, serving and drinking coffee, usually after a big meal. It is one of the most recognizable parts of Ethiopian culture, which is offered to visiting friends, during **festivities**, or as a daily staple of life. If coffee is politely declined by the guest, then most likely tea will be served.

Making

First the host or hostess roasts the green coffee beans over hot coals in a **braizer**, right in front of guests. Once the coffee beans are roasted ready, each participant is given an opportunity to sample the aromatic scent by **wafting** the roasting smoke throughout the whole room. This is followed by the grinding of roasted coffee beans in a wooden **mortar** and **pestle**. **Coffee grounds** are then put into a clay boiling pot "**jebena**", with a **spherical** base, a neck and a pouring **spout**, and a handle where the neck connects with the base. When

Jebena-clay coffee pot
(Photographer: Sun Lihua)

the coffee boils up through the neck, it is poured in and out of another container to cool down, and then is put back into the boiling pot until next boiling. To pour the coffee from the boiling pot, a **filter** made from **horsehair** or other materials is placed in the spout of the boiling pot to prevent coffee grounds from escaping.

Unit IX African Foods

Serving

The host or hostess pours out coffee for all participants by moving the **tilted** boiling pot over a tray with small, handleless cups without stop until each cup is full. One extra cup is poured each time. The grounds are brewed three times: the first round of coffee is called "awel", the second "kalei", and the third "bereka" (meaning "to be blessed").

Drinking

People add sugar to their coffee, or in the countryside, sometimes salt and/or traditional butter. Snacks, such as popcorns, **toasted** barleys, or peanuts, are often served. The whole coffee ceremony may be accompanied by burning various traditional **incenses** such as **frankincense** or **gum arabic**. In most households, a dedicated coffee area is surrounded by fresh grass, with special furniture for the coffee maker.

2. West Africa

West African cuisine **encompasses** a diverse range of foods that are split between its 16 countries. The history of west Africa plays a critical role in their

A woman in the middle carrying plantains on her head
(Photographer: Sun Lihua)

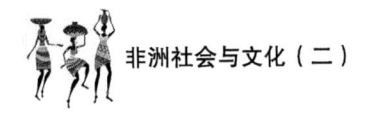

cuisines and recipes, as interactions with different cultures (particularly the Arab world and later Europe) over the centuries have introduced many foreign ingredients that would go on to become key **components** today.

The local cuisines and recipes of West Africa continue to remain deeply **entrenched** in the local customs and traditions, with ingredients like native rice, millet, sorghum, and **groundnuts**, **black-eyed beans**, brown beans, and root vegetables such as yams, **cocoyams**, sweet potatoes, and cassava.

A typical West African meal is heavy with starchy items, meat, spices and flavors. A wide array of staples are eaten across the region, including "fufu", "kenkey"[11] (a kind of maize dough), "couscous"[12], and "garri"[13] (cassava dough) which are all served alongside stews and soups. "Fufu" is often made from cereal grains like millet and sorghum; starchy root vegetables like yams and cassavas; or fruits like plantains. The staple grain varies from region to region and ethnic group to ethnic group, although corn has gained significant ground as it is cheap, **swells** to greater volumes and creates a beautiful white final product that is desired. Rice dishes are also widely eaten in the region, especially in the dry Sahel belt[14] inland.

Centuries before the influence of Europeans, West African people were trading with the Arab world, and spices like cinnamon, cloves, and **mint** were not unknown and became part of the local **flavorings**. Centuries later, the Portuguese, the French and the British influenced the regional cuisine, but only to a limited extent. However, it was European explorers who introduced peanuts, corn, cassavas, and plantains, along with chili peppers or chilies and tomatoes from the New World, and both of them have become **ubiquitous** components in West African cuisines.

Dietary pattern and cooking techniques of West Africa are changing. In the past, people ate much less meat and used native oils (palm oil on the coast and shea butter in Sahel belt). Baobab[15] leaves and numerous local green vegetables were everyday staples during certain times of the year. Today's diet is much heavier in meat, salt, and fats. Many dishes combine meat and fish, including dried and fermented fish. **Flaked** and dried fish is often fried in oil, and sometimes with hot peppers, onions, tomatoes and various spices to prepare a highly flavored stew. In some areas, chicken, eggs, beef, mutton, and goat meat are preferred. "Suya"[16], a popular **grilled** spicy meat "kebab"[17] flavored with peanuts and other spices, is sold by street **vendors** as a tasty snack or evening meal and is typically made with beef or chicken.

With regard to beverages, water has a very strong ritual significance in many West African nations (particularly in dry areas), and water is often the first thing an African host or hostess will offer his or her guest. Palm wine is also a common beverage made from fermented sap of various types of palm trees and is usually sold in sweet (less-fermented, retaining more sap sugar) or sour (fermented longer, making it stronger and less sweet) varieties. Millet beer is another common beverage.

Groundnut stew

Groundnut stew or "maafe" is a peanut-based stew common to much of west Africa and central Africa, particularly since the huge expansion of groundnut cultivation during the colonial period. Recipes for the stew vary wildly, but groundnut stew at its core is cooked with a sauce based on groundnut paste, tomatoes, onions and chilies, and common protein components are mutton, lamb, beef or chicken. In the coastal regions of **Senegal**, it is frequently made with fish. It is traditionally served with white rice, "couscous" or "fufu" and sweet potatoes in the more tropical areas.

Jollof rice

Jollof rice, also called "benachin", is a popular dish all over West Africa. It was **originated** in Senegal but has since spread to the whole of West Africa, especially **Nigeria** and **Ghana** among members of the "**Wolof**" ethnic group, from whom the word "jollof" originated. There are many variations of jollof rice. The most common basic ingredients are rice, tomatoes and/or tomato paste, onions, salt, red or chili peppers, and spices (such as nutmeg, ginger, **Guinea pepper**, or cumin). Beyond that, nearly any kind of meat, fish, vegetables, or spices can be added.

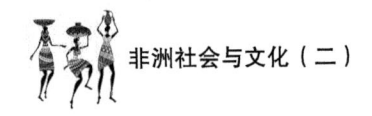

3. Southern Africa

The cooking of Southern Africa is sometimes called "rainbow cuisine", as the food in this region is a **blend** of many cultures—the indigenous African tribal societies, Europe, Asia and America. To understand indigenous cuisine, it is important first to understand the various native peoples of southern Africa.

The indigenous people here are roughly divided into 2 groups and several sub-groups. The largest group consisted of **Bantu-speakers**, whose **descendants** today may identify themselves by various sub-groups. They arrived in the region around 2 000 years ago, who grew grain crops extensively and raised cattle, sheep and goats. They also grew pumpkins, beans and leafy vegetables.

A smaller group is the **primeval** residents of the region, the **Khoisan**, who some **archaeologists** believe, had lived in the region for at least 10 000 years. The Khoisan originally were hunter-gatherers (who came to be known as "**San**" by the Bantu-speakers and as "**Bushmen**" by Europeans). After the arrival of Bantu-speakers, however, some Khoisans adopted Bantu-speakers' cattle raising, but did not grow crops. The Khoisans who raised cattle called themselves "**Khoi-Khoi**".

People were, in other words, defined to some extent by the kinds of food they ate. The Bantu-speakers ate grains, meat, milk, dairy products and vegetables, while the Khoi-Khois ate meat and milk, and the Sans hunted wild animals and gathered wild tubers and vegetables. The Khoisans ate roasted meat, and they also dried meat for later use. The influence of their diet is reflected in the Southern African love of **barbecue**.

The basic ingredients involve meat products (including wild game meat: **venison**, **ostrich**, **impala**, **poultry**, and seafood, as well as grains, vegetables and fresh fruits. **Desserts** may simply be fruits, but there are some more western style **puddings**.

Traditional beer is ubiquitous in Southern African diet, and it is a traditional **obligation** for any family to offer a visitor **copious** amount of beer. Beer brewing is done by women, and the status of a housewife in pre-colonial Southern Africa depended significantly on her skill at brewing delicious beer.

Milk is historically one of the most important components of Southern African diet. Because there is no **refrigeration**, most milk is soured into a kind of yogurt. Today, many Southern Africans enjoy drinking sour milk products that are sold in the supermarkets. On weekends they will have a meal of maize porridge and grilled meat.

Potjiekos

Seafood in a coastal restaurant
(Photographer: Sun Lihua)

In South Africa, "potjiekos", literally translated into "small pot food", is a stew prepared outdoors. It is traditionally cooked in a round, three-legged iron pot, **"potjie"**, so "potjieko" refers to the food cooked in it. It **descended from** the Dutch oven brought from the Netherlands to South Africa in the 17th century and found in the homes and villages of people throughout Southern Africa. The pot is heated using small amounts of wood or **charcoal** or, if fuel is scarce, grass, or even dried animal **dungs**.

"Potjiekos" originated with the Voortrekkers[18] during their long journey, evolving as a stew made of venison and vegetables (if available) cooked in the pot, "potjie". As trekkers (pioneers) shot wild games, they were added to the pot. The large bones were included to thicken the stew. Each day when the **wagons** stopped, the pot was placed over a fire to **simmer**. New bones replaced old, and fresh meat replaced meat eaten. Games included venison, poultry like **guinea fowls**, bushpigs, and **hares**.

The pot, with a bit of cooking oil inside, is placed on a fire until the oil has been sufficiently heated. Meat is added first, which can be anything from lamb or pork to "biltong"[19]. The meat is spiced and often a form of alcohol is added for better flavor–mostly beer, or wine (especially **sherry**). When the meat is lightly browned, vegetables like potatoes, carrots, **cabbages**, **cauliflowers** or pumpkins are added, along with whatever fruits and spices, depending on the preference of the **chef**. Little sauce or water is used, so that cooking is done by steaming and not boiling. The lid is then closed and the contents left to simmer slowly without **stirring**, so that the flavors of different ingredients could mix as little as possible. A "potjie" is usually accompanied by rice or **pasta**.

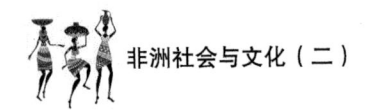

A "potjie" is not only a dish but also a relaxing social gathering, with guests sitting around chatting while the chef cooks.

4. Central Africa

Central Africa had remained largely free of culinary influences from the outside world until the late 19th century, with the exception of the widespread adaptation of cassavas, peanuts, and chili peppers which arrived along with the slave trade during the early 16th century. Central African cooking has remained mostly traditional.

The basic ingredients are plantains and cassavas. "Fufu"-like starchy foods (usually made from fermented cassavas) are served with grilled meat and sauces. Groundnut stew is also prepared here, containing chicken, okra, ginger, and other spices. Another favorite is "bambara", a porridge of rice, peanut butter and sugar. Beef and chicken are favorite meat dishes, but game meat including crocodiles, monkeys, antelopes and bushpigs are also served occasionally.

Fufu

It is often made by boiling maize, cassavas, yams or plantains, and then pounding it in a giant wooden mortar using a wooden pestle. In between blows from the pestle, the mixture is turned by hand and water is gradually added till it becomes sticky **slurry**. The mixture is then formed into a ball and served. The traditional method of eating "fufu" is to **pinch off** some of it in one's right hand fingers and form it into a small easily **ingested** ball. The ball is then dipped in soup or sauce and swallowed whole.

"Fufu" is a staple food in most parts of Sub-Saharan Africa. Foods made in this manner are known by different names in different regions. A similar staple in East Africa is called "ugali", which has been mentioned above.

IV. HOW IS FOOD PREPARED?

Africa is such an immense and diverse continent with a long history that its cooking traditions are not only native but also include imports from the Muslim world, India, and Europe as well.

1. Food Preparation

In African households, women play the key role in preparing and serving foods. They **tend** gardens; gather vegetables, fruits, and grasses; and pound grains, tubers, and nuts into usable form. Besides, they fetch water and firewood for cooking, which normally takes much longer than actual cooking time. Hunting is generally men's responsibility, although both men and women may engage in fishing. In some cultures, people of both genders own and tend flocks of domestic fowls. Young boys may be given responsibility for raising their own poultry.

In much of Africa, the staple food is prepared by using a long pestle and a standing mortar to pound grains or tubers. Porridge, eaten throughout Sub-Saharan Africa, is usually prepared by adding the pounded grain or tuber to boiling water and stirring frequently until it thickens. Cassavas, yams, or other tubers can also be **peeled** and boiled, then pounded into a thick dough. Other techniques include steaming in leaves, simmering, frying in oil, toasting or grilling over a fire, roasting, and baking in hot coals. As many African dishes are cooked over an open fire, cooking a meal often involves gathering fuel for the fire as well as preparing the ingredients. The main fuel for cooking in most households is wood, supplemented with crop **residues** and sometimes animal dungs.

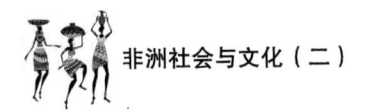

Africans use a variety of techniques to preserve foods for future use. Farmers often keep plants such as cassavas in the ground until needed to prevent **spoilage**. Fish is usually salted for long-term storage, and meat is dried. People also dry some vegetables and fruits, such as tomatoes and mango slices.

2. What's Not Used?

A few things are generally missing from African cooking. Western style **yeast-raised** breads, **white potatoes**, eggs and cheese have little place in cookbooks. Because huge groups of the continent are Muslims, pork is not as prominent in the diet as it is in the rest of the world. And sweet baked **pastry** desserts, like cakes, cookies or pies, usually don't end an African meal. Plentiful and cheap fresh fruits serve that purpose instead.[20]

V. EATING CUSTOMS

In all societies, food is both a source of nutrition and a part of culture. The customs that groups of people have for preparing, serving, and consuming food form an essential part of their shared tradition.

Foods served in Two Oceans Restaurant in the Cape of Good Hope Nature Reserve, South Africa
(Photographer: Sun Lihua)

Unit IX African Foods

1. Eating Habits

Throughout Africa, learning the rules of eating and sharing foods within the household is an essential experience for children. In strict Muslim families, and in many non-Muslim agricultural societies, family members will not always eat together from the same dish. Sometimes there are three eating groups: one consisting of men and older boys; one of women and very young children; and a third of older children, **supervised** by an older sister. A group that eats together may share a large bowl of food, each person taking his or her food with the right hand. Foods are not always equally **distributed**, and men often get the best part of the food, such as a good piece of meat or fish. A study in **Malawi** indicates a **priority** in food **allocation** to adult males over adult females. Boys and girls are equally fed, however. In some societies where **polygamy** exists, a man's wives take turns cooking meals for the entire household. Among other groups, each wife cooks separately for her own children and sends cooked foods to the husband.

2. Food Taboos

Food avoidance or food taboos do exist, permanently or temporarily. Individuals or groups may avoid eating particular foods for a variety of reasons. For example, Muslims do not consume pork or alcohol. Nomadic **livestock** herders have an **aversion** to fish out of their **contempt** for the way of life in fishing communities. History sometimes plays a certain role in food taboos, some foods, such as antelopes and dogs, may be avoided when they are closely associated with the history of someone's **clan**. A royal clan of the **Mamprusi** people in northern Ghana has refused to eat pigeons, believing that a pigeon once helped an ancestor to win a particular battle in the distant past.

Besides these permanent avoidances, some foods are not consumed during certain critical periods of the life cycle, such as **infancy**, pregnancy and **lactation**, or when suffering from various diseases. In some cultures, pregnant women avoid green leafy vegetables, eggs or honey out of fear that they could harm unborn children.

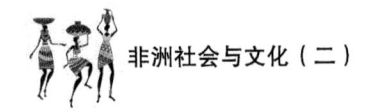

3. Colonial Influence

European influence on African food habits prior to colonialism was generally limited to the introduction of new crops or plants, such as maize and tomatoes. Colonization led to significant changes both in what foods Africans produced and what foods were available to purchase.

Imported foods intended for European settlers also made their way into African diet. Initially only a small minority of Africans, mostly the educated urban **elites**, purchase foreign and costly foods, such as bread, pasta, **margarine**, and soft drinks. In some circles, the ability to buy and serve European cuisines became a marker of social status, just like wearing western-style clothing. Certain foods, however, eventually became a part of the working-class diet. Men who **migrated** to urban areas were among the earliest regular consumers of foods like bread and tea, partly because they were cheap and convenient. Migrant laborers also helped introduce these foreign foods to rural regions by bringing them back to share with their families.

Today, regional variations in some popular European food stuffs reflect the influence of the colonial power. In the cities of Francophone West Africa, for example, people eat **baguettes** and drink coffee with milk, while in the former Italian colonies they eat pasta, and in the former British colonies square bread **loaves** and tea predominate. Although these foreign foods are no longer consumed only by an elite few, during times of economic hardship they are too expensive for the vast majority of common people.

4. Changing Food Habits

Population growth has had 2 main effects on African food habits. First, there are more mouths to be fed. Some countries have shifted from native crops such as millet and yam to cassava and maize, which produce more foods per **acre** but are less nutritious. The result is that more people can be fed, but their diet is lower in quality.

Supplies of meat and fish have also **diminished**.

The second effect of population growth is the growing demand for wood, which is the main fuel for cooking in most households. As the supply of wood declines, women must spend more time collecting wood—and perhaps change their methods of food preparation. In Malawi, for example, people **economizing on** fuel have replaced **legumes** with vegetables, which require less cooking time but provide less protein than legumes.

Other changes in food habits are the result of urban growth. In the years to come, the urban factor in African society will increase considerably; in 2000, 38% of the population lived in cities and that percentage is expected to increase to 55% by 2030, according to a United Nations study.

New food habits often develop in cities, and are likely to spread into rural areas subsequently. The urban diet is influenced by the richness of food culture of various ethnic groups, the colonial past, and the effects of modern globalization. There has been a shift since mid-1970s in dietary pattern from **coarse** grains to nontraditional grains, mainly wheat and rice. One trend is an increased demand for imported foods such as wheat (bread, pasta, biscuits, etc.), **canned** products (meat, fish, and condensed milk), hard liquor, **powdered milk** and dairy products, bottled beer and soft drinks.

Spaghetti with tomato sauce served in Samrat Hotel, Dire Dawa, Ethiopia
(Photographer: Han Hong)

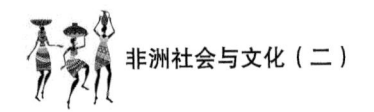

City dwellers generally enjoy a more varied diet than people who live in the country. They have access to a greater **assortment** of fruits and vegetables, more meat, and less seasonal variation, meanwhile they are also exposed to foods from other cultures. The situation may differ from country to country, however, and between those living in the **shantytowns** and in the planned urban districts. But although new food habits and new kinds of food are constantly being incorporated into urban culture, the typical diet of city people remains basically the same as that of country folks.

Another is greater individual freedom for food choices, including food consumed outside the household. One response to this new pattern is the development of street foods, especially in cities–foods and beverages served ready to eat by vendors in streets and public places. Poor urban households may find it less expensive to purchase street foods than to cook at home.

St. George Beer, a popular beer in Ethiopia
(Photographer: Han Hong)

Modern fast-food restaurants and supermarkets are **prevalent** in major African cities. The fast-food restaurant Mr. Bigg's has 130 locations in Nigeria and 2 in Ghana. Similar in concept to McDonald's, it specializes in **meat pies**. McDonald's opened its first restaurant in Africa in 1995; as of 2006, South Africa had 89 McDonald's locations. Fast food can be considered the modern but more expensive **successor** to street foods.

Unit IX African Foods

Explanations

［1］**injera**:"英吉拉"是东非埃塞俄比亚和厄立特里亚的主食。它的原材料"苔麸"是埃塞俄比亚高原的特产，颗粒小，产量低。英吉拉的做法通常是：把磨成粉末的苔麸加水和成面糊，放在容器中发酵。大约三天后，用木勺舀满面糊，均匀地浇到已经加热、抹好一层油的平底大锅上，盖上锅盖，过一会儿翻个个儿，再过三四分钟英吉拉薄饼就做好了。松软的薄饼一面光滑，另一面呈海绵状。人们把英吉拉（或者英吉拉卷）整齐地摆放在一个大篮子里，上面浇上用肉和蔬菜做成的各种配菜。大家围坐在大篮子周围，用右手揪下一小块薄饼，蘸上配菜送入口中。英吉拉的配菜叫"沃特"（wat），种类丰富，通常用小火将牛、羊或鸡肉加洋葱、西红柿、辣椒粉等调料煨制而成。

［2］**Nothing could be further from the truth**: 这种看法大错特错。

［3］**Milk and dairy products are absent in the humid tropics, because the climate is unfavorable for cattle, while they are part of the cattle-owning nomads and farmers of the Sahel and East African highlands**: 高温高湿的气候条件不利于牛的生长，所以潮湿的热带地区不产牛奶和奶制品。另一方面，在萨赫勒地带和东非高原上，牧民和农民可以养很多牛。

［4］**cassava**: 木薯是根茎类蔬菜，原产美洲，现在是非洲大部分地区的主食。其淀粉含量高，很容易有饱腹感。而且易于烹饪，可以加工成各种食物。此外，木薯叶也可以食用。

［5］**mead**:"蜂蜜酒"是把蜂蜜和水混合后，发酵成的黄色饮料，有时还含有水果、香料和谷物等成分。

［6］**Anglophone countries**：讲英语的国家。英语是非洲很多国家的官方语言，例如博茨瓦纳、加纳、肯尼亚、尼日利亚、塞拉利昂、南非、赞比亚和津巴布韦等。尽管20世纪60年代以后，曾经被英国殖民的非洲国家纷纷独立，但是前宗主国的语言却保留下来。

［7］**Francophone countries**: 讲法语的国家。同样由于历史原因，法语作为前宗主国的语言在非洲很多国家依然被广泛使用，包括中非共和国、

乍得、刚果（布）、刚果（金）、马里、毛里塔尼亚、尼日尔和塞内加尔等国。

[8] **halal**: "清真"一词源于阿拉伯语，意为"合法的"，这里指符合伊斯兰教教规的饮食。伊斯兰教的食物禁忌包括自死物、血液、猪肉、以及非诵真主之名宰杀的动物。

[9] **Ramadan**: "拉马丹"俗称"斋月"。伊斯兰教法规定，穆斯林成年男女在伊斯兰教历每年9月期间封斋1个月，每日从黎明前到日落后，禁绝饮食、房事和一切非礼行为，以省察己躬，洗涤罪过。

[10] **ugali**: "乌伽黎"是东非和南非地区流行的一种主食。用玉米粉（主要是白玉米粉）加水和成面团，然后上锅蒸制而成。配菜是用肉和蔬菜做成的炖菜。西非类似的食物富富（fufu）是用木薯粉加水和成面团做成的。

[11] **kenkey**: 在西非地区流行的一种主食，配以各种肉类、蔬菜、酱汁或汤同吃。一般是把玉米粉加水合成面团制成，有些地区也用芭蕉或木薯代替玉米粉。kenkey和ugali有相似之处，差别在于前者的面团需要两三天发酵时间，有时人们还用香蕉叶、玉米叶或锡纸裹住面团然后上锅蒸。

[12] **couscous**：" 古斯古斯"是流行于摩洛哥、阿尔及利亚、突尼斯、毛里塔尼亚和利比亚等国，以及意大利西西里岛的一种食物。它的主要食材是磨碎的、北非特有的硬粒小麦（durum wheat），这种黄黄亮亮的主食质地松散，口味独特，容易入味。上面通常浇上不同的炖菜，很像盖浇饭的吃法。

[13] **garri**: 西非地区流行的一种主食。人们把木薯剥皮捣成泥，加上棕榈油，放在透气的袋子里风干，在锅里煎熟以后食用。

[14] **Sahel belt**: 萨赫勒地带位于非洲撒哈拉沙漠南部和苏丹草原之间，横贯非洲，从大西洋东岸一直延伸到非洲东部的非洲之角。横跨9个国家，属于半干旱的草原地区，当地居民主要从事农牧业生产。

[15] **baobab**: 猴面包树是大型落叶乔木，主要分布在马达加斯加、非洲大陆以及澳洲北部地区。树干短，树冠巨大，分枝众多且姿态千奇百怪。猴面包树果实硕大，甘甜多汁，是猴子、猩猩、大象等动物最喜欢的

Unit IX　African Foods

食物。每当果实成熟的时候，猴子就会成群结队爬上树去摘果子吃，因此得名。猴面包树的果实养分充足，因而受到越来越多的青睐。

[16] **suya:** 一种在西非国家流行的辣味烤肉串，尤其深受尼日利亚人的喜爱，在尼国很多地方的大街小巷都有这种路边快餐。烤串的食材可以是牛肉、羊肉和鸡肉，也可以是腰子、肝和牛百叶等动物内脏。食材被切成块、穿成串，用盐、植物油和花生酱等调料（因地区和个人口味而异）腌制一会儿，然后上火烤。肉串的配菜通常是辣椒粉拌洋葱和西红柿。

[17] **kebab:** "土耳其烤肉"通常的做法是将切成小块的牛肉、羊肉或鸡肉穿到一根扦子上，放到炭火上烤，一边烤一边转，外层熟了就切下一层和卷饼一起吃，还可以添加蔬菜和酱料。

[18] **Voortrekkers:** 大迁徙的阿非利卡先民。阿非利卡人旧称"布尔人"（Boer），主要是荷兰移民的后代，一开始主要居住在南非沿海的开普殖民地（Cape Colony）。1835年年初开始，不满英国殖民政策，但是又无力反抗的阿非利卡人陆续离开开普殖民地，开始了一系列有组织的、大规模的迁徙，他们从南部沿海地区居家搬迁到东部、北部的内陆大草原。这场颠沛流离的旅程陆陆续续持续了4年之久，被布尔人称为"大迁徙"（Great Trek）。位于南非行政首都比勒陀利亚（Pretoria）的"先民纪念馆"（Voortrekker Monument）对这段历史有专门记载。

[19] **biltong:** 生肉干"比尔通"外层坚硬内里柔软，是南非人喝红酒时最喜欢吃的零食。做"比尔通"的食材通常是牛肉，也有用鸡肉、鱼肉、野味或者鸵鸟肉的。肉被切成小条，加上调味料（如香菜、黑胡椒、盐、醋、辣椒、洋葱末等），然后风干而成。

[20] **And sweet baked pastry desserts, like cakes, cookies or pies, usually don't end an African meal. Plentiful and cheap fresh fruits serve that purpose instead:** 非洲人饭后不吃甜点（如油酥糕点、蛋糕、曲奇饼干或者水果馅饼），他们吃充足的、价格低廉的新鲜水果。

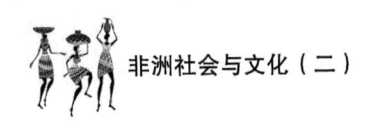

Exercises

I. Read the following statements and decide whether they are true (T) or false (F).

____ 1. Religion and custom play a crucial role in determining dietary patterns.

____ 2. Africa is rich in food resources but lack in diversity.

____ 3. African food culture is dynamic, which has constantly incorporated new foods into the farming system and diet.

____ 4. African cuisine is basically a rural one, derived from a rural way of life.

____ 5. Most African diets are based on bread and cheese.

____ 6. The core of most meals in Sub-Saharan Africa is a starchy porridge made from cereals or tubers, accompanied by a soup or stew of cooked vegetables or crushed peanuts.

____ 7. Maize is now cultivated in few parts of Africa.

____ 8. African vegetables and fruits are eaten fresh, and seldom used as an ingredient in cooking.

____ 9. Sub-Saharan Africa has an age-old beer tradition, and beer plays an indispensable role in ceremonies and certain social gatherings.

____ 10. Colonization led to significant changes both in what foods Africans produced and what foods were available to purchase.

II. Fill in the following blanks with words that best complete the sentences.

1. Tomato was brought from the New World by _____ in the 16th century, and is now cultivated and consumed throughout much of Africa.

2. Common grains in Africa include _____ (or corn), millet, sorghum, barley, and wheat, which are usually ground into _____.

3. In Ethiopia a staple pancake-like bread "injera" is made from a kind of grain in

Unit IX African Foods

_____ with limited production called "_____".

4. Plantains, which are similar to bananas, but _____ and _____, can also be easily processed into flour, which are often boiled or fried.

5. African traditional alcoholic beverages are _____ and have to be consumed soon after being made, which shapes its drinking customs.

6. "Ugali" is the east Africa's version of west Africa's "_____".

7. The cooking of southern Africa is sometimes called "_____ cuisine", as the food in this region is a _____ of many cultures–the indigenous African tribal societies, Europe, Asia and America.

8. In South Africa, "potjiekos", literally translated into "small pot food", is a _____ prepared outdoors. It is traditionally cooked in a round, three-legged iron _____, so "potjiekos" refers to the food cooked in it.

9. Food avoidance or food _____ do exist, permanently or temporarily.

10. Regional variations in some popular European food stuffs reflect the influence of the _____ power.

Review and Reflect

✧ There are many misconceptions about African food. Africa is frequently viewed as a place with nothing to offer but starvation, misery and strife. Did you have any misconceptions about African food before learning this unit? What were they?

✧ "The way people live influences what they eat." Do you agree with this saying? Try to find some examples about African foods to support your point.

✧ Nowadays, African eating habits are changing as more people begin to live in cities. Imported and fast foods become more widely available, and the urban diet is featured by being multi-cultural. Do you think it is a way of losing tribal tradition? What's your comment on the relationship between modernization and tradition?

Unit X African Arts

在非洲大陆上，浓厚的宗教气息为历史悠久的雕刻艺术蒙上了一层神秘的面纱。在20世纪的现代视觉革命中，无数西方前卫艺术家从非洲雕刻作品和面具中汲取养分，掀起了野兽主义、立体主义、表现主义、抽象主义以及超现实主义等一波又一波的现代、当代艺术思潮，其中就包括20世纪最伟大的艺术家毕加索、马蒂斯和布拉克等等。

Colors of Africa
(Photographer: Sun Lihua)

"Matisse was mostly influenced by Islamic and North African art while Picasso appreciated Sub-Saharan sculpture for its physicality and tragic power.... African art appealed to these masters because of its strong simplification and abstraction of form."

——Francoise Treuttel-Garcias, an art commenter at Louvre, Orsay and Picasso museums

Unit X   African Arts

> ◎ **Think and Talk**
> ☆ Have you heard of any African artist? What do you think of his/her works?
> ☆ When talking about African arts, what comes to your mind first?
> ☆ If you travel in Africa, what kinds of souvenirs do you want to buy?

I. OVERVIEW OF AFRICAN ART

Each of the hundreds of different cultures in Africa has its own artistic traditions and its own ideas of what is beautiful or important. Differences in the style and form of artworks, as well as in the materials used to produce them, reflect such factors as a region's geography and climate, its social customs, and the available technology. Of course, the skills and tastes of individual artists, and the purpose for which the work is created, also play a role in shaping the final product.

African art takes many forms, from sculpture and paintings to masks, **textiles**, baskets, jewelry, and **utensils**. Artistic style also covers a wide range, from lifelike representations of people or animals to **abstract geometric** patterns. The **Yoruba** of Nigeria and the **Bamiléké** of Cameroon, for example, believe that sculptures should resemble their **subjects** and must also show certain ideal qualities such as youth and beauty. The **Bambara** of Mali favor geometric shapes and

A copper statue of a drummer from Cameroon
(Photographer: Han Hong)

A carved entrance door in Zanzibar, Tanzania
(Photographer: Du Fengyan)

idealized images over **realistic** portrayals of people or animals.

In **Sub-Saharan Africa**, many art objects are created to serve a particular purpose. These purposes include dealing with the problems of life, marking the passage from childhood to adulthood, communicating with spirits, and expressing basic beliefs. Artists carve figures to honor **ancestors**, rulers, and gods. They make masks for use in **rituals** and funerals and for entertainment. They design jewelry and body painting that often function as a sign of wealth, power, and social position.

1. Meaning in African Art

The subject of a work of art and the way in which it is made often have an influence on its meaning. In some cases, objects of great social and ritual significance have to be assembled according to certain procedures. Following the rules ensures that the piece will be filled with the appropriate "power". If the rules are broken, the artwork loses its power and becomes an ordinary object. In other cases, the power is given to the object after it is completed.

Some objects serve as a base for materials that add to their significance. For example, when a carver makes a mask, village elders may contribute medicines or herbs to give the mask power. The resulting piece is considered to have a personality of its own.

Design and decoration play a major role in the meaning of an object. An artist may make a mask large to indicate that it is important and add an important forehead to suggest that the mask is rich in spiritual power. Certain patterns have particular significance, perhaps standing for water, the moon, the earth, or other ideas. Objects that represent spirits or spiritual powers are often abstract because the things they represent are abstract. Figures that represent living rulers tend to be more realistic to make it possible to recognize the individual's features. Some objects include symbols that represent powerful animals.

In one type of African art, forms that have known meanings are used in creating images of figures and ideas. The purpose is to portray rulers or ancestors as superhuman and, at the same time, to communicate a sense of permanence. Another category of art includes sculptures and masks that represent the visible world but refer as well to an unseen world behind them. These objects may be used in activities such as healing ceremonies and **divination**.

A third type of African art consists of everyday objects, such as spoons, pots, doors, cloths, and so on. Some of these items have elaborate decorations, such as the intricate human faces carved into the handles of wooden **ladles** from Ivory Coast.[1] Often reserved for the wealthy, these objects can also be markers of social position.

2. Collecting African Art

Europeans began collecting African artworks as early as the 1600s, and by the 1800s, interest in these objects was high. However, the first African pieces brought to Europe were regarded as **curiosities** rather than works of arts. While admiring the workmanship, some people considered African art to be "**primitive**" and without artistic value. Nevertheless, by the end of the 1800s, many European museums had acquired African pieces for their collections, usually to show everyday life in their countries' colonies.

African works did not attract much attention as art until the 1920s, when interest focused mainly on sculptures in wood and **bronze**. Since the 1950s, Western collectors, scholars, and museums have come to recognize more and more African objects as valuable works of art. Prices of these works have risen accordingly.

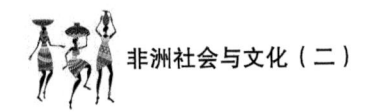

In the early years, European museums often displayed African objects with exhibits of animals, rather than with other works of art. Today, museums present African pieces in their art collections. Furthermore, collectors now understand that, although individual works are not signed, many African artists are well-known in the continent by name and reputation.

Art collecting has also changed in Africa. In the past, Africans sometimes threw objects away when they were thought to have lost their power. Without a specific function, the items had little value. Recently, however, more Africans have begun to collect works of art and a number of museums have been established on the continent with collections of African art.

3. Recent African Art

Over the centuries, African art has changed with the times. Not surprisingly, modern African society and culture are reflected in the recent works of African artists. Some of the religious rituals and other traditional activities for which African art was created no longer exist. Furthermore, new traditions, such as those connected to the practice of **Christianity**, have been introduced. Some artists have combined African ideas and Christian themes in their work. Others have produced pieces with African **motifs** and designs that are not intended for use in rituals. Yet, though much of the current art reflects modern concerns and issues, traditional art forms continue to play a meaningful role in the lives of ordinary people.

Styles of art change as well. Traditional designs often appear in new ways, such as using body painting designs in paintings on **canvas**. Perhaps one of the most notable features of recent African art is its role in the modern objects specifically for Western tourists and collectors.[2] Such "tourist art" may include copies of older art forms as well as modern designs.

II. SCULPTURE

For sculpture, perhaps Sub-Saharan Africa's greatest art form, the most commonly used materials are wood, **clay** and metals such as iron, bronze, and gold. Unfortunately, wood **decomposes** and is easily destroyed, so few pieces of early wooden sculpture have survived.

1. West Africa

Sculpture is one of the major art forms in West Africa. Scholars divide the artistic traditions of the region into two broad geographical areas: the western Sudan[3] and the Guinea Coast. Although some common themes appear in the art of these areas, the most **striking** feature of West African sculpture is its diversity.

The western Sudan, a **savanna** region that extends across West Africa, includes several well-defined sculptural traditions. Figures from this region often have **oval** bodies, **angular** shapes, and facial features that represent an ideal rather than an individual, and they often have dull surfaces **encrusted** with materials placed on them in ceremonial offerings.

The **Mandé-speaking** peoples of the western Sudan create wooden figures with broad and flat surfaces. The body, arms, and legs are shaped like **cylinders**, while the nose

Ebony sculpture of a man carrying bananas on his head from Côte d'Ivoire
(Photographer: Han Hong)

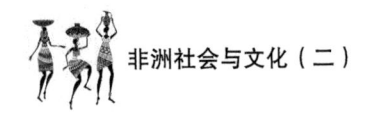

may be a large vertical **slab**. Artists often burn patterns of **scars**—a common type of body decoration—into the surface of figures with a hot **blade**. Scar patterns also consist of large geometric shapes. The Mandé wooden figures are usually dark brown and black.

Another important sculptural tradition of this region is that of the **Dagon** people of Mali. Much Dagon sculpture is linked to ancestor worship. The Dagon carve figures meant to house the spirits of the dead which they place on family **shrines**. Their designs feature raised geometric patterns, such as black-and-white **checkerboards** and groups of circles in red, white and black.[4]

A chess set presented to Deng Xiaoping by president of the Republic of the Congo, Denis Sassou Nguesso in 1987
(Photographer: Han Hong)

The Guinea Coast extends along the Atlantic Ocean from **Guinea-Bissau** through central Nigeria and Cameroon. Sculptural figures of this region tend to be more realistic in design than those from other parts of West Africa. The arms, legs, and bodies of figures are curved and smooth. Detailed patterns representing body scars, also typical of this region, rise above the surrounding surface. Many figures are **adorned** with rings around the neck. A common form of body adornment, the rings are symbols of prosperity and well-being.

Two **noteworthy** sculptural traditions of the Guinea Coast are those of the

Asante[5] and the **Fon**. The Asante carve dolls that represent their idea of **feminine** beauty. They also produce swords and **staffs**, covered in gold **foil**, for royal officials. The Fon people are known for their large copper and iron sculptures of **Ogun**, the god of iron and war.

The artistic traditions of Nigeria are very old indeed. Among the earliest sculptures from northern Nigeria are realistic clay figures of animals made by the Nok culture[6] as early as the 400s B.C. The human figures produced by the Nok, with their tube-shaped heads, bodies, arms, and legs, are less realistic. The ancient kingdom of Bénin in Nigeria was renowned for its magnificent **brass** sculptures. Dating from about the 1400s, these include images of groups of animals, birds and people.

Another important sculptural tradition is that of Ife[7], an ancient city of the Yoruba of southwestern Nigeria. Between 1100 and 1450, the people of Ife were creating realistic figures in brass and clay, and some of these probably represent **royalty**. Life-sized Yoruba brass heads from this time may have played a role in funeral ceremonies. Yoruba carvings typically portray human figures in a **naturalistic** style. The sculptural traditions of Ife are still followed, but individual **cults** often have their own distinct styles.

2. Central Africa

Central Africa, a vast area of forest and savanna that stretches west from Cameroon to Angola and east to the Democratic Republic of the Congo, contains a great diversity of cultures and arts. Yet, in most cases, the differences in artistic styles are so striking that experts have no trouble in identifying the area where an object was produced.

A number of groups in central Africa have ancient sculptural traditions, and some of the most impressive carvings in Africa come from this region. Pieces range from the wooden heads made by the **Fang** people to the royal figures carved by the **Kuba** to guard boxes of ancestral **relics**. The Kuba figures are decorated with geometric patterns and objects symbolizing each king's accomplishments.

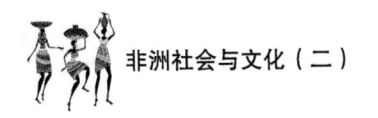

The varied sculpture of central Africa does have some characteristic features, such as heart-shaped faces that curve inward and patterns of circles and dots. Some groups prefer rounded, curved shapes, while others favor geometric, angular forms. Specific details are often emphasized. Particularly striking are the richly carved **hairdos** and **headdresses**, intricate scar patterns and **tattoos**, and necklaces and **bracelets**. Although wood is the primary material used in carving, the people of this region also create figures from ivory, bone, stone, clay and metal.

3. Eastern Africa

Although sculpture is not a major art form in eastern Africa, a variety of sculptural traditions can be found in the region. An unusually sculptural form in some parts of eastern Africa is the **pole**, which is carved in human shape and decorated. Usually associated with death, pole sculptures are placed next to graves or at the entrances to villages. Among the **Konso** of Ethiopia, for example, the grave of a wealthy, important man may be marked by a group of carved wooden figures representing the **deceased**, his wives, and the people or animals he killed during his lifetime.

Sculpture is mainly associated with the dead in parts of Madagascar as well. Figures are often placed on tombs or in shrines dedicated to ancestors. The tombs of important **Mahafaly** individuals may be covered with as many as 30 wooden sculptures. Carved from a single piece of wood, each sculpture stands about 2 meters high. The lower parts are often decorated with geometric forms, while the tops are carved with figures of animals, people, and various objects.

4. Southern Africa

Sculpture does not have a particularly strong tradition in southern Africa. The oldest known clay figures from South Africa, dating from between 400 and 600 A.D., have **cylindrical** heads, some with human features and some with a combination of human and animal features.

Among the more notable carved objects found in southern Africa are wooden **headrests** in various styles from geometric designs to more realistic carvings of animal figures. Some headrests were buried with their owners, and some were handed down from one generation to the next.

III. MASKS

Masks are one of the most important and widespread art forms in Sub-Saharan Africa. They may be used in **initiation** ceremonies,

A double-horned crest mask inlaid with shells from Togo
(Photographer: Han Hong)

such as the one marking the passage from childhood to adulthood. Masks also serve as symbols of power to enforce the laws of society.

Masks are usually worn as **disguises** in ceremonies and rituals, along with a costume of leaves, cloth, feathers, and other materials. Although masks may represent either male or female spirits, they are almost always worn by men. The person wearing the mask in the ceremony is no longer treated as himself or herself but as the spirit that the mask represents.

In addition to face masks (which just cover the face), there are **helmet** masks (which cover all or most of the head) and **crest** masks (worn on top of the head like a headdress). Made of wood, clay, metal, leather, **fabric**, or other materials, masks may be painted and decorated with such things as animal skins, feathers, **beads**, and shells.

1. Western Africa

Many different forms and styles of masks can be found in western Africa. The

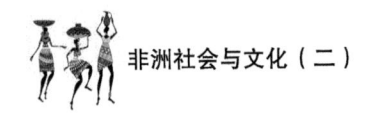

Bambara people of Mali have specific masks for their various male societies. Many of these masks represent animals that stand for imaginary characters. The masks are decorated with **antelope** horns, **porcupine quills**, bird **skulls**, and other objects. The characteristics of several animals are combined in masks of the **Senufo** people of Ivory Coast.

Masks play a role in rituals and ceremonies related to death or ancestors. Once a year, in elaborate performances honoring their ancestors, the Yoruba people of Nigeria put on masks made of colorful fabrics and small carved wooden heads. In other parts of Nigeria, masks representing both human and animal characters are worn at the funerals of important elders as a way of honoring the deceased.

The **Igbo** people of Nigeria have two types of masks to mark the **transition** from childhood to adulthood. Dark masks represent "male qualities" such as power and strength, prosperity, and impurity, while delicate white masks symbolize "female qualities" of beauty, gentleness, and purity. Among the **Mende** people of Sierra Leone, elaborate black helmet masks representing the Mende ideals of feminine beauty are used in rituals **initiating** young girls into womanhood. This is the only case of women wearing masks in Africa.

2. Central and Eastern Africa

Many central African masks signify rank and social position, representing the authority and privilege of kings, chiefs, and other individuals. Some also function as symbols of identity for specific groups. While certain masks are considered the property of individuals, others are owned collectively by the group. Used in a variety of situations, masks may inspire fear, fight **witchcraft**, or entertain. As elsewhere in Africa, many masks are linked with initiation and funeral rituals.

Among the most notable masks of central Africa are large helmet masks with figures of humans, animals and scenes on top. Too heavy to be carried or worn, they are displayed during important ceremonies. The masks of the **Pende** people of Angola and Democratic Republic of the Congo are among the most **dramatic** works of art in Africa. These large helmet masks have faces with angular patterns and heavy **triangular eyelids**. Topped by plant fibers that represent hair, they are thought to possess mysterious powers. The Pende make smaller versions of these masks in ivory or wood for use as **amulets**. In nearby Zambia, various materials are used to create ceremonial masks. The **Mbundu** work in wood, and the **Luvale** and **Chokwe** attach pieces of painted **bark** cloth to a **wicker** frame.

Masks do not play an important role in the art of eastern Africa. However, the **Makonde** of Mozambique and southeastern Tanzania create distinctive face masks and body masks.

IV. PAINTING

Painting on canvas is a recent development in Africa. Although Africans have always painted, they have done so primarily on rock surfaces or on the walls of houses and other buildings. Africans also apply paint to carved figures, masks, and their own bodies.

1. Rock Painting

The earliest known African paintings are on rocks in southern Africa. Made by the **Khoisan** people about 20 000 years ago, these rock paintings portray human and animal figures, often in hunting scenes. The paintings may have had ritual or social significance, though no one knows for sure. Other ancient rock paintings are found in eastern and southern Africa.

2. Body Painting

The people of eastern Africa have traditionally painted and marked their bodies in various ways. Such decoration has been considered a sign of beauty as well as a form of artistic expression. Some of it is temporary, as in the case of body painting with various natural **pigments** and other coloring agents. The patterns and designs used often signify group identity, social status, and passage through important stages in life.

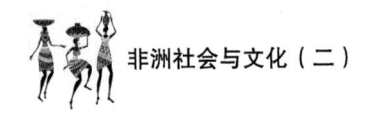

3. Wall Painting

Wall painting on the interiors or exteriors of buildings is an important art form in southern Africa. Some very striking examples can be found in this region. Among the best-known are those of the **Ndebele** of South Africa and Zimbabwe. Almost **exclusively** the work of women, these paintings were traditionally done in natural earth colors using bold geometric shapes and **symmetrical** patterns. In recent years, Ndebele women have also used commercial paints, and their designs have become more varied, incorporating lettering and objects such as **light bulbs**, as well as abstract designs.

Traditions of painting are found in several other areas of eastern Africa as well. The **Dinka** and **Nuer** people of southern Sudan, for example, paint pictures of cattle and people on the walls of huts. Members of the secret **snake charmer** society of the **Sukuma** people in Tanzania decorate the interior walls of their meeting houses with images of humans, snakes, and **mythological** figures. The **Luo** of western Kenya paint geometric designs on fishing boats, and Mahafaly of Madagascar paint scenes on the sides of tombs.

4. Tinga Tinga

Tinga Tinga (also spelt Tingatinga or Tinga-tinga) painting was originated by Edward Saidi Tingatinga (1937—1972) and developed in the second half of the 20th century in the Oyster Bay area in **Dar es Salaam** and later spread to most East Africa. He drew on modern Makonde sculpture and contemporary painting from the Congo to create a new art form consisting of an invented and stylized **imagery** of animals and plants, which he painted on hardboard squares using brightly colored house paints. Its roots could also be found in local tradition of decorating hut walls in eastern Africa.

Unit X African Arts

A Tingatinga painting entitled Kilimanjaro drawn by Mustapha Abdallah
(Photographer: Han Hong)

Edward Tingatinga began painting around 1968 in Dar es Salaam. He employed low cost materials such as **masonite** and bicycle paint and attracted the attention of tourists for their colorful, both **naïve** and **surrealistic** style. When Tingatinga died in 1972, his style was so popular that it had started a wide movement of imitators and followers, sometimes informally referred to as the "Tingatinga school". Because of his short artistic life, Tingatinga left only a relatively small number of paintings, which are sought-after by collectors. Today it is known that **fakes** were produced from all famous Tingatinga paintings like *The lion, Peacock on the **Baobab** Tree, **Antelope, Leopard, Buffalo,** or Monkey*.

The first generation of artists from the Tingatinga school basically reproduced the works of the school's founder. In the 1990s new trends emerged within the Tingatinga style, in response to the transformations that the Tanzanian society was undergoing after independence. New subjects related to the new urban and multi-ethnic society of Dar es Salaam (e.g. crowded and busy streets and squares) were introduced, together with occasional technical **novelties**. One of the most well-known 2nd generation Tingatinga painters is Simon George Mpata (1942—1984), younger half-brother of Edward Tingatinga.

Tingatinga paintings are traditionally made on masonite, using several layers of bicycle paint, which makes for brilliant and highly **saturated** colors. The drawings themselves can be described as both naïve and **caricatural**, and humor and **sarcasm** are often explicit.

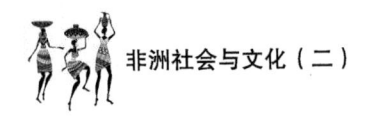

As with the modern **Kamba** and Makonde traditions, Tingatinga painting proved very successful commercially and was taken up by many people. Tingatinga paintings are one of the most widely represented forms of tourist-oriented art in Tanzania, Kenya and neighboring countries. Many elements of the style are related to requirements of the tourist-oriented market; for example, the paintings are usually small so they can be easily transported, and subjects are intended to appeal to the Europeans and Americans (e.g. the big five[8] and other wild **fauna**). In this sense, Tingatinga paintings can be considered a form of "airport art".

5. Others

There are also other forms of painting in Africa. For example, in Ethiopia, Christian influence has been strong for centuries, and around 1100s, Ethiopian artists began painting religious scenes on the walls of churches. Since the 1600s, Ethiopians have also produced religious pictures on canvas, wood **panels**, and **parchment**.

V. DECORATIVE ARTS

The decorative arts include such items as textiles, jewelry, **pottery**, and **basketry**. While viewed as **crafts** in some Western cultures, these objects can also be seen as works of art because of the care and level of skill that goes into their creation.[9]

Many useful objects are carved from wood or other hard materials and then decorated. The **Swahili** of eastern Africa used ivory and **ebony** to build elaborate "chairs of power" with **footrests** and removable backs.

A tribal chief chair carved in wood presented to Mao Zedong by Togo President Gnassingbe Eyadema
(Photographer: Han Hong)

Unit X African Arts

In West Africa, some Nigerian **artisans** make musical instruments and food containers from round fruits known as **gourds**. The outer surfaces of the gourds are covered with delicately carved and painted geometric designs.

1. Basketry

Both men and women make many kinds of baskets and mats out of plant materials such as wood, **palm** leaves, **reeds**, grasses, and roots. They decorate their **handiwork** with patterns of differently colored and **textured** materials or with leather **stitched** onto the basketwork. There are two basic basket-making techniques. In **plaited** basketry, **strands** of plant fiber are soaked and then **twined**, woven, or twisted together. In sewn basketry, a thin **strip** of continuous material—usually grass—is stitched onto itself in a **coil.** Some baskets made this way are so tightly sewn that they hold liquid.

Baskets serve a wide range of practical purposes. Most are used as containers for serving food, storing items, or carrying goods. Some baskets function as tools, such as traps for fish and animals and **strainers** for flour or homemade beer. Basketry techniques are applied to other tasks, including fashioning the framework for **thatched** roofs and **wattle-and-daub** walls.

A basket from Botswana
(Photographer: Han Hong)

African baskets have decorative and social purposes as well. Hats are often made of basketwork adorned with fiber **tufts**, feathers, fur, and leather. The traditional beaded **crowns** of the Yoruba people of Nigeria, for example, have basketry foundations. Groups such as the Chokwe of Angola and Zambia create dance masks of basketry or bark cloth on wicker frame. Over much of eastern Africa, baskets ornamented with shells, beads, dyed leather, and metal **dangles** are presented as special gifts. They may also be included among a bride's wedding decorations.

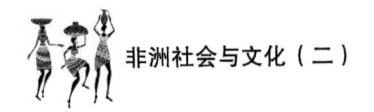

Flat mats, another form of basketry, often serve as ground covering on which to sit or sleep. The **nomadic** Somali people use mats to roof their temporary shelters. In the Congo region, traditional houses are often walled with rigid mats, patterned in black on a background of natural yellow.

2. Beads and Jewelry

Beads

Africans use beads to adorn their bodies, their **furnishings**, and their burials. Nigerians had developed a glass bead industry by 1000 B.C., and ancient trade routes circulated beads of bone, stone, ivory, seed, **ostrich** eggshell, metal, and shell. **Cowry** shells from the Indian Ocean were highly valued. Once used as money, they still serve as symbols of wealth in many places.

Western and central Africans traditionally used beads to cover furniture, sculpture, and clothing. Groups in Nigeria and Cameroon fashioned complicated pictures out of tiny colored beads. For many nomadic peoples, beadwork, which could be carried with them, was the main form of visual art. In eastern Africa, beadwork ornaments displayed the wearer's social position through a complex system of color and design. In many regions, children wore beads to bring good health and luck. Foreign contact and modern materials have changed the types of beads used in Africa. Glass beads from India were imported into Sub-Saharan Africa more than 1000 years ago. By the late 1800s, colored glass beads manufactured in Europe were being shipped by the ton to Africa, where they served as trade goods. Despite the widespread use of these imported beads, native African bead-making techniques survived. However, craftspeople began using new materials in their work, for example, **Maasai** groups have recently incorporated blue plastic pen caps into their beadwork in place of traditional feather **quill** pens. Today people produce beads and other kinds of jewelry from coins, buttons, **wire**, and discarded **aluminum** and plastic, working these materials into their traditional styles.

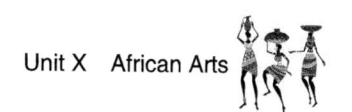

Jewelry

African artists and craftspeople also make metal ornaments and jewelry. Many parts of western Africa have a long history of producing fine gold jewelry. The country that is now Ghana was formally named Gold Coast. The name came from the fact that the local Asante kings wore so many gold necklaces, bracelets, crowns, rings, and **anklets**. The **Tuareg** people of northeastern Africa specialize in making silver jewelry.

African artists create jewelry for adornment, as symbols of social position, and even to bring good health and luck. They use materials such as gold, silver, and various types of beads to make necklaces, bracelets, crowns, rings, and anklets. In the **Kalahari Desert** in southern Africa, artisans fashioned adornment with beads and made from glass or ostrich eggshell. In West Africa, the Asante are famous for their gold jewelry and gold-handled swords. Today many Africans produce jewelry and beadwork to sell to tourists.

Yoruba beads-a most intricate art form

Of the diverse art forms of the Yoruba, beads are an **integral** part of everyday lives. Their beadwork is considered to be among the most intricate and complex of the world. For the Yoruba people, beads are not only used to decorate ceremonial items such as headpieces, necklaces, and **sheaths**, but also used for spiritual purposes, by those who know how to polish them properly such as priests and **diviners**. What's more, beadwork is used to decorate jewelry, belts, shoes, **cushions**, furniture, sculptures, paintings, clothing, and head coverings. The **veil** on many beaded head coverings covers the face of a chief to protect **commoners** from looking directly at a so powerful being. Beadwork in metal, glass, and stone is used to distinguish its owner in both life and death.

A stool with beadwork and Adinkra symbols on top in the Embassy of the People's Republic of Ghana in China
(Photographer: Han Hong)

Beads were originally made from shell, bone, wood, seeds, and clay. Later they were made from metal, ivory, glass, and stone. There is evidence of Yoruba beadwork dating back to the 6th century, about 300 years before the beginning of mass glass bead importation from Europe. Beads made from certain materials represented specific wants, beliefs, and status. The grant land snail is one of the oldest, most easily attained and abundant food sources for the Yoruba. Wearing its shell symbolizes the hope of a long and peaceful life.

And evidence has shown that glass beads were used as a status symbol since at least 800 A.D. as well as for economic exchange. Before the European beans began flooding African markets to trade for ivory and gold, Yoruba people made their beads using recycled glass and **staining** it to the desired color, and stones were also used. They also used **coral**, which they believe is provided by their protector, the goddess of the sea.

As decorative items, beads carry heavy symbolism. Everything from colors to shapes has meaning and purposeful calculations and design. The colors used by the Yoruba people fall into 3 main different categories: funfun is associated with cold and includes colors such as silver, white and gray; pupa is associated with warmth and includes colors such as red, orange and pink; and dudu, associated with the extremes of warmth and cold and includes colors such as black, dark brown and purple. Careful balancing of colors depicts "balance and **restraint**" on the part of the orisha[10], which is reached through the beads which act as "an **ambassador** of heaven" and serve the purpose of uniting heaven and earth. In addition to the symbolism of the bead colors, shape and design play a major role in the meaning, history and power of the beadwork. The designs of Yoruba beadwork can range anywhere from geometric shapes to animals to the faces of their ancestors. These patterns can be used on all sorts of ceremonial items, such as the King's crowns, sword sheaths, chairs and masks, all of which are designed to please their particular orisha.

The simple act of creating beadwork in a step-by-step or one-by-one manner is considered sacred because **concentration** is required and repetition places the artist in a **trance** like state that further heightens the spiritual value of the beadwork. The art of beading, or **stringing**, follows a serial process and composition of Yoruba art, an extension of the fundamental principle of Àṣẹ[11]. When threaded together, beads represent **solidarity**, togetherness and unity. Bead **embroidery** is practiced by extremely skilled men in a number of Nigerian centers.

As they encircle and adorn parts of the body (head, neck, arms, wrists, waist, legs, ankles, and toes), beads secure the spiritual essence of the person, conceal and protect a person's Àṣẹ and, through their symbolic meaning, may also reveal essential characteristics of that person.

3. Pottery

Pottery is among Africa's oldest crafts. **Archaeologists** have discovered evidence that people in the Sahara desert were making pottery more than 10 000 years ago. **Deposits** of clay are found throughout the continent. This **versatile** material is used to make containers for cooking, storing, and measuring foodstuffs, as well as for jewel, furniture, **coffins**, toys, **beehives**, musical instruments, household utensils, and **tiles**. Even broken pottery has value in Africa—as game pieces, floor tiles, and raw material for making new pottery.

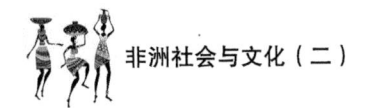

Traditionally, each piece of African pottery was made by hand. Potters, some of whom were traveling craftspeople, developed a variety of techniques that could produce **sturdy** pottery quickly and inexpensively. They baked it over open **bonfires**, in fire pits, or in **kilns**. Although these methods remain in use, some African manufacturers now make pottery by pressing or pouring clay into **molds** for mass production.

Africans often decorate their pottery with **texture**. They carve or raise patterns and designs on the surface of the clay. Craftspeople in Islamic cultures, especially in North Africa, paint clay tiles with elaborate geometric patterns and designs inspired by Arabic **script**. These are generally used to decorate **mosques** and Muslim religious schools.

Africans tend to draw a line between clay sculpture and functional pottery vessels. Traditionally, in much of the continent, sculpture is produced by men and the pottery by women. This division of labor came in part from a belief that making clay images of people or animals was considered similar to a woman's ability to have children. However, in many cultures, powerful women and women beyond childbearing age may create **figurines**.

Yellow-glazed pottery vessel with painted figures from the Republic of the Congo
(Photographer: Han Hong)

African pottery vessels sometimes carry meanings beyond their everyday functions. The style of a pot may reflect a person's position in society. A **widow**, a married man, and a child might each be expected to use a **pitcher** of a different shape. A flour jar marking a tomb may indicate that a fertile mother is buried within. Pottery vessels may also act as containers of spiritual forces. A dead woman's spirit could be thought to inhabit the pot that she used for years to **haul** water.

4. Textiles

Textiles are clothes woven of threads. Africans produce many distinctive clothes woven from cotton, wool, wild silk, **raffia** fibers or man-made threads. In Africa, they have great cultural as well as practical significance. People offer textiles as gifts on important social occasions and often bury them with the dead. Textiles may indicate the wearer's importance in the community. Their patterns or color combinations sometimes carry symbolic messages. Textiles remain an important item in the economy, especially in West Africa, where more workers are engaged in the production and trade of cloth than in any other craft profession.

African textile makers have traditionally used at least five types of hand-operated **looms** to weave their cloth. Some types are worked on only by men, others by women. All of these looms produce long, narrow strips of material, ranging from less than an inch (2.54cm) to about 10 inches (25.4cm) in width. When sewn together, the strips make **rectangular** clothes. Today African textiles are often manufactured on automatic looms in factories.

Bark cloth, traditionally used throughout much of central and eastern Africa, is not a true textile. It is pounded from the bark of the **fig** tree. However, Africans have long used bark cloth in the same way they use textiles. Textile weaving and the production of bark cloth rarely occur in the same area.

Many groups of people in western and central Africa have developed their own weaving traditions, using particular types of looms and decorative techniques such as embroidery, patchwork, painting, stenciling, or tie-dyeing.[12] Weavers use cotton, wool, wild silk, raffia, or man-made threads to create their designs. In Niger, the **Zerma** weave large cotton covers in vivid red and black patterns.

The **Fulani** people of Mali are known for their **kaasa** covers, a tightly woven wool fabric that offers protection against cold and insects. **Berber** women produce colorful wool rugs in unique geometric designs. Manufactured fibers such as **rayon** play an important part in the modern textile trade of Africa.

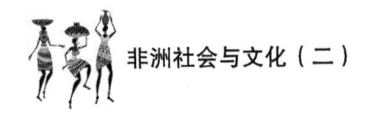

Kente cloth-a treasured textile

The **icon** of African cultural heritage around the world, Asante Kente is identified by its **dazzling**, multicolored patterns of bright colors, geometric shapes and bold designs.

According to **Ghanaian mythology**, Kente cloth was first created when two friends watched how a spider wove its web. By imitating its actions, they created Kente cloth the same way. This story, whether true or not, shows the harmony between Ghanaians and the mother nature.

As we look back in history, the Kente cloth was reserved for the kings and associated with royalty and sacredness. One Kente cloth called wonya wo ho a, wonye dehyee (meaning "you may be rich, but you are not of royal **descent**") was apparently worn by the royals to distinguish themselves from the emerging class of rich traders. Even in today's world, it is worn only during important times. Though the cloth has widespread acceptance and usage, it is still held in high esteem among the Akan[13] tribe and the Ghanaians in general.

An ebony sculpture with strips of Kente around the necks of human figures
(Photographer: Han Hong)

However, Kente cloth is more than just clothing to be worn. For the Ghanaians, this represents the history, philosophy, oral literature, religious beliefs, political thought and **aesthetic** principles of life. It is hand woven on wooden looms and is of very high value. It comes in a variety of patterns, colors and designs, each of which has different meanings. The various colors in the cloth symbolize various aspects of life. For example, blue symbolizes peace and harmony. Pink and purple colors are associated with women. White and grey colors symbolize **holiness**, **cleansing** rituals and are mostly used by priests and holy people.

VI. ROLES OF ART IN AFRICAN SOCIETY

The multiple roles that art plays in African communities are as diverse as the forms of **patronage**. These include social, political, economic, historical, and **therapeutic** functions.

1. Social Role

One of the most important functions of African art is distinctly social. In fulfilling this role, African art frequently depicts women as mothers, usually nursing or holding their young gently. Men, on the other hand, are often presented both as elders—the traditional community leaders—and as successful warriors, appearing on horseback or with weapons. Social themes are prevalent in many African **masquerade** performances as well. In these masquerades, animal and human characters, in appropriate masks and clothing, assume a variety of roles

A wood mask decorated with color drawings from Gabon
(Photographer: Han Hong)

in demonstrating proper and improper forms of societal behavior. Performances of the **Ijaw** and southern Igbo of Nigeria include diverse antisocial characters, such as the **miser**, the greedy person, the **prostitute**, the incompetent physician, and the **unscrupulous** lawyer. In the **Egungun** performances of the nearby Yoruba, the gossip, the **glutton**, and the strange-mannered foreigner have key parts as negative social models.

2. Political Role

Political control is another major concern displayed through art in Africa. Among the **Dan**, **Kota**, Pende, and others, special masks are worn by persons serving as community judges and policemen. The Gon (**gorilla**) maskers of Gabon are a particularly good example of this type of masked community official. Because of their **anonymity** and perceived special powers, these Gon masked figures are able to break normal societal codes and **prescriptions** as a means of redistributing scarce food and animals at times of great community need.[14] A different type of societal control is achieved by certain African figures and architectural designs. The **reliquary** figures of the Kota and Fang of Gabon, for example, are used as guardian images to protect the sacred ancestral relics of the community from theft or harm. The **Dogon** of Mali and the **Senufo** of Côte d'Ivoire carve elaborate doors that ritually protect the community food supplies and sacred objects.

Chi Wara antelope headdress of the Bambara of Mali
(Photographer: Han Hong)

3. Economic Role

Art in Africa fulfills an important economic role. The elegant wooden Chi Wara[15] antelope headdresses of the Bambara of Mali are worn in planting and harvest ceremonies. Chi Wara, the **mythical** Bambara inventor of agriculture, is said to have buried himself in the earth as an act of self-sacrifice. The dance of the Chi Wara maskers on the agricultural fields (Chi Wara's grave) serves to honor this great being and to remind the young Bambara farmers of Chi Wara's sacrifice that they in turn must make each year. Among the Senufo of Côte d'Ivoire, delicately carved figures are used in a similar way to encourage farmers in their difficult work. The Senufo secure staffs in the ground at the end of cultivation rows; these staffs use bird or female images and serve as goals, markers, and prizes for the field-planting competitions.[16]

4. Historical Role

African art fulfills an important historical role through its memorialization of important persons and events of the past. With this in mind, the Dogon of Mali have carved numerous images of their famous ancestors, the Nommo[17], who descended from the sky at the beginning of time. Such Nommo figures occupy important places on **granary** doors, in cave paintings, and on sacred architectural supports. Some of these figures have upraised hands pointing to the sky and their village of origin.

Bénin plaque: the Oba with Europeans in British Museum
(Photographer: Han Hong)

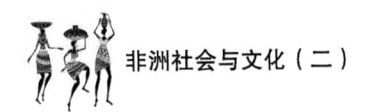

In the powerful kingdom of Bénin in Nigeria, elaborate **relief plaques** cast in bronze similarly carried images of important persons and events of the past. The images represent the meetings of foreign **dignitaries**, battle scenes, court **pageants**, nobles in state dress, religious ceremonies, musicians, and other historical figures and events.

5. Therapeutic Role

Some traditional African **therapies** have required special forms of art. Divination, the means by which problems and their potential resolutions could be determined, was particularly important in the production of artworks. Yoruba Ifa[18] diviners used elaborately carved divination boards, bowls, and other items as an essential part of their ritual equipment. Similarly, the **Baule** of Côte d'Ivoire used elaborate divination vessels for similar purposes. Among the **Kongo** of the Democratic Republic of the Congo, powerful wooden **fetish** figures stuck through with iron nails were employed therapeutically as a means of repelling personal danger and suffering.

VII. CONTEMPORARY AFRICAN ART

Many of the so-called traditional arts of Africa are still actively being **commissioned**, carved, and used in traditional contexts. As in all art periods, important innovations coexist with significant elements of established styles and modes of expression. In recent years, with the changes in transportation and mass communications within the continent, a number of art forms have been widespread among diverse African cultures. For example, today some Nigerian-style masks are being used in Ghana and other coastal centers on the eastern Guinea Coast.

In addition to distinct African influences, a number of changes also have originated from the outside. For example, **Islamic** architecture and design patterns are evident in many of the arts of the northern regions of Nigeria, Mali, Burkina

A modern African studio
(Photographer: Liang Zi)

Faso, and Niger. East Indian[19] print designs have similarly found their way into sculptures and masks of the **Ibibio** and **Efik** artists living along the southern coast of Nigeria. Some contemporary artists have taken up Christian themes in their designs for panels, doors, and **baptismal fonts** for Africa's Christian churches and **cathedrals**. In recent years, artists have also found important sources of patronage for various art forms in the banks, commercial establishments, government offices, and other official institutions of some nations. Tourists have been responsible for still other art demands, particularly for decorative masks and ornamental African sculptures made of ebony or ivory.[20]

A souvenir market on Gorée Island, Senegal
(Photographer: Chen Yong)

The development of schools of art and architecture in Sub-Saharan African cities has pushed artists to work in new media such as **cement**, oil and other paints, ink, stone, aluminum, and a variety of **graphic** modes. The images and designs they have created reflect a **vibrant** combination of African and contemporary Western traditions.

Unit X　African Arts

Explanations

［1］**Ivory Coast:** "象牙海岸"的官方名称是"科特迪瓦共和国"。

［2］**Perhaps one of the most notable features of recent African art is its role in the modern objects specifically for Western tourist and collectors:** 也许，当代非洲艺术一个非常显著的特点就是要迎合西方游客和收藏家的口味。

［3］**western Sudan:** "西苏丹"是个历史概念，位于今天西非的北部地区。过去，西苏丹的范围西至大西洋，东到乍得盆地，包括西非雨林以北的亚热带稀树草原和萨赫勒地区。该地区有源自富塔贾隆高原（Fouta Djallon）的塞内加尔河（Senegal River）、冈比亚河（Gambia River）和尼日尔河（Niger River）等水系，曾经孕育过很多伟大的帝国。

［4］**Their designs feature raised geometric patterns, such as black-and-white checkerboards and groups of circles in red, white and black:** 多贡人的设计特点是凸出的几何图形，例如，黑白相间的国际象棋棋盘，以及成组的红色、白色和黑色圆圈。

［5］**Asante:** 阿散蒂人生活在加纳，是阿坎族（Akan）众多支系当中人数最多、最著名的一支。

［6］**Nok culture:** 诺克文化是尼日利亚中部乔斯高原（Jos Plateau）以及周围地区在从石器时期向铁器时期过渡期间所拥有的灿烂文化。人们在这里发现了大量石器和铁器，其中的铁器代表了撒哈拉以南非洲地区迄今为止发现的最早的铁器文化。其繁盛时期在公元前500年至公元200年之间，当时的制陶工艺已经达到很高的水平。伊费和贝宁的雕塑艺术据说都源自诺克文化。

［7］**Ife:** 伊费位于尼日利亚西南部，始建于12世纪，是约鲁巴人的宗教中心。历史上以制作精美的青铜器和赤土陶器闻名于世。伊费现在是金矿开采中心，还有纺织工业以及可可和油棕加工工业。

［8］**the big five:** "非洲五大兽"指的是生活在非洲的五种动物：大象（elephant）、狮子（lion）、豹子（leopard）、犀牛（rhinoceros）和野牛（buffalo）。

[9] **The decorative arts include such items as textiles, jewelry, pottery and basketry. While viewed as crafts in some Western cultures, these objects can also be seen as works of art because of the care and level of skill that goes into their creation:** 非洲的装饰艺术包括织物、饰品、陶器和篮筐等等。尽管在一些西方文化中，它们属于手工艺品的范畴，但是由于非洲工匠们高超的技艺以及倾注的大量心血，这些工艺品堪称艺术品。

[10] **Orisha:** 奥瑞莎（also Orisa or Orixa）是约鲁巴传统宗教中的小神。该宗教有一套复杂的神祇体系，上有造物主，下有约400个等级不同的小神和精灵，它们与其本身的宗派及祭司密切相关。

[11] **Àṣẹ:** "阿斯"是约鲁巴人的一个概念，象征促使事情发生和改变的力量。根据约鲁巴神话，上帝奥罗伦（Olorun）给天地间万事万物赋予了这种力量。

[12] **Many groups of people in western and central Africa have developed their own weaving traditions, using particular types of looms and decorative techniques such as embroidery, patchwork, painting, stenciling, or tie-dyeing:** 西非和中非的许多部族都有各自独特的编织传统。他们先在织布机上织布，然后用刺绣、拼贴、绘画、刻版印花或扎染等技术对布料加以装饰。

[13] **Akan:** "阿坎人"（也译作"阿肯人"）是西非多个民族的总称，主要生活在几内亚湾沿岸的加纳和科特迪瓦境内，是两国最重要的部族。分布在世界各地的阿坎人总数据估计在2 000万至4 000万。

[14] **Because of their anonymity and perceived special powers, these Gon masked figures are able to break normal societal codes and prescriptions as a means of redistributing scarce food and animals at times of great community need:** 在大猩猩面具的掩盖下，没有人知道佩戴者的真实身份，而且人们对他们的特殊能力深信不疑，因此这些佩戴面具的人就可以在集体需要的时候打破社会规则和规范，重新分配稀缺的食品和动物。

[15] **Chi Wara:** "奇瓦拉"象征着农业丰收。奇瓦拉羚羊顶饰是马里班巴拉人的象征，当地青年男女在欢庆节日时，喜欢用这种饰物来装饰自己。

人们佩戴着奇瓦拉面具，跳起有关农业的舞蹈，并且举行和农业相关的仪式，以此来向年轻人传授社会价值以及农业技术。

[16] **The Senufo secure staffs in the ground at the end of cultivation rows; these staffs use bird or female images and serve as goals, markers, and prizes for the field-planting competitions:** 播种时，塞努福人在农田里每排农作物的尽头都插一根棍子，这些有鸟类和女性形象的棍子起到了划界和标记的作用，还是播种比赛赢家的奖品。

[17] **Nommo:** "诺默"或"鱼人"是马里多贡人崇拜的祖先的灵魂。在多贡族的神话传说中，诺默是天空神创造的第一个生物。

[18] **Ifa:** "伊发"是约鲁巴人的智慧神，代表着"智力的发展"。每当需要做出重大的个人或集体决定时，人们就会使用"伊发占卜体系"。该体系不依靠灵媒，而是由一位占卜师对一套符号体系进行诠释。

[19] **East Indian:** "东印度"与"西印度群岛"相对，都是西方人在寻找通往印度的航线过程中产生的名称。"东印度"有两种解释，一说是"印度的西孟加拉邦、比哈尔邦、恰尔肯德邦、奥里萨邦和安达曼以及尼科巴群岛"；另一说是"今天印度、中南半岛和马来群岛的泛称"。

[20] **Tourists have been responsible for still other art demands, particularly for decorative masks and ornamental African sculptures made of ebony or ivory:** （此外，）一些非洲艺术家为了满足游客的需要，用乌木或象牙雕刻出非洲特色的装饰性面具和雕塑。

Exercises

I. Read the following statements and decide whether they are true (T) or false (F).

____ 1. Objects that represent spirits or spiritual powers are often realistic although the things they represent are abstract.

____ 2. The first African pieces brought to Europe were regarded as works of arts.

____ 3. Wood decomposes and is easily destroyed, so few pieces of early wooden sculpture have survived.

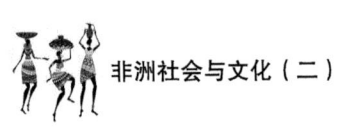

_____ 4. Among the earliest sculptures from northern Nigeria are realistic clay figures of animals made by the Ifa culture as early as the 400s B.C.

_____ 5. The human figures produced by the Nok, with their tube-shaped heads, bodies, arms, and legs, are realistic.

_____ 6. Masks are one of the most important and widespread art forms in Sub-Saharan Africa.

_____ 7. The Igbo people of Nigeria have two types of masks to mark the transition from childhood to adulthood–dark masks and delicate white masks.

_____ 8. The earliest known African paintings are on rocks in South Africa.

_____ 9. The country that is now Ghana was formerly named Ivory Coast.

_____ 10. The multiple roles that art plays in African communities are as diverse as the forms of patronage. These include social, political, economic, historical, military and therapeutic functions.

II. Fill in the following blanks with words that best complete the sentences.

1. The Asante carve dolls that represent their idea of _____ beauty.
2. Among the Konso of Ethiopia, the grave of a wealthy, important man may be marked by a group of carved wooden figures representing the _____, his wives, and the people or animals he killed during his lifetime.
3. Masks are usually worn as _____ in ceremonies and rituals, along with a _____ of leaves, cloth, feathers, and other materials.
4. In addition to face masks, there are _____ masks and _____ masks.
5. Some central African masks function as symbols of _____ for specific groups.
6. Rock paintings by the Khoisan people about 20,000 years ago portray human and animal figures, often in _____ scenes.
7. Tinga tinga paintings have attracted the attention of tourists for their colorful, both _____ and _____ style.
8. Of the diverse art forms of the Yoruba, beads are an _____ part of everyday

lives.

9. The simple act of creating beadwork in a step-by-step or one-by-one manner is considered sacred because _____ is required and repetition places the artist in a _____ like state that further heightens the spiritual value of the beadwork.

10. The _____ of African cultural heritage around the world, Asante Kente is identified by its dazzling, multicolored patterns of bright colors, geometric shapes and bold designs.

Review and Reflect

- Which African art form impresses you most?
- What do you think of African art on the whole?
- What roles do tourists play in African art?

Unit XI　African Literature I

　　在世人的印象当中，非洲是一片文化荒漠。事实上，非洲文学的成就不可小觑。非洲悠久的口述文学传统包含了神话、史诗、民间歌谣、寓言和谚语等多种文学形式。文学与宗教信仰、社会生活、意识形态等方面息息相关，成为非洲作家在叙述中构建自我意识的重要方式。

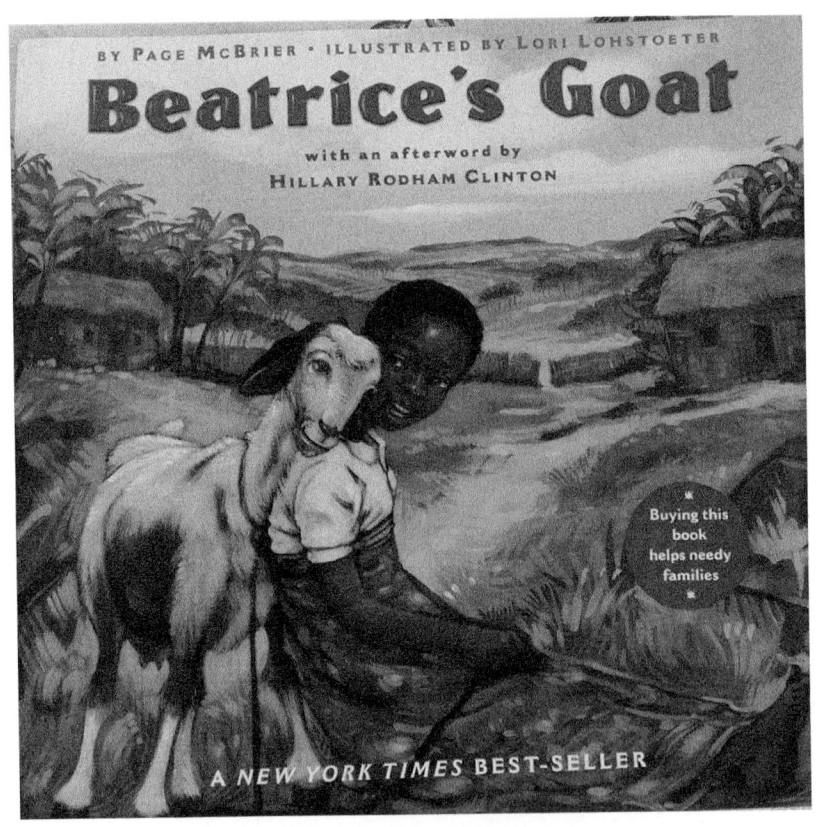

The front cover of an illustrated book
(Photographer: Han Hong)

　　"The African continent has so many stories to tell, it's about time they are told, by them-not us."

　　—Akilnathan Logeswaran, Digital Strategy Consultant of Deloitte Digital

Unit XI African Literature I

> ◎ **Think and Talk**
> ☆ Have you read any African folk tales?
> ☆ What are the forms of African literature?
> ☆ What do you think about African literature?

I. Background and Introduction of African Literature

Africa has a long and complex literary history. Indeed, to suggest that one historical account can represent all of the literature, across time, from all of the regions of Africa is misleading. Deciding when African literature first appeared, or when the tradition began, are questions that are ultimately unanswerable, and determining which literary forms originated in Africa and which were borrowed from elsewhere are issues over which literary critics continue to debate. Nevertheless, scholars of African literature have put forth a general historical overview that allows readers to gain a sense of the literary history of Africa.

African literature is, as we know, the body of traditional oral and written literature in **Afro-Asiatic** and African languages together with works written by Africans in European languages. **Oral literature**, including stories, dramas, **riddles**, histories, myths, songs, **proverbs**, and other expressions, is frequently employed to educate and entertain children. Oral histories, myths, and proverbs additionally serve to remind whole communities of their ancestors' heroic deeds, their past, and the **precedents** for their customs and traditions. Essential to oral literature is a concern for presentation and **oratory**. Folktale tellers use call-response techniques. A **griot** (praise singer) will accompany a **narrative** with music.

Traditional written literature, which is limited to a smaller geographic area than oral literature, is most characteristic of those Sub-Saharan cultures that have participated in the cultures of **the Mediterranean**. In particular, there are written literatures in both **Hausa** and Arabic, created by the scholars of what is now northern

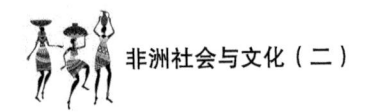

Nigeria, and the Somali people have produced a traditional written literature. There are also works written in **Ge'ez** (**Ethiopic**) and **Amharic**, two of the languages of Ethiopia, which is the one part of Africa where Christianity has been practiced long enough to be considered traditional.[1] Works written in European languages date primarily from the 20th century onward.

Many Africans began writing in European languages during the 1950s in response to colonialist **anthropology**, history, **fiction**, and travel narratives. **Intellectuals** throughout Africa thought their cultures were being misrepresented in these European texts, so they wrote their own perspectives.[2] Westerners then began using those texts because they were widely available and written in the languages of Europe.

The relationship between oral and written traditions and in particular between oral and modern written literatures is one of great complexity and not a matter of simple evolution. Modern African literatures were born in the educational systems imposed by colonialism, with models drawn from Europe rather than existing African traditions. But the African oral traditions exerted their own influence on these literatures.

II. Oral Literatures

Oral literatures have flourished in Africa for many centuries and take a variety of forms, including **epics**, tales, riddles, **poetry** and proverbs.

The African oral tradition **distills** the essence of human experience. Performers of these oral forms take ancient **images** and shape them into spoken texts that influence audiences in **contemporary** societies.[3] Some African performers have used the oral tradition to document centuries of history and to pass on cultural practices over several generations. "When those of us in my generation awakened to earliest consciousness," said Nongenile Masithathu Zenani,[4] a contemporary **Xhosa** storyteller from South Africa, "we were born into a tradition that was already flourishing." Ikabbo,[5] a **San** performer in South Africa in the nineteenth century, also recognized the long history of the oral tradition: "A story is like the wind; it comes from a distant place, and we feel it." However, the African oral tradition is more than simply a means of recording history and maintaining cultural continuity.[6] In these oral art forms, storytellers remember past experiences and the wisdom of ancient times; their stories, epics, and poems become an artistic medium that organizes, examines, and interprets an audience's experiences of the present.[7]

The African oral tradition is not simply a spoken art; it is also an event, a **ritual**, and a performance. Performers use **metaphor** to take an audience's routine experiences and link them to ancient, often fantastic, images from the artistic tradition. When the storytellers bring the two sets of images together, audiences are brought to see the connections between them. This enables the members of the audience to understand their daily experiences at the same time that they are rooted in history. An important theme in some oral traditions is the connection between all living things.

1. Riddle

The riddle establishes a model for all African oral art. The relationship between images in a riddle always contains at least the potential for metaphor and complexity. When a **Lingala** riddle poses the riddle, "A chief who only sits among **thorns**", the answer "the tongue" reveals a description not only of the tongue but also of the chief. The **paradox** of the riddle—in this case, how a chief can sit only among thorns— challenges the audience to solve the puzzle by relying on the **intellect**. Riddles also rely on imagination. In this case, the audience imagines a tongue as a chief and teeth as thorns. This reliance on **imagery** encourages the members of the audience to use their imagination to find answers. By engaging audience in this way, the riddle brings the members of the audience into the center of the riddle, the metaphor that is at its core, allowing them to learn from it by becoming part of the process.

In the riddle, two unlike, and sometimes unlikely, things are compared. The obvious thing that happens during this comparison is that a problem is set, then solved.

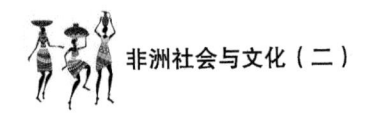

But there is something more important here, involving the riddle as a **figurative** form: the riddle is composed of two sets, and, during the process of riddling, the aspects of each of the sets are transferred to the other. On the surface, it appears that the riddle is largely an intellectual rather than a poetic activity. But through its imagery and the tension between the two sets, the imagination of the audience is also engaged. As they seek the solution to the riddle, the audience itself becomes a part of the images and therefore—and most significantly—of the **metaphorical** transformation.

This may not seem a very complex activity on the level of the riddle, but in this **deceptively** simple activity can be found the essential core of all storytelling, including the interaction of imagery in **lyric** poetry, the tale, and the epic. In the same way as those oral forms, the riddle works in a **literal** and in a figurative mode. During the process of riddling, the literal mode interacts with the figurative in a **vigorous** and creative way. It is that play between the literal and the figurative, between reality and **fantasy**, which characterizes the riddle: in that relationship can be found metaphor, which explains why it is the riddle that **underlies** other oral forms. The images in metaphor by their nature **evoke** emotion; the **dynamics** of metaphor trap those emotions in the images, and meaning is caught up in that activity. So meaning, even in such seemingly simple operations as riddling, is more complex than it may appear.

2. Lyric Poem

People were those who broke for me the string.
Therefore,
The place became like this to me,
On account of it,
Because the string was that which broke for me.
Therefore,
The place does not feel to me,
As the place used to feel to me,

On account of it. For,

The place feels as if it stood open before me,

*Because the **string** has broken for me.*

Therefore,

The place does not feel pleasant to me,

On account of it.

— A San poem, from Specimens of Bushman Folklore[8]

The images in African lyric interact in a dynamic fashion, establishing metaphorical relationships within the poem, and so it is riddling that is the motor of the lyric. And, as in riddles, so also in lyric: metaphor frequently involves and **invokes** paradox. In the lyric, it is as if the singer were **stitching** a set of riddles into a single richly **textured** poem, the series of riddling connections responsible for the ultimate experience of the poem. The singer organizes and controls the emotions of the audience as he systematically works his way through the levels of the poem, carefully establishing the connective threads that bring the separate metaphorical sets into the poem's **totality**. None of the separate **riddling** relationships exists divorced from those others that compose the poem[9]. As these riddling relationships interact and **interweave**, the poet brings the audience to a close, intense sense of the meaning of the poem. Each riddling relationship provides an emotional clue to the overall design of the poem. Further clues to meaning are discovered by the audience in the **rhythmical** aspects of the poem, the way the poet organizes the images, the riddling organization itself, and the sound of the singer's voice as well as the movement of the singer's body. As in the riddle, everything in the lyric is directed to the **revelation** of metaphor.

3. Proverb

Work the clay while it is fresh.

Lack of money is lack of friends; if you have money at your disposal, every dog and goat will claim to be related to you. (Yoruba proverb)

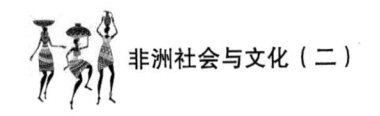

When two elephants fight, it is the grass that gets trampled. (Swahili proverb)
A fight between grasshoppers is a joy to the crow.[10]

The African proverb seems initially to be a **hackneyed** expression, a **trite leftover** repeated until it loses all force. But proverb is also performance, it is also metaphor, and it is in its performance and metaphorical aspects that it achieves its power. In one sense, the experience of a proverb is similar to that of a riddle and a lyric poem: different images are brought into a relationship that is **novel**, which provides insight. When one experiences proverbs in appropriate contexts, rather than in isolation, they come to life. In the riddle the poser provides the two sides of the metaphor. In lyric poetry the two sides are present in the poem but in a complex way; the members of the audience derive their **aesthetic** experience from comprehending that complexity. The words of the proverb are by themselves only one part of the metaphorical experience. The other side of the riddle is not to be found in the same way as it is in the riddle and the lyric. The proverb establishes ties with its metaphorical equivalent in the real life of the members of the audience or with the wisdom of the past. The words of the proverb are a riddle waiting to happen. And when it happens, the African proverb ceases to be a group of tired words.

4. The Tale

The riddle, lyric, and proverb are the materials that are at the dynamic center of the tale. The riddle contains within it the possibilities of metaphor; and the proverb **elaborates** the metaphorical possibilities when the images of the tale are made lyrical–that is, when they are rhythmically organized. Such images are drawn chiefly from two **repertories**: from the contemporary world (these are the realistic images) and from the ancient tradition (these are the fantasy images). These diverse images are brought together during a storytelling performance by their rhythmic organization. Because the fantasy images have the capacity to **elicit** strong emotional reactions from members of the audience, these emotions are the raw material that is woven into the image organization by the patterning. The audience thereby becomes an **integral** part of the story by becoming a part of the metaphorical process that moves to meaning. And meaning, therefore, is much more complex than an obvious **homily** that may be readily available on the surface of the tale.

This patterning of imagery is the main instrument that shapes a tale. In the simplest tales, a model is established, and then it is repeated in an almost **identical** way. In a Xhosa story, an **ogre** chases a woman and her two children. With each part of the story, as the ogre moves closer and as the woman and her children are more intensely **imperiled**, a song organizes the emotions of helplessness, of **menace**, and of terror, even as it moves the story on its **linear** path:

Qwebethe, Qwebethe, what do you want? I'm leaving my food behind on the prairie, I'm leaving it behind, I'm leaving it behind.

With little more than a brief introduction and a quick close, the storyteller develops this tale. There is an uninterrupted linear movement of a realistic single character fleeing from a fantasy ogre—from a conflict to a **resolution**.[11] But that fantasy and that reality are controlled by the lyrical center of the tale, and that seemingly simple mechanism provides the core for complexity. That linear movement, even in the simplest stories, is **subverted** by a **cyclical** movement—in this case, the song—and that is the engine of metaphor. It is the cyclical movement of the tale that makes it possible to experience linear details and images in such a way that they become equated one with the other. So it is the simplest tale that becomes a model for more complex narratives. That lyrical center gives the tale a potential for development.

In a more complex tale, the storyteller moves two characters through three worlds, each of those worlds seemingly different. But by means of that lyrical pulse, the rhythmical ordering of those worlds brings them into such **alignment** that the members of the audience experience them as the same. It is this **discernment** of different images as identical that results in complex structures, characters, events, and meanings. And what brings those different images into this alignment is poetry–more specifically, the metaphorical character of the lyrical poem. The very **composition** of tales makes it possible to link them and to order them metaphorically.

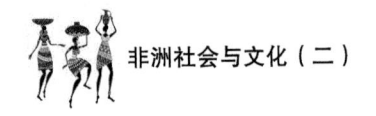

The possibilities of epic are visible in the simplest of tales, and so are the possibilities of the novel.

The **trickster** tale, as it does with so much of the oral tradition, provides insights into this matter of the construction of stories.[12] Masks are the weapons of the trickster: he creates **illusions**, bringing the real world and the world of illusion into temporary and **shimmering proximity**, convincing his **dupe** of the reality of metaphor. That trickster and his **antic** activities are another way of describing the metaphorical motor of storytelling.

5. Heroic Poetry

Hero who surpasses other heroes! **Swallow** *that disappears in the clouds, others disappearing into the heavens! Son of Menzi!* **Viper** *of Ndaba!* **Erect**, *ready to strike. It strikes the* **shields** *of men! Father of the cock! Why did it disappear over the mountains? It* **annihilated** *men! That is* **Shaka**, *son of Senzangakhona, of whom it is said, Bayede! You are an elephant!*

— From a heroic poem dedicated to the Zulu chief Shaka

It is in heroic poetry, or **panegyric**, that lyric and image come into their most obvious union. As in the tale and as in the lyric, riddle, and proverb, the essence of panegyric is metaphor, although the metaphorical connections are sometimes somewhat **obscure**. History is more clearly evident in panegyric, but it remains **fragmented** history, rejoined according to the poetic intentions of the **bard**. Obvious metaphorical connections are frequently made between historical personages or events and images of animals, for example. The fantasy aspects of this kind of poetry are to be found in its construction, in the merging of the real and the animal in metaphorical ways. It is within this metaphorical context that the hero is described and assessed. As in other forms of oral tradition, emotions associated with both historical and non-historical images are at the heart of meaning in panegyric. It is the lyrical rhythm of panegyric that works such emotions into form. In the process, history is reprocessed and given new meaning within the context of contemporary experience. It is a **dual** activity: history is thereby redefined at the same time that it shapes experiences of the present.

The images vary, their main organizing **implement** being the subject of the poem. It is the **metrical** ordering of images, including sound and motion, that holds the poem together, not the narrative of history.

6. Epic

In an epic can be found the merging of various frequently unrelated tales, the metaphorical **apparatus**, the controlling mechanism found in the riddle and lyric, the proverb, and heroic poetry to form a larger narrative. All of this centers on the character of the hero and a gradual revelation of his **frailty**, uncertainties, and torments; he often dies, or is deeply troubled, in the process of bringing the culture into a new **dispensation** often **prefigured** in his **resurrection** or his coming into knowledge. The mythical transformation caused by the creator gods and culture heroes is reproduced precisely in the acts and the cyclical, tortured movements of the hero.

An epic may be built around a **genealogical** system, with parts of it developed and **embellished** into a story. The epic, like the heroic poem, contains historical references such as place names and events; in the heroic poem these are not greatly developed. When they are developed in an epic, they are built not around history, but around a **fictional** tale.[13] The fictional tale ties the historical episode, person, or place name to the cultural history of the people. In an oral society, oral **genres** include history (the heroic poem) and imaginative story (the tale). The epic combines the two, linking the historical episode to the imaginative tale. Sometimes, myth is also a part of epic, with emphasis on origins. The tale, the heroic poem, history, and myth are combined in the epic. In an echo of the tale—where the emphasis is commonly on a central but always non-historical character—a single historical or non-historical character is the center of the epic. And at the core of the epic is that same engine composed of the riddle, the lyric, and the proverb. The tale and myth lend to the epic a magical, supernatural atmosphere: all of nature is touched in the west African *Epic of Sundiata*[14].

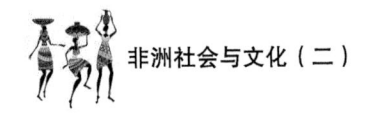

Much is frequently made of the psychology of this central character when he appears in the epic. He is given greater detail than the tale character and given deeper dimension. The epic performer remembers the great events and turning points of cultural history. These events change the culture. In the epic, these elements are tied to the ancient images of the culture (in the form of tale and myth), an act that thereby gives these events cultural **sanction**. The tale and myth lend to the epic (and, by **inference**, to history) a magical, and supernatural atmosphere.

The heroic epic is a grand blending of tale and myth, heroic poetry and history. These separate genres are combined in the epic, and separate epics contain a greater or lesser degree of each. Oral societies have these separate categories: history, the imaginative tale, heroic poetry, myth, and epic. Epic, therefore, is not simply history. History exists as a separate genre. The essential characteristic of epic is not that it is history but that it combines history and tale, fact and fancy, and worlds of reality and fantasy. The epic becomes the grand **summation** of the culture because it takes major turning points in history (always with **towering** historical or non-historical figures who symbolize these turning points) and links them to tradition, giving the changes their sanction. The epic hero may be revolutionary, but he does not signal a total break with the past. Continuity is stressed in epic—in fact, it is as if the shift in the direction of the society is a return to the **paradigm envisioned** by ancient cultural wisdom. The effect of the epic is to mythologize history, to bring history to the essence of the culture, to give history the **resonance** of the ancient roots of the culture as these are expressed in myth, imaginative tale (and **motif**), and metaphor. In heroic poetry, history is fragmented, made discontinuous.[15] In epic, these discontinuous images are given a new form, that of the imaginative tale. And the **etiological** aspects of history (that is, the historical alteration of the society) are tied to the **etiology** of mythology—in other words, the acts of the **mortal** hero are tied to the acts of the **immortals**.

Unit XI　African Literature I

A reader in a bookstore in Dar es Salaam, Tanzauia
(Photographer: Sun Lihua)

History is not the significant genre involved in the epic. It is instead tale and myth that organize the images of history and give those images their meaning. History by itself has no significance: it achieves significance when it is **juxtaposed** to the images of a tradition grounded in tales and myths.[16] This suggests the great value that oral societies place on the imaginative traditions: they are entertaining, certainly, but they are also major organizing devices. As the tales take routine, everyday experiences of reality—by placing them in the **fanciful** context of conflict and resolution with the emotion-evoking motifs of the past—give them a meaning and a completeness that they do not actually have, so in epic is history given a form and a meaning that it does not possess. This imaginative environment revises history, takes historical experiences and places them into the context of the culture, and gives them cultural meaning. The epic is a blending, then, of the ancient culture as it is represented through imaginative tradition with historical events and **personages**. The **divine** trickster links heaven and earth, god and human; the epic hero does the same but also links fancy and reality, myth and history, as well as cultural continuity and historical **disjunction**.[17]

Storytelling is the myths of a society: at the same time that it is conservative, at the heart of nationalism, it is the **propelling** mechanism for change. The struggle between the individual and the group, between the traditions that support and defend the rights of the group and the sense of freedom that argues for undefined horizons of the individual—this is the contest that characterizes the hero's **dilemma**, and the hero in turn is the **personification** of the **quandary** of the society itself and of its individual members.[18]

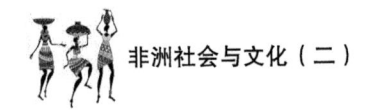

III. The Nature of Storytelling

The storyteller speaks, time collapses, and the members of the audience are in the presence of history. It is a time of masks. Reality, the present, is here, but with explosive emotional images giving it a context. This is the storyteller's art: to mask the past, making it mysterious, seemingly **inaccessible**. But it is inaccessible only to one's present intellect; it is always available to one's heart and soul as well as one's emotions. The storyteller combines the audience's present waking state and its past condition of **semi-consciousness**, and so the audience walks again in history, joining its **forebears**. And history, always more than an academic subject, becomes for the audience a collapsing of time. History becomes the audience's memory and a means of reliving of an **indeterminate** and deeply obscure past.

Storytelling is a **sensory** union of image and idea, a process of recreating the past in terms of the present; the storyteller uses realistic images to describe the present and fantasy images to evoke and embody the substance of a culture's experience of the past. These ancient fantasy images are the culture's heritage and the storyteller's **bounty**: they contain the emotional history of the culture, its most deeply felt **yearnings** and fears, and they therefore have the capacity to elicit strong emotional responses from members of audiences. During a performance, these **envelop** contemporary images—the most unstable parts of the oral tradition, because they are by their nature always in a state of **flux**—and thereby visit the past on the present.

It is the task of the storyteller to forge the fantasy images of the past into masks of the realistic images of the present, enabling the performer to pitch the present to the past, to **visualize** the present within a context of—and therefore in terms of—the past. Flowing through this **potent** emotional **grid** is a variety of ideas that have the look of **antiquity** and ancestral sanction. Story occurs under the **mesmerizing** influence of performance—the body of the performer, the music of her voice, the complex relationship between her and her audience. It is a world unto itself, whole, with its own set of laws. Images that are unlike are juxtaposed, and then the storyteller reveals—to the delight and instruction of the members of the audience—the linkages between them that render them **homologous**. In this way the past and the present are blended; ideas are thereby generated, forming a conception of the present. Performance gives the images their context and ensures the audience a ritual experience that bridges past and present and shapes contemporary life.

Storytelling is alive, ever in transition, never hardened in time. Stories are not meant to be temporally frozen; they are always responding to contemporary realities, but in a **timeless** fashion. Storytelling is therefore not a memorized art. The necessity for this continual transformation of the story has to do with the regular **fusing** of fantasy and images of the real and contemporary world. Performers take images from the present and wed them to the past, and in that way the past regularly shapes an audience's experience of the present. Storytellers reveal connections between humans—within the world, within a society, within a family—emphasizing an **interdependence** and the disaster that occurs when obligations to one's **fellows** are **forsaken**. The artist makes the linkages, the storyteller forges the bonds, tying past and present, joining humans to their gods, to their leaders, to their families, to those they love, to their deepest fears and hopes, and to the essential core of their societies and beliefs.

The language of storytelling includes, on the one hand, image, the patterning of image, and the **manipulation** of the body and voice of the storyteller and, on the other, the memory and present state of the audience. A storytelling performance involves memory: the **recollection** of each member of the audience of his experiences with respect to the story being performed, the memory of his real-life experiences, and the similar memories of the storyteller. It is the rhythm of storytelling that **welds** these

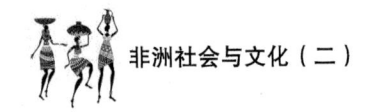

disparate experiences, yearnings, and thoughts into the images of the story. And the images are known, and familiar to the audience. That familiarity is a crucial part of storytelling. The storyteller does not **craft** a story out of whole cloth: she recreates the ancient story within the context of the real, contemporary and known world. It is the metaphorical relationship between these memories of the past and the known images of the world of the present that constitutes the essence of storytelling. The story is never history; it is built of the **shards** of history. Images are removed from historical contexts, then reconstituted within the demanding and authoritative frame of the story. And it is always a sensory experience, an experience of the emotions. Storytellers know that the way to the mind is by way of the heart.[19] The interpretative effects of the storytelling experience give the members of the audience a refreshed sense of reality, a context for their experiences that has no existence in reality. It is only when images of contemporary life are woven into the ancient familiar images that metaphor is born and experience becomes meaningful.

Stories deal with change: mythic transformations of the **cosmos**, heroic transformations of the culture, transformation of the life of every man. The storytelling experience is always ritual, always a rite of passage; one relives the past and, by so doing, comes to insight about present life. Myth is both a story and a fundamental structural device used by storytellers. As a story, it reveals change at the beginning of time, with gods as the central characters. As a storytelling tool for the creation of metaphor, it is both material and method. The heroic epic **unfolds** within the context of myth, as does the tale. At the heart of each of these genres is metaphor, and at the core of metaphor is riddle with its associate, proverb. Each of these oral forms is characterized by a metaphorical process, the result of patterned imagery. These universal art forms are rooted in the **specificities** of the African experience.

IV. Influence and Connection

African storytelling traditions have had a wide-ranging influence on other parts of the world. In the United States, African American oral traditions and storytelling dating from the slavery era have profoundly shaped American culture as a whole, an influence reflected in jazz, **rap**, and **ballads**. Outside the United States, the influence of African oral traditions is also apparent. A common African storytelling character, the trickster, is found in oral traditions in Brazil, **Haiti**, and **Jamaica**—all countries with sizable populations of African **descent.** Of equal significance is the fact that the oral traditions of Africa find their **counterparts** in cultures around the world. *** The Epic of Odysseus*** in Greece and *the Epic of Sundiata* in West Africa correspond to the story of ***Ramayana*** in India. We tell the same stories, and sing the same songs.

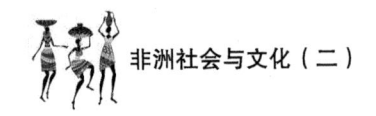

Explanations

［1］**There are also works written in Ge'ez (Ethiopic) and Amharic, two of the languages of Ethiopia, which is the one part of Africa where Christianity has been practiced long enough to be considered traditional:** 还有用埃塞俄比亚的吉兹语和阿姆哈拉语完成的著作。埃塞俄比亚人对基督教的信仰历史悠久，信仰上帝早已成为该国传统。

［2］**Intellectuals throughout Africa thought their cultures were being misrepresented in these European texts, so they wrote their own perspectives:** 非洲学者普遍认为欧洲作家的著作歪曲了非洲文化，因此他们选择从自己的视角来阐述本土文化。

［3］**The African oral tradition distills the essence of human experience. Performers of these oral forms take ancient images and shape them into spoken texts that influence audiences in contemporary societies:** 非洲口述传统以人类历程的精华为内容源泉。讲故事的人利用古代的形象，通过口口相传的方式，对当代听众产生影响。

［4］**Nongenile Masithathu Zenani:** 泽娜妮是南非科萨族人（生卒年不详），生前居住在南非东南部的西斯凯地区（Ciskei）。1967年，她结识了研究非洲语言和文学的美国人哈洛德·斯科伍布（HaroldScheub,1931—）。在1967—1982年期间，他们数次合作，《世界和单词：来自科萨口述传统的故事和观察》（*The World and the Word: Tales and Observations from the Xhosa Oral Tradition*）一书由泽娜妮口述，哈洛德记录完成。为了收集非洲故事、诗歌和口述历史，哈洛德曾到南非、斯威士兰、津巴布韦、莱索托采风，总行程接近1万公里，他用录音带和胶卷记录下大量的非洲故事。他的著作包括《讲故事的非洲人》（*The African Storyteller*）和《非洲形象》（*African Images*, 1972）等等。

［5］**Ikabbo:** 伊卡波1810年左右出生在南非，是个会讲故事的桑人。他认为写作和讲故事具有同样的功能。在被监禁在开普敦期间，他用文字记录下来曾经讲述过的故事。

［6］**However, the African oral tradition is more than simply a means of recording history and maintaining cultural continuity:** 然而，非洲口述传统不仅仅是一种记录历史、保护文化传承的方式。

［7］**In these oral art forms, storytellers remember past experiences and the wisdom of ancient times; their stories, epics, and poems become an artistic medium that organizes, examines, and interprets an audience's experiences of the present:** 通过这些口头艺术表现形式，讲故事的人追溯了古人的经历和智慧。他们利用故事、史诗和诗歌，把观众当前的经历串联起来，审视并且诠释它们。

［8］*Specimens of Bushman Folklore:*《布须曼民俗的标本》由德国语言学家韦尔海姆·布里克（Wilhelm Bleek, 1827—1875）和英格兰语言学家露西·劳埃德（Lucy Lloyd, 1834—1914）合作完成。通过采访会讲故事的布须曼人的方式，他们记录并翻译了87个传奇人物故事、神话传说和其他传统故事。书中还包括一些素描，描绘对象据说是由布须曼人创作的岩画（rock painting）。1875年，韦尔海姆去世，露西将他未竟的事业继续下去，直到1911年该书出版。《布须曼民俗的标本》被视为研究布须曼人及其宗教信仰的基石。

［9］**None of the separate riddling relationships exists divorced from those others that compose the poem:** 除了构成诗歌的关系以外，并不存在任何独立的、令人摸不着头脑的其他关系。

［10］**Work the clay while it is fresh:** 趁热打铁。

Lack of money is lack of friends; if you have money at your disposal, every dog and goat will claim to be related to you (Yoruba proverb): （约鲁巴族谚语）穷在闹市无人问，富在深山有远亲。

When two elephants fight, it is the grass that gets trampled (Swahili proverb): （斯瓦希里谚语）城门失火，殃及池鱼。

A fight between grasshoppers is a joy to the crow: 鹬蚌相争，渔翁得利。

［11］**There is an uninterrupted linear movement of a realistic single character fleeing from a fantasy ogre—from a conflict to a resolution:** 一个真实人物从一个虚构的恶魔身边逃走的过程构成了一个不间断的线性运动，

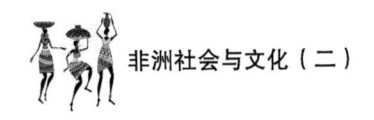

表现了从矛盾到决心的转变。

［12］**The trickster tale, as it does with so much of the oral tradition, provides insights into this matter of the construction of stories**：骗子故事和口述传统的大部分内容都有助于人们了解故事的构成。

［13］**The epic, like the heroic poem, contains historical references such as place names and events; in the heroic poem these are not greatly developed. When they are developed in an epic, they are built not around history, but around a fictional tale**：史诗和英雄诗篇都包含地点和历史事件。在英雄诗篇中，对于地点和事件只是点到为止。史诗对地点和事件有更多阐述，但是并不围绕历史，而是围绕一个虚构的故事展开。

［14］***Epic of Sundiata:*** 长篇英雄史诗《松迪亚塔》歌颂了13世纪西非马里帝国（Mali Empire）的奠基人松迪亚塔（Sundiata Keita, 1230—1255年在位）创建国家的英雄业绩。这部史诗由说唱诗人世代口口相传，有很多不同的版本。

［15］**In heroic poetry, history is fragmented, made discontinuous**：在英雄诗歌中，历史是支离破碎的、不连续的。

［16］**History by itself has no significance: it achieves significance when it is juxtaposed to the images of a tradition grounded in tales and myths**：历史本身并没有任何意义。只有在把它和根植于故事与神话中的传统形象做比照时，历史才具备了重要性。

［17］**The divine trickster links heaven and earth, god and human; the epic hero does the same but also links fancy and reality, myth and history, and cultural continuity and historical disjunction**：骗术出神入化的骗子会把天与地、人与神扯上关系。而史诗中的英雄会进一步把虚幻和现实、神话和历史、文化传承和历史脱节联系在一起。

［18］**The struggle between the individual and the group, between the traditions that support and defend the rights of the group and the sense of freedom that argues for undefined horizons of the individual—this is the contest that characterizes the hero's dilemma, and the hero in turn is the personification of the quandary of the society itself and of its individual members**：个人

与团体之间的斗争，支持和捍卫团体权利的传统与争取个人无限自由之间的斗争让英雄人物左右为难。另一方面，英雄所处的状况也代表了社会和个人进退两难的处境。

[19] **Storytellers know that the way to the mind is by way of the heart:** 讲故事的人知道，只有先打动听众，才能对他们产生影响。

Exercises

I. Read the following statements and decide whether they are true (T) or false (F).

____ 1. Oral literature, including stories, dramas, riddles, histories, myths, songs, proverbs, and other expressions, is frequently employed to educate and entertain adults.

____ 2. Traditional written literature, which is limited to a smaller geographic area than oral literature, is most characteristic of those Sub-Saharan cultures that have participated in the cultures of the Mediterranean.

____ 3. The relationship between oral and written traditions and in particular between written traditions and modern written literatures is one of great complexity and not a matter of simple evolution.

____ 4. On the surface, it appears that the riddle is largely an intellectual rather than a poetic activity.

____ 5. When one experiences proverbs in appropriate contexts, rather than in isolation, they come to life.

____ 6. The proverb establishes ties with its metaphorical equivalent in the real life of the members of the audience or with the wisdom of the past.

____ 7. By means of that lyrical pulse, the rhythmical ordering of those worlds brings them into such alignment that the members of the audience experience them as the same.

____ 8. *The Epic of Sundiata* is about east African history.

_____ 9. In heroic poetry, history is fragmented, made discontinuous.

_____ 10. Stories deal with change: mythic transformations of the cosmos, heroic transformations of the culture, transformations of the lives of every man.

II. Fill in the following blanks with words that best complete the sentences.

1. There are also works written in Ge'ez (Ethiopic) and Amharic, two of the languages of _____, which is the one part of Africa where _____ has been practiced long enough to be considered traditional.

2. During the process of riddling, the literal mode interacts with the figurative in a _____ and _____ way.

3. The African proverb seems initially to be a _____ expression, a trite leftover repeated until it loses all _____.

4. Masks are the weapons of the trickster: he creates illusions, bringing the real world and the world of illusion into temporary and shimmering _____, convincing his _____ of the reality of metaphor.

5. It is in heroic poetry, or panegyric, that _____ and _____ come into their most obvious union.

6. The essential characteristic of epic is not that it is history but that it combines history and tale, fact and fancy, and worlds of _____ and _____.

7. Story occurs under the _____ influence of performance–the body of the performer, the music of her voice, the complex _____ between her and her audience.

8. Stories are not meant to be _____ frozen; they are always responding to contemporary realities, but in a _____ fashion.

9. The interpretative effects of the storytelling experience give the members of the audience a refreshed sense of reality, a _____ for their experiences that has no _____ in reality.

10. Of equal significance is the fact that the _____ of Africa find their _____ in cultures around the world.

Unit XI African Literature I

Review and Reflect

- How do you understand the saying "Oral literature is a necessary and important part in African literature"?
- What do you think of the relationship between epics and traditional religions in Africa?
- What in your opinion is the future of oral literature in Africa? Will it die out?

Unit XII　African Literature II

　　在非洲各国摆脱殖民统治，赢得独立以后，许多国家都面临政治纷争、经济崩溃、传统文化丧失的问题。后殖民时代，用非洲各门语言创造的民族文学相继崛起，反对殖民主义、呼唤民族意识、歌颂本土文化，成为这一时期非洲文学的主旋律。一大批优秀作家和诗人应运而生，创造出许许多多反映非洲各族人民生活和斗争的佳作。以阿契贝和索因卡等为代表的世界级文学大师以其鲜明的民族情感、深刻的思想和独特的非洲韵味感动了世人，向世界展示了非洲人眼中家园的今昔对比，描绘出一个多姿多彩的独特非洲。

The front cover of Things Fall Apart
(Photographer: Han Hong)

"Among the Igbo the art of conversation is regarded very highly, and proverbs

Unit XII　African Literature II

are the palm-oil with which words are eaten."

　　—Chinua Achebe, Nigerian novelist and author of *Things Fall Apart*

> ⊙ **Think and Talk**
> ☆ Have you heard of any African novels?
> ☆ Have you heard of any African literary figures?
> ☆ Have you heard of any African Noble laureates in literature?

I. Literacy in Africa

African literature consists of a body of works in different languages and various **genres**, ranging from oral literature to literature written in colonial languages—English, French and Portuguese.

Some of the first African writings to gain attention in the West were the **poignant** slave **narratives**, such as *The Interesting Narrative of the Life of Olaudah Equiano*[1] *or Gustavus Vassa, the African, Written by Himself* (1789), which described vividly the horrors of slavery and the slave trade. As Africans became literate in their own languages, they often reacted against colonial **repression** in their writings. Others looked to their own past for subjects. Thomas Mofolo,[2] for example, wrote *Chaka* (tr. 1931), about the famous **Zulu** military leader, in Susuto.

Since the early 19th century, writers from western Africa have used newspapers to air their views. Several founded newspapers that served as vehicles for expressing **nascent** nationalist feelings. French-speaking Africans in France, led by Léopold Sédar Senghor, were active in the négritude movement[3] from the 1930s, along with Léon Damas and Aimé Césaire, French speakers from French Guiana and Martinique. Their poetry not only **denounced** colonialism, it proudly **asserted** the **validity** of the cul-

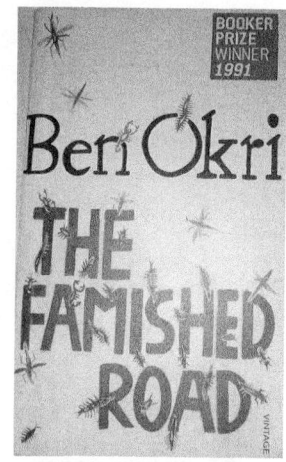

The front cover of The Famished Road by Ben Okri
(Photographer: Han Hong)

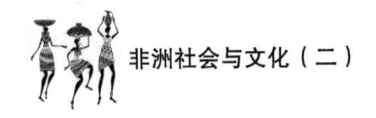

tures that the **colonials** had tried to crush.

After World War II, as Africans began demanding their independence, more African writers published their books. Such writers as, in west Africa, Wole Soyinka, Chinua Achebe, Ousmane Sembène, Kofi Awooner, Agostinho Neto, Tchicaya U Tam'si, Camera Laye, Mongo Beti, Ben Okri, and Ferdinand Oyono and, in east Africa, Ngũgĩ wa Thiong'o, Okot p'Bitek, and Jacques Rabémananjara[4] produced poetry, short stories, novels, essays, and plays. All were writing in European languages, and often they shared the same themes: the clash between **indigenous** and colonial cultures, **condemnation** of European **subjugation**, pride in the African past, and hope for the continent's independent future.

In South Africa, the horrors of **apartheid** have, until the present, dominated the literature. Much of contemporary African literature reveals **disillusionment** and **dissent** with current events. For example, V. Y. Mudimbe in *Before the Birth of the Moon* (1989) explores a doomed love affair played out within a society **riddled** by deceit and corruption. In Kenya, Ngũgĩ wa Thiong'o was jailed shortly after he produced a play, in **Kikuyu**, which was perceived as highly critical of the country's government. Apparently, what seemed most offensive about the drama was the use of songs to emphasize its messages.

Works by Nigerian author Chimamanda Ngozi Adichie
in a bookstore
(Photographer: Sun Lihua)

The weaving of music into the Kenyan's play points out another characteristic of African literature. Many writers incorporate other arts into their work and often weave oral **conventions** into their writing. Achebe's characters **pepper** their speech with proverbs in *Things Fall Apart* (1958). Others, such as **Senegalese** novelist Ousmane Sembène, have moved into films to take their messages to people who cannot read.

A discussion of written African literatures raises a number of complicated and complex problems and questions that only can be briefly sketched out here. The first problem concerns the small readership for African literatures in Africa. Over 50% of Africa's population is illiterate, and hence many Africans cannot access written literatures. The **scarcity** of books available, the cost of those books, and the scarcity of publishing houses in Africa **exacerbate** this already critical situation. Despite this, publishing houses do exist in Africa, and in countries such as Ghana and Zimbabwe, African publishers have produced and sold many impressive works by African authors, many of which are written in African languages.

Many of the works identified by teachers and researchers in North America and Europe as African literature, Chinua Achebe's *Things Fall Apart*, for example, are texts published by presses outside Africa. Some of these works are not even available to African readers. Likewise, what an American teacher might recognize as an African novel might be very different from the locally produced, popular novels that are sold to and read **exclusively** by people living in Africa.

Scholars have identified three waves of literacy in Africa. The first occurred in Ethiopia where written works have been discovered that appeared before the earliest literatures in the **Celtic** and **Germanic** languages of Western Europe. The second wave of literacy moved across Africa with the spread of **Islam**. Soon after the emergence of Islam in the 7th century, its believers established themselves in North Africa through a series of **jihads**, or holy wars. In the 11th and 12th centuries, Islam was carried into the kingdom of Ghana. The religion continued to move eastward through the 19th century.

Remnants of narrative poetry in **Swahili** have been recovered from as early as the 18th century. The poems, in **epic** form, describe the life of **Mohammed** and his **exploits** against Christians. In West Africa, **manuscripts** in Arabic **verse** have been dated to the 14th century. Several literatures, known as **ajami**, written in the Arabic **script** for non-Arabic languages have been discovered from the 18th century. The literatures were written in **Fulani** (West Africa), **Hausa** (northern Nigeria), and **Wolof** (Senegal).

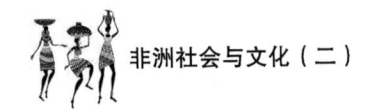

The encounter with Europe through trade relationships, missionary activities, and colonialism **propelled** the third wave of literacy in Africa. In the 19th and 20th century, literary activity in the British colonies was conducted almost entirely in **vernacular** languages. Missionaries found it more useful to translate the Bible into local languages than to teach English to large numbers of Africans. This resulted in the production of **hymns**, morality tales, and other literatures in African languages concerned with **propagating** Christian values and morals. The first of these "Christian-inspired African writings" emerged in South Africa. Thomas Mofolo studied **theology** at the Bible School of the Paris **Evangelical** Mission at Morija (in present-day **Lesotho**). He worked as a teacher and clerk, and was a **proofreader** for the Morija Printing Press. The Press published his novel, Moeti Oa Bocha'bella (The Traveler of the East) as a **serial** in the newspaper in 1906. The novel reveals the influence of **John Bunyan**'s *the Pilgrim's Progress from This World, to That Which Is to Come,* and tells the story of Fekesi, who, tired of all of the **sinfulness** he sees around him, tries to find a perfect kingdom to the East. West African writers, such as Daniel Olorunfemi Fagunwa who wrote in **Yoruba**, produced similar works in African languages. Writers also recorded proverbs, praise-poems, and other pieces of oral literature during this period.

II. NÉgritude

Although Africans had been writing in Portuguese as early as 1850 and a few volumes of African writing in English and French had been published, an explosion of African writing in European languages occurred in the mid-20th century. In the 1930s, black intellectuals from French colonies living in Paris initiated a literary movement called Négritude. Négritude emerged out of a sudden grasp of racial identity and of cultural values and an awareness of the wide **discrepancies** which existed between the promise of the French system of **assimilation** and the reality. The movement's founders looked to Africa to rediscover and **rehabilitate** the African values that had been erased by French cultural superiority.[5] Négritude writers wrote poetry in French in which they presented African traditions and cultures as **antithetical**, but equal, to European culture. Out of this philosophical literary movement came the creation of Présence *Africaine* by **Alioune Diop** in 1947. The journal, according to its founder, was an endeavor to help define African **originality** and to hasten its introduction into the modern world. Other Négritude authors include Léopold Sédar Senghor, Aimé Césaire, and Léon Damas. Below is an excerpt from Senghor's poem *Prayer to Masks:*

Masks! Masks!

Black mask, red mask, you black-and-white masks,

Masks of the four points from which the Spirit blows

In silence I salute you!

Nor you the least, Lion-headed Ancestor

You guard this place forbidden to all laughter of women, to all smiles that fade

*You **distill** this air of **eternity** in which I breathe the air of my Fathers.*

Masks of unmasked faces, stripped of the masks of illness and the lines of age

You who have fashioned this portrait, this my face bent over the alter of white paper

In your own image, hear me!

In the mid-1960s, Nigeria replaced French West Africa as the largest producer and consumer of African literature, and literary production in English surpassed that in French. Large numbers of talented writers in **Francophone** Africa came to occupy important political and diplomatic posts and gave up creative writing. Furthermore, the **tenets** of Négritude seemed far less relevant after independence, as newly independent nations found themselves facing civil wars, military **coups** and corruption.

The vastness in size and population of Nigeria gave it an advantage over smaller countries. In the 1950s, a large readership made up of clerks and small traders and a steadily increasing number of high school students developed in Nigeria, and this readership enabled the emergence of Onitsha market literatures[6]. **Ibadan** College, founded in 1957, produced some of the writers that came to the forefront in the 1960s. East Africa followed West Africa, and in the 1960s, **Makerere College** became a productive center for East African literature. By the mid-1970s, after the coup that brought General **Idi Amin** to power in Uganda, Kenya became the literary center in East Africa.

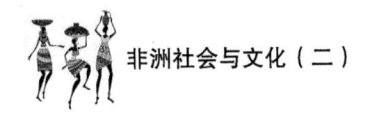

III. Pre-colonial African Literature

Examples of pre-colonial African literature are numerous. Oral literature of West Africa includes the "*Epic of Sundiata*" composed in **medieval** Mali, and the older "*Epic of Dinga*" from the old Ghana Empire [7]. In Ethiopia, there is a substantial literature written in **Ge'ez** going back at least to the 4th century AD; the best-known work in this tradition is *the Kebra Negast*, or "*Book of Kings.*" One form of traditional African folktale is the "**trickster**" story, where a small animal uses its wits to survive encounters with larger creatures. Examples of animal tricksters include Anansi, a spider in the folklore of the **Ashanti** people of Ghana; Àjàpá, a tortoise in Yoruba folklore of Nigeria; and Sungura, a hare found in central and East African folklore. Other works in written form are abundant, namely in North Africa, the **Sahel** regions of West Africa and on the Swahili coast. From **Timbuktu** alone, there are an estimated 300,000 or more manuscripts **tucked away** in various libraries and private collections, mostly written in Arabic but some in the native languages Cuamely Fulaanel Songhai.[8] Many were written at the famous University of Timbuktu. The material covers a wide array of topics, including **Astronomy**, Poetry, Law, History, Faith, Politics, and Philosophy among other subjects. Swahili literature similarly, draws inspiration from Islamic teachings but develops under indigenous circumstances. One of the most **renowned** and earliest pieces of Swahili literature is *Utendi wa Tambuka* or *The Story of Tambuka*[9].

In Islamic times, North Africans such as **Ibn Khaldun** attained great **distinction** within Arabic literature. Medieval North Africa boasted universities such as those of **Fes** and Cairo, with **copious** amounts of literature to supplement them.

IV. Colonial African Literature

The African works best known in the West from the period of colonization and slave trade are primarily slave narratives, such as Olaudah Equiano's *The Interesting Narrative of the Life of Olaudah Equiano or Gustavus Vassa, the African, Written by Himself*.

In the colonial period, Africans exposed to Western languages began to write in those tongues. In 1911, Joseph Ephraim Casely Hayford of the Gold Coast published what is probably the first African novel written in English, *Ethiopia Unbound: Studies in Race* **Emancipation**. Although the work moves between fiction and political **advocacy**, its publication and positive reviews in the Western press mark a **watershed** moment in African literature.

During this period, African plays began to emerge. H. I. E. Dhlomo of South Africa published the first English-language African play, *The Girl Who Killed to Save: Nongqawuse the Liberator* in 1935. In 1962, Ngũgĩ wa Thiong'o of Kenya wrote the first East African drama, *The Black Hermit*, a **cautionary** tale about "tribalism" (racism between African tribes).

Among the first pieces of African literature to receive significant worldwide critical **acclaim** was *Things Fall Apart*, by Chinua Achebe. Published in 1958, late in the colonial era, *Things Fall Apart* analyzed the effect of colonialism on traditional African society.

African literature in the late colonial period (between the end of World War I and independence) increasingly showed themes of liberation, independence, and (among Africans in French-controlled territories) négritude. One of the leaders of the négritude movement, the poet and eventual President of Senegal, Léopold Sédar Senghor, published in 1948 the first **anthology** of French-language poetry written by Africans, *Anthology of the New Black and **Malagasy** Poetry in the French Language*, featuring a **preface** by the French **existentialist** writer **Jean-Paul Sartre**.

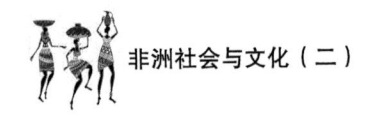

For many writers, this emphasis was not restricted to their publishing. Many, indeed, suffered deeply and directly: **censured** for casting aside his artistic responsibilities in order to participate actively in warfare, **Christopher Okigbo** was killed in battle for **Biafra** against the Nigerian movement of the 1960s' civil war;[10] Mongane Wally Serote was **detained** under South Africa's Terrorism Act No. 83 of 1967[11] between 1969 and 1970, and subsequently released without ever having stood trial; in London in 1970, his **countryman** Arthur Norje committed suicide; Malawi's **Jack Mapanje** was **incarcerated** with neither charge nor trial because of an **off-hand** remark at a university pub; and, in 1995, **Ken Saro-Wiwa**.

V. Postcolonial African Literature

Post-colonialism in Africa refers in general to the era between 1960 and 1970, during which period many African nations gained political independence from their colonial rulers. Many authors writing during this time, and even during colonial times, saw themselves as both artists and political activists, and their works reflected their concerns regarding the political and social conditions of their countries. As nation after nation gained independence from their colonial rulers, beginning in the mid-twentieth century, a sense of **euphoria** swept through Africa as each country celebrated its independence from years of political and cultural domination.[12] Much of early postcolonial writing reflects this sense of freedom and hope. In the years that followed, as many African nations struggled to **reinvigorate** long-**subservient** societies and culture, writers of postcolonial Africa began reflecting the horrors their countries suffered following **decolonization**, and their writing is often **imbued** with a sense of despair and anger, at both the state of their nations and the leaders who replaced former colonial **oppressors**. Critics, including Neil Lazarus, have proposed that this sense of disillusionment, reflected in the works of such authors as Ayi Kwei Armah, marked the beginning of a major change in African intellectual and literary development. Beginning in the 1970s, Lazarus, writes the direction of African fiction began to change, with writers **forging** new forms of expression reflecting more clearly their own thoughts about culture and politics in their works. The writing of this period and later moves away from the subject matter of postcolonial Africa, and moves into the **realm** of new and **realistic** texts that reflect the concerns of their respective nations.

Postcolonial studies gained popularity in England during the 1960s with the establishment of Commonwealth[13] literature–in the United States, this phenomenon did not reach its **zenith** until the 1990s. Because postcolonial writers are studied by and read most often by Western audiences, their works are often seen as being representative of the Third World and studied as much for the **anthropological** information they provide as they are as works of fiction. This, notes Bart Moore-Gilbert in his Postcolonial Theory, has led to the creation of a criticism that is unique in its set of reading practices, which are "preoccupied principally with analysis of cultural forms which **mediate**, challenge, or reflect upon relations of domination and **subordination**." In his study of postcolonial African fiction, Graham Huggan also comments on this phenomenon, theorizing that Western critics need to make an increased effort to expand their **interpretive** universe in order to study African texts as fiction, rather than as windows into the cultures they represent. This difficulty is further **compounded** by the fact that many indigenous African authors in the postcolonial era and beyond remain un-translated, and are thus unavailable to Western critics. In the meantime, the **canon** of translated or European-language works that are available, although but a minor part of African literature in general, have come to

The front cover of Indaba My Children by Credo Mutwa
(Photographer: Han Hong)

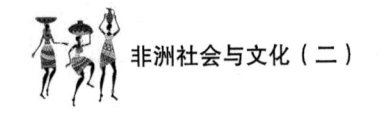

define postcolonial literature and its critical response.

African writers themselves are very conscious of this gap between texts that are accessible to the West and those that remain in Africa. In fact, the language issue became a central concern with many African writers in the years following decolonization, and some, including Ngũgĩ wa Thiong'o, have chosen in the years following independence to reject English and other European languages in favor of native African writing. Ngũgĩ and his supporters were opposed by several African writers, including Chinua Achebe, Wole Soyinka, and others, who challenged the usefulness of such a **stance**. In contrast, Ngũgĩ theorized that by writing in English or French and other European languages, African authors are continuing to enrich those cultures at the expense of their own.[14] Writers who support African-language literature are also concerned that European languages are unable to express the complexity of African experience and culture in those languages, along with the fact that they exclude a majority of Africans, who are unable to read in these languages, from access to their own literary success. In contrast, critics such as Jeannine DeLombard have pointed out that while African-language literature is popular among indigenous African populations, such writing tends to be **formulaic** and **stereotypical**. While the language debate continues, many authors, including **playwrights** Penina Muhando Mlama, Ngũgĩ, and several others, have expanded their literary horizons by collaborating with African people to produce writing that is popular in both origin and destination.

In the present age, a literary **metamorphosis** is taking place within the African continent. There is an observable shift in way of writing (by different authors) and expression by African literary writers. Issues and concerns affecting the African continent, some of which were earlier on thought as "unspeakable" are now gaining audience. Breaking unrealistic conventions and existing **paradigms** of African literary way of writing, while at the same time, borrowing-a-page from the old stock of African writers, is characteristic of the new direction adopted by African literature.

In the **dynamics** of modern-day living, African literature comes in handy in giving directions and ensuring that order prevails in society, mainly through appealing to the society's conscience. African literature is a "**mine** field" that still boasts of rich deposits of values, entertainment and knowledge. Reviewing and researching on African literature reveals all the "hidden treasure".

VI. Women Writers and Issues in Women's Literature

The development of African literature during the 1800s and early 1900s was largely restricted to male writers. **Sexism** made it difficult for women to write and to be recognized. But as the movement for African liberation gained strength after World War II, women writers joined the struggle and made significant contribution to African literature and politics. They wrote from their special experience as victims of both colonialism and sexism, and they did not spare their home countries from criticism.[15] Especially since the appearance of **Flora Nwapa**'s famous novel *Efuru* in 1966, women writers have become leading literary voices on the continent and outspoken voices for change.

The late development of female literature in Africa has its roots in the attitude of African cultures toward women. Women in traditional societies are often excluded from decision making and are limited to defined roles as wives and mothers, despite significant contributions in farming, housework, and child rearing. Practices such as **polygyny**, in which a man has more than one wife, also serve to emphasize the power of males over females in such societies. Motherhood is considered the greatest achievement for a woman, and women are often judged by their ability to produce **offspring**. These **bounds** on the world of traditional African women severely

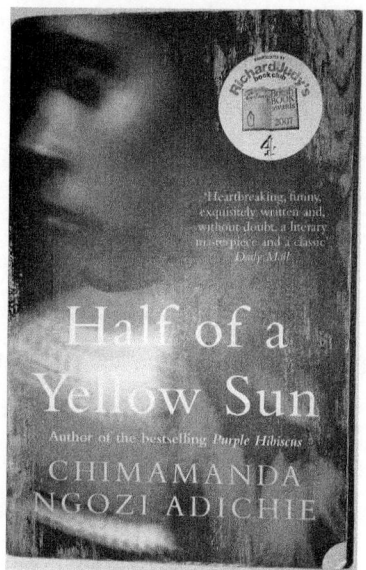

The front cover of Half of a Yellow Sun by Chimamanda Ngozi Adichie
(Photographer: Han Hong)

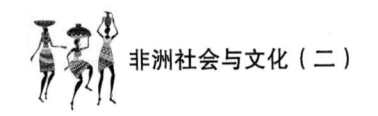

limit their ability to express their identities, experiences, and hopes.

The work of many male African authors has focused on the conflict between the traditional and colonialism, and the corruption of modern African rulers. Many look back on Africa's precolonial past as a kind of glorious golden age. Many women writers, however, have taken a less romantic view of traditional society. For them, the fight for independence meant not only freedom from European domination, but also from a male-dominated world that did not allow them to have a voice of their own.

Meanwhile, in criticizing African society after independence, women have typically been less concerned with political change at the high levels of government and more concerned with the individual's role in the society. Many male authors blame corrupt political leaders for the moral breakdown in African society. Women writers, however, often point out that the average person bears much of the blame–and much of the responsibility for the progress.[16]

Much writing by African women has focused on male behavior, not only on traditional male practices such as **polygamy**, but also on the sexist attitudes of modern African men. Female writers accuse African men of allowing the corrupt social structure to continue because it preserves male advantages. This theme runs through **Mariama Bâ**'s novel *So Long a Letter* (1979). It tells the tale of Ramatoulaye, an African woman whose husband takes a very young second wife after 20 years of marriage. He dies, leaving Ramatoulaye to raise 12 children by herself. The book explores her growth as an independent person.

Female writers examine other aspects of the tension between modern and traditional society. Many do not seek to destroy or abandon African culture, they often emphasize that they are African women. But in trying to change their society for the better, they do not **disregard** all western influence. For example, many male authors portray western-style education as a form of colonial domination, but female authors tend to see it as a liberating force for women. Books such as Bâ's *Scarlet Song* (1981) explore the dilemma of educated women in traditional African society, women who find themselves valued by their husbands mainly as wives and mothers.

African women writers see the modern Africa as neither a paradise nor a land without hope. Instead they see a continent still struggling to throw off the oppressions of colonialism and sexism. They work for social change that will allow all Africans, men and women, to reach their potential.

VII. African Nobel Laureates

Since 1974, the Nobel Committee has disallowed the awarding of the prize **posthumously**, but with the passing of Chinua Achebe in March, 2013, the demand that he be awarded the prize **rekindled** a furious debate in his home country. Anyone from Nigerian politicians in search of a cause to everyday readers of Achebe, felt he had been done by while still alive. Wole Soyinka was, however, not convinced, insisting that the call for awarding a Nobel to the late Achebe was "**obscene**", "**hypocritical**", and a "gross **disservice** to Achebe". Anyone from Nigerian politicians in search of a cause to everyday readers of Achebe all felt an African genius had been unacceptably overlooked. Indeed, in the eyes of many, the work of Achebe–from his **seminal** novel *Things Fall Apart*, stories of Biafra collected in *Girls at War*, and essays such as *"English and the African Writer,"* published in 1965–deserved and still deserves, the Swedish award, especially given his impact on the English literary canon, global literature, and postcolonial studies.

That said, if **the Swedish Academy** were to reverse its stance on posthumous awards in the future, Zimbabwe's **Yvonne Vera**, whose death at 40 in 2005 was a devastating loss for the African literary community, deserves a mention on this dream-list. Primarily a writer of fiction, Vera's novels and short stories make **legible** the often-silenced narratives of Black urban life in colonial **Rhodesia** and postcolonial Zimbabwe. Her piercingly **lyrical** novels such as *Nehanda*, *Butterfly Burning*, and *The Stone Virgins* describe the **paradoxes inherent** to nationalism, modernity, and revolution, especially as experienced by African women. Her work has encouraged not only a fierce following by literary scholars, but has inspired a new **cadre** of exceptionally talented female writers from Zimbabwe such as **Petina**

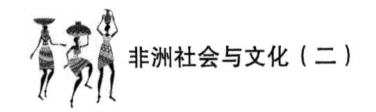

Gappah and **No Violet Bulawayo**.

But this is unlikely to happen soon.

Thus, turning our sights to the living, Ngũgĩ wa Thiong'o is perhaps the most realistic **contender** for the prize. From *Weep Not, Child*, his **semi-autobiographical** novel about the **Mau Mau Struggle** in settler-colonized Kenya to his more recent epic **satire** *Wizard of the Crow*, essays in *Decolonizing the Mind: the Politics of Language in African Literature* and his controversial drama *Ngaahika Ndeenda (I will Marry when I Want)* and as well as many other works across genres, the work of wa Thiong'o represents the **heft**, depth, and breadth that should mark a Nobel laureate's output.

While he was imprisoned for his socialist-**inflected** writing, he **infamously** turned from writing in English to Kikuyu. Despite or because of this, wa Thiong'o has **garnered** a worldwide readership, even as he continues to challenge the **hegemony** of the English language. His **unabashed** commitment to writing an African-centered vision of social transformation for Kenyans, Africans, and all people who have **contended** with physical and cultural forms of violence, domination, and **marginalization**, makes him an especially relevant choice for the prize in the **aftermath** of the Westgate attack[17].

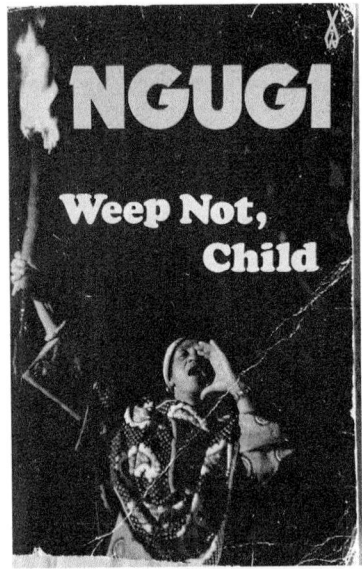

The front cover of Weep Not, Child by Ngũgĩ wa Thiong'o (Photographer: Han Hong)

It is ironic that **Nurrudin Farah**, who could be announced as the Nobel **awardee** on 2013,10,10 by The Nobel Committee for Literature, also reminds us of the recent violence and loss of life in Kenya, via his **vantage point** on the other side of the border. Still, the work of this Somalian writer should not be said to only give context to what political analysts have described as state collapse, civil war, and the rise of **piracy** in Somalia. Instead, Farah's **highly-acclaimed** fiction, which includes three sets of **trilogies**, (the best-known being the one which includes the novels *Maps, Secrets,* and *Gifts*) tells how the **fragility** and power of the nation is affirmed and challenged by the stories of cities, communities, and individual people. Indeed, his masterful and complex **renditions** of **coming-of-age**, **exile**, and return narratives capture in colorful detail the failures, triumphs, impossibilities, and dreams which make up everyday life in the Horn of Africa[18]. It would be well-deserved good news for both Kenya and Somalia, and all of Africa, if perhaps tomorrow, we hear his name.

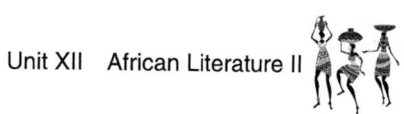

Lastly, and, certainly not the least, is Algerian **feminist** writer **Assia Djebar**, whose name has often floated around the Nobel for the last several years. Djebar, a **prolific** writer of the French language, was **inducted** into the elite **Académie Française** in 2005 and awarded, like Nurrudin Farah, the prestigious **Neustadt International Prize for Literature.** As a very strong contender for the Nobel Prize, Djebar's work **unsettles** the **Anglophile**, **Sub-Saharan**, and **masculinist preoccupations** within the African literary reading public. Her work **topples singular** geographic, political, and formal borders as it can be read as Islamic, **secular**, feminist, anti-colonial, Arab, French, (North) African and covers multiple forms including poetry, fiction, drama, essay, as well as, film screen plays. Author of over ten novels, including *Vaste est la prison* (*So Vast the Prison*), 2013 may very well be her year to **pluck** the Nobel Prize for Literature. Only five African writers have been awarded the prize since its **inception**: Wole Soyinka (1986), Naguib Mahfouz (1988), Nadine Gordimer (1991), J. M. Coetzee (2003) and Doris Lessing (2007).[19]

1. Albert Chinualumogu Achebe

Chinua Achebe was a Nigerian novelist, poet, professor, and critic. His first novel *Things Fall Apart* (1958) was considered his **magnum opus**, and is the most widely read book in modern African literature. He gained worldwide attention for *Things Fall Apart* in the late 1950s; his later novels include *No Longer at Ease* (1960), *Arrow of God* (1964), *A Man of the People* (1966), and *Anthills of the Savannah* (1987). Achebe wrote his novels in English and defended the use of English, a "language of colonisers", in African literature. In 1975, his lecture *An Image of Africa: Racism in* **Joseph Conrad's** *"****Heart of Darkness****"* featured a famous criticism of Joseph Conrad as "a **thoroughgoing** racist"; it was later published in *The Massachusetts Review* amid some controversy.

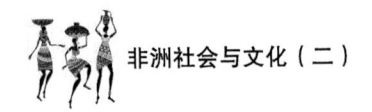

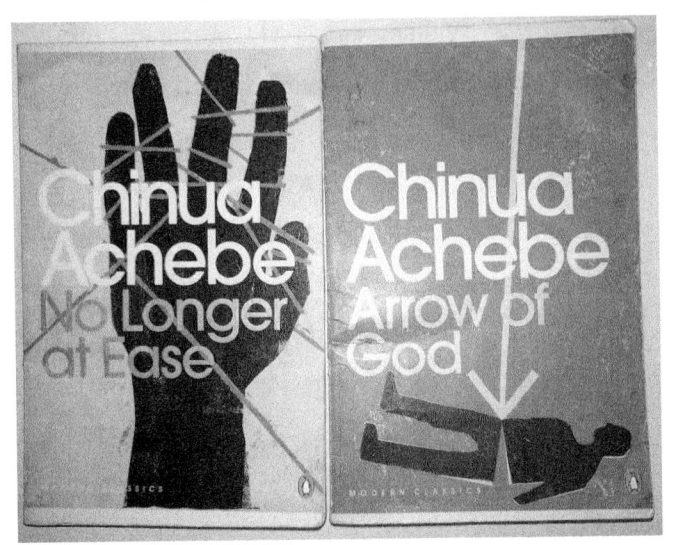

The other 2 books of the African Trilogy by Chinua Achebe
(Photographer: Han Hong)

Back in Nigeria, Achebe set to work revising and editing his novel *Things Fall Apart*, after a line in the poem *"****The Second Coming****"* by **William Butler Yeats**. He cut away the second and third sections of the book, leaving only the story of a **yam** farmer named Okonkwo who lives during the colonization of Nigeria. He added sections, improved various chapters, and restructured the **prose**.

In 1958, Achebe sent his novel to the agent recommended by Gilbert Phelps in London. It was sent to several publishing houses; some rejected it immediately, claiming that fiction from African writers had no market potential. Finally it reached the office of **Heinemann**, where executives hesitated until an educational adviser, Donald MacRae just back in England after a trip through West Africa read the book and forced the company's hand with his **succinct** report: "This is the best novel I have read since the war".

Heinemann published 2,000 **hardcover** copies of *Things Fall Apart* on 17 June

1958. The book was received well by the British press, and received positive reviews from critic Walter Allen and novelist **Angus Wilson**. Three days after publication, *The Times Literary Supplement* wrote that the book "genuinely succeeds in presenting tribal life from the inside". *The Observer* called it "an excellent novel", and the literary magazine *Time and Tide* said that "Mr. Achebe's style is a model for **aspirants**".

Things Fall Apart went on to become one of the most important books in African literature. Selling over eight million copies around the world, it was translated into 50 languages, making Achebe the most translated African writer of all time.

Nigerian Nobel laureate Wole Soyinka has described the work as "the first novel in English which spoke from the interior of the African character, rather than portraying the African as an **exotic**, as the white man would see him."

2. Akinwande Oluwole "Wole" Babatunde Soyinka

Soyinka is a Nigerian playwright and poet. He was awarded the 1986 Nobel Prize in Literature, the first African to be honored in that category. Soyinka was born into a Yoruba family in Abeokuta. After study in Nigeria and the UK, he worked with the **Royal Court Theatre** in London. He went on to write plays that were produced in both countries, in theatres and on radio. He took an active role in Nigeria's political history and its struggle for independence from Great Britain. In 1965, he seized the Western Nigeria Broadcasting Service studio and broadcast a demand for the cancellation of the Western Nigeria Regional Elections. In 1967 during the Nigerian Civil War, he was arrested by the federal government of General **Yakubu Gowon** and put in **solitary confinement** for two years.

Soyinka has been a strong critic of successive Nigerian governments, especially the country's many military **dictators**, as well as other political **tyrannies**, including the **Robert Gabriel Mugabe regime** in Zimbabwe. Much of his writing has been concerned with "the **oppressive** boot and the irrelevance of the colour of the foot that wears it". During the regime of General **Sani Abacha**, Soyinka escaped from Nigeria via the "National Democratic Coalition (**NADECO**) Route" on a motorcycle. Living abroad, mainly in the United States, he was a professor first at **Cornell University** and then at **Emory University** in Atlanta, where in 1996 he was appointed **Robert W. Woodruff** Professor of the Arts.

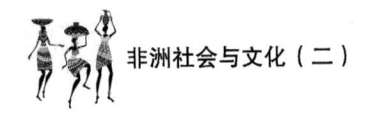

Abacha proclaimed a death sentence against him "**in absentia**". With civilian rule restored to Nigeria in 1999, Soyinka returned to his nation. He has also taught at the universities of Oxford, Harvard and Yale.

From 1975 to 1999, he was a Professor of Comparative Literature at the **Obafemi Awolowo University**, then called the University of **Ife**. With civilian rule restored to Nigeria in 1999, he was made **professor emeritus**. Soyinka has been a Professor of Creative Writing at the University of Nevada, Las Vegas. In the fall of 2007 he was appointed Professor in Residence at **Loyola Marymount University** in Los Angeles, California, US.

A Dance of the Forests is one of the most recognized of Wole Soyinka's plays. The play "was presented at the Nigerian Independence celebrations in 1960, it **denigrated** the glorious African past and warned Nigerians and all Africans that their energies **henceforth** should be spent trying to avoid repeating the mistakes that have already been made." At the time of its release, it was an **iconoclastic** work that angered many of the elite in Soyinka's native Nigeria. Politicians were particularly **incensed** at his **prescient** portrayal of post-colonial Nigerian politics as aimless and corrupt. Despite the **deluge** of criticism, the play remains an influential work. In it, Soyinka **espouses** a unique vision for a new Africa, one that is able to forge a new identity free from the influence of European imperialism.

A Dance of the Forests is regarded as Soyinka's theatrical **debut** and has been considered the most complex and difficult to understand of his plays. In it, Soyinka **unveils** the rotten aspects of the society and demonstrates that the past is no better than the present when it comes to the **seamy** side of life. He lays bare the fabric of the Nigerian society and warns people as they are on the brink of a new stage in their history; independence[20].

Unit XII　African Literature II

Explanations

［1］**Olaudah Equiano:** 奥拉达·艾奎亚诺在其代表作《一个非洲黑奴的自传》(*The Interesting Narrative of the Life of Olaudah Equiano or Gustavus Vassa, the African, Written by Himself*)中，无情揭露了万恶的奴隶制度以及奴隶贸易。曾经为奴的悲惨经历促使他参与了英国的废奴运动（Anti-slavery Movement）。

［2］**Thomas Mofolo**：托马斯·莫夫洛被认为是巴索托（Basotho）最伟大的作家。其代表作《夏卡》(*Chaka*)讲述了一个祖鲁国王的故事：在19世纪初的20多年中，夏卡通过武力扩张的方式迅速建立了一个强大的帝国，但是他的野心和欲望最终导致了帝国的灭亡。

［3］**négritude movement:** 法语单词négritude的意思是"黑人文化运动"。1934年，塞内加尔的利奥波德·赛达尔·桑戈尔（Léopold Sédar Senghor, 1906—2001）、法属圭亚那的莱昂·达马（LéonDamas,1912—1978）和马提尼克的艾梅·塞泽尔（Aimé Césaire, 1913—2008）在巴黎创办刊物《黑人大学生》(*L'Étudiant Noir*)时发起了该运动，旨在复兴黑人价值。

［4］① **Wole Soyinka:** 尼日利亚剧作家、诗人、小说家、评论家沃莱·索因卡（1934—）有"非洲的莎士比亚"之称。1986年，他荣膺诺贝尔文学奖。其代表作有《狮子与珠宝》(*The Lion and the Jewel,* 1959)、《森林之舞》(*A Dance of the Forests,* 1960)、《孔其的收获》(*Kongi's Harvest,* 1964)和《死亡与国王的侍从》(*Death and the King's Horseman,* 1975)等等。

② **Chinua Achebe:** 钦努阿·阿契贝（1930—2013）是尼日利亚著名小说家、诗人、评论家，被誉为"非洲现代文学之父"。他的代表作《非洲三部曲》(*the African Trilogy*)包括《瓦解》(*Things Fall Apart,* 1958)、《再也不得安宁》(*No Longer at Ease,* 1960)以及《神箭》(*Arrow of God,* 1964)。继《非洲三部曲》之后，阿契贝又陆续出版了长篇小说《人民公仆》(*A Man of the People,* 1966)和《荒原蚁丘》(*Anthills of the Savannah,* 1987)等等。

③ **Ousmane Sembène:** 乌斯曼·塞姆班（1923—2007）是塞内加尔作家兼电影导演，他用法语和沃洛夫语创作，被誉为"非洲电影之父"。在2004年戛纳电影节（Festival de Cannes）上，他凭借电影《割礼龙凤斗》（*Moolaadé*）获得"天主教人道精神奖"（Prize of the Ecumenical Jury）。

④ **Kofi Awooner:** 科菲·阿武诺（1935—2013）是加纳诗人、剧作家、演员、政治家、外交家和哲学家。他的诗歌深受其所属埃维部族（Ewe）口述文学传统的影响，内容经常围绕寻根、生死，以及殖民主义展开。

⑤ **Agostinho Neto:** 阿戈什蒂纽·内图（1922—1979）不仅是安哥拉著名诗人，而且是安哥拉解放运动（Angolan Liberation Movement）领袖、安国首任总统。

⑥ **Tchicaya U Tam'si:** 契卡雅·乌·塔姆西（1931—1988）是刚果诗人、记者。他的诗基本上采用超现实主义手法完成。1962年，他出版了诗集《历史概要》（*Épitomé*）。1966年，该诗集在达喀尔（Dakar, Senegal）举办的第一届世界黑人艺术节（The First World Festival of Black Arts）上荣获"诗歌大奖"。从1989年起，在摩洛哥海滨小镇阿西拉（Asilah），以他的名字命名的非洲诗歌奖（the Tchicaya U Tam'si Prize for African Poetry）每两年颁发一次。

⑦ **Camera Laye:** 几内亚作家卡马拉·莱伊（1928—1980）的法语自传体小说《黑孩子》（*L'Enfant noir*, 1953）用回忆的方式描述了非洲的风土人情，成功吸引了世人的眼光。1954年，在第2部小说《国王的目光》（*Le Regard du roi*）中，他描写了一个穷困潦倒的白人在非洲被同化的过程。

⑧ **Mongo Beti:** 蒙戈·贝蒂（1932—2001）对喀麦隆，乃至整个非洲都有深远影响。1956年，他的小说《可怜的蓬巴基督》（*Le pauvre Christ de Bomba*）引起了广泛重视。这部小说挖苦一名白人传教士，指出他和殖民主义之间不可分割的密切联系。贝蒂的其他两部小说《完成的使命》（*Mission terminée*, 1957）和《死里逃生的国王》（*Le roi miraculé: chronique des Essazam*, 1958）也是讽喻性作品。

⑨ **Ben Okri:** 尼日利亚诗人及小说家本·奥克瑞（1959—）被认为是非洲后现代以及后殖民时期最著名的作家。代表作包括《饥饿的路》（*The*

Famished Road, 1991）、《非洲挽歌》（An African Elegy, 1992）、《迷魂之歌》（Songs of Enchantment, 1993）、《神灵为之惊异》（Astonishing the Gods, 1995）、《危险的爱》（Dangerous Love, 1996）以及《无尽的财富》（Infinite Riches, 1998）等。在《饥饿的路》一书中，奥克瑞将现实主义、现代主义与非洲口述传统，尤其是约鲁巴文化巧妙结合，评论界将这一独特的写作手法称为"非洲的魔幻现实主义"，甚至将它与加西亚·马尔克斯（Gabriel García Márquez）的《百年孤独》（Cien Años de Soledad）相提并论。1991年，该书荣获布克奖（the Man Booker Prize）。此外，奥克瑞还撰写了许多文论和短篇小说。他曾荣膺多个文学奖项，近年来在世界文坛备受瞩目。

⑩ **Ferdinand Oyono：** 费尔南德·奥约诺（1929—2010）是喀麦隆外交家、政治家以及作家。他的作品经常含有讽刺意味，其反对殖民主义的文学作品被认为是20世纪非洲文学的典范。1956年，奥约诺发表的两部反殖民主义小说《家童的一生》（Une vie de boy）与《老黑人和奖章》（Le Vieux Nègre et la médaille）揭露了欧洲殖民者的虚伪和暴虐，反映了黑人觉悟的提高。

⑪ **Ngũgĩ wa Thiong'o：** 肯尼亚作家恩古吉·瓦·提安哥（1938—）是一位具有民族独立意识以及本土文化保护意识的作家兼评论家。1964年，恩古吉毕业于乌干达马凯雷雷大学（Makerere University College），后进入英国利兹大学（University of Leeds）续修文学。1967年回国，在内罗毕大学任教，改英国文学系为非洲文学和语言系。他的代表作有小说《黑隐士》（The Black Hermit, 1963）、《孩子，你别哭》（Weep Not, Child, 1964）、《大河两岸》（The River Between, 1965）、《一粒麦种》（A Grain of Wheat, 1967）、《血染的花瓣》（Petals of Blood, 1977）、《十字架上的魔鬼》（Devil on the Cross, 1982），以及《乌鸦魔法师》（Wizard of the Crow, 2006）等等。《血染的花瓣》和剧本《我想结婚时就结婚》（I Will Marry When I Want, 1977）得罪了当权者，恩古吉因此被捕入狱，获释后与家人过着流亡生活，直到肯尼亚第二任总统丹尼尔·阿拉普·莫伊（Daniel arap Moi, 1978—2002在位）下台，才终于安全回国。除了小说创作，恩古吉还写剧本、政论、儿童文学，虽然他的大多数

英语作品都获得了世界性的美誉，但是在肯尼亚独立以后，他开始坚决反对继续使用殖民语言进行文学创作。他认为"语言就像刀枪火炮，是殖民者摧毁本土民族文化最有力的武器"。在恩古吉看来，后殖民时代的作家作为人民的启蒙者，恢复母语写作是本民族斩断殖民奴性的唯一出路。恩古吉认为"文学应该反哺滋养它的土地和人民"。1977年以后，他放弃英语，直接采用母语——基库尤语（Kikuyu）进行文学创作。与此同时，他通过聘请他人或者亲力亲为的方式把自己的新作翻译成英文出版，从而继续保持了自己在非洲乃至世界的影响力。

⑫ **Okot p'Bitek:** 奥考特·庇代克（1931—1982）是乌干达诗人。1966年，他发表了用卢奥语（Luo）完成的代表作《拉维诺之歌》（*Song of Lawino*）。不少评论家认为《拉维诺之歌》是"东非历史上第一部真正的文学作品，开创了新的非洲形式的文学之先河"。

⑬ **Jacques Rabémananjara:** 雅克·拉贝马南雅拉（1913—2005）是马达加斯加政治家、剧作家和诗人。他的长诗《朗巴》（*Lamba*, 1956）和《解毒剂》（*Antidote*, 1961）反映了马达加斯加人民争取自由的艰苦卓绝的斗争。

[5] **The movement's founders looked to Africa to rediscover and rehabilitate the African values that had been erased by French cultural superiority:** 这个运动的发起人将目光投向非洲，期望重新发现并且复兴那些在强势法国文化大举入侵的情况下，已经被遗忘的非洲价值观。

[6] **Onitsha market literatures:** 奥尼查是尼日利亚东南部一个重要的商业城镇，也是伊博族（Igbo）聚居区。20世纪60年代，大量由普通人创作的低俗文学作品以及道德说教手册摆放在奥尼查的书摊上进行销售，从而形成了所谓的"奥尼查市场文学"。

[7] **Ghana Empire:** 加纳帝国是西非历史上有文字记载的最古老、最强大的帝国，它位于塞内加尔河和尼日尔河的上游地区，也就是今天的马里共和国和布基纳法索。在极盛时期，加纳帝国的版图曾经到达今天加纳共和国的西北部，但是两者之间并没有任何直接联系。从11世纪下半叶起，信奉伊斯兰教的柏柏尔人（Berber）大举入侵加纳帝国，很多拒绝

改变宗教信仰的民族被迫向南迁徙，阿肯（Akan）和莫西（Mossi）等部族迁居到今天的加纳共和国境内，成为其主要民族。因此，1957年，当黄金海岸（Gold Coast）在西非率先独立以后，便将国名改为"加纳共和国"。

[8] **From Timbuktu alone, there are an estimated 300,000 or more manuscripts tucked away in various libraries and private collections, mostly written in Arabic but some in the native languages (namely Fula and Songhai):** 仅仅在廷克巴图这一个地方，保存在图书馆中或被私人收藏的手稿就约有30万件之多。除一部分使用本地语言（富拉语和桑海语）以外，大部分手稿都是用阿拉伯语创作完成的。

[9] **Utendi wa Tambuka or The Story of Tambuk:** 《通布卡人的故事》是用斯瓦希里语创作的史诗，完成于1728年，是已知最古老的斯瓦希里文献之一。

[10] **Nigerian movement of the 1960s' civil war:** "尼日利亚内战"是指1967年7月至1970年1月间，发生在尼日利亚联邦共和国的内战，又名"比夫拉战争"（the Biafran War）。历史上的尼日利亚并非一个统一体。在尼日利亚的250多个部族中，最有影响的有3个：北部信奉伊斯兰教的豪萨—富拉尼族（Hausa-Fulani）、西南部的约鲁巴族（Yoruba）和东南部尼日尔河三角洲地带的伊博族（Igbo）。在殖民时期，英国殖民统治者将不同种族和不同文明糅合在一起。独立后的尼日利亚深受殖民问题后遗症所累，国家发展举步维艰。为了保住伊博人的资源和财富，1967年5月30日，尼日利亚东区军事总督伊梅卡·奥杜梅格伍·奥朱古（Chukwuemeka Odumegwu Ojukwu）在其政治中心埃努古（Enugu）发表了《比夫拉独立宣言》，宣布脱离尼日利亚联邦，成立独立的"比夫拉共和国"。这个"国家"的领土面积有12万平方公里，人口高达1,350万。1970年1月，"比夫拉共和国"战败投降，尼日利亚恢复统一。300万人付出了生命的代价，绝大多数死于饥饿和疾病。"比夫拉共和国"经济被彻底摧毁。

[11] **South Africa's Terrorism Act No. 83 of 1967:** 1967年，推行种族隔离政策的前南非政府通过了《反恐怖主义法83号》。该法律名义上反对一

切形式的恐怖主义、依法取缔恐怖活动和组织。但是警方利用该法律追捕和迫害反对种族隔离政策的组织以及个人。很多被羁押的人遭到毒打，很多人从此下落不明。

[12] **As nation after nation gained independence from their colonial rulers, beginning in the mid-twentieth century, a sense of euphoria swept through Africa as each country celebrated its independence from years of political and cultural domination:** 从20世纪中期开始，非洲各国陆续摆脱殖民统治，获得政治独立。在遭受多年的政治和文化统治之后，整个非洲都洋溢着欢声笑语。

[13] **Commonwealth:** "英联邦"是一个松散的国际组织，其全称是the Commonwealth of Nations，由53个独立的主权国家以及属地组成。成员大多数都是前英国殖民地或保护国，包括澳大利亚、加拿大、印度等等。成员国中既有共和国，又有君主国。英王是"英联邦"的名义元首。

[14] **In contrast, Ngũgĩ theorized that by writing in English or French and other European languages, African authors are continuing to enrich those cultures at the expense of their own:** 相比之下，恩古吉认为：用英语、法语或者欧洲其他语言进行创作的非洲作家在不断丰富该语言的同时，削弱了本族语言。

[15] **They wrote from their special experience as victims of both colonialism and sexism, and they did not spare their home countries from criticism:** 深受殖民主义和男性至上主义两座大山的压迫，非洲的女性作家以自己独特的人生经历为素材进行创作。与此同时，对于祖国存在的种种问题，她们也会毫不留情地加以批评。

[16] **Women writers, however, often point out that the average person bears much of the blame–and much of the responsibility for the progress:** 女性作家经常会进一步指出：除了腐败的政客以外，普通人也是造成非洲社会道德沦丧的重要推手。每个人都应该为社会的发展进步承担责任。

[17] **the Westgate attack:** 当地时间2013年9月21日，肯尼亚首都内罗毕的西门商场内（Westgate Shopping Mall）发生了恐怖袭击事件。袭击分子来自肯尼亚邻国索马里，是原教旨主义极端组织"索马里青年党"

（al-Shabab）的成员。他们训练有素，武器精良，弹药充足，依靠地利和劫持的人质与肯尼亚安全部队展开斗争。恐怖袭击一共持续了三天半，造成了惨重的人员伤亡和财产损失。西门商场位于驻肯尼亚的联合国办公机构附近，2007年开业时号称是"东非最好的现代化购物中心"，里面有餐厅、咖啡馆、银行、大型超市和电影院，每天熙熙攘攘，不但是许多肯尼亚富豪、外交官和普通外国人喜欢光顾的地方，而且是新闻机构和媒体人密集的地方。尽管恐怖袭击发生在肯尼亚，但是因为涉及很多国家的公民而成为重大的国际事件。据不完全统计，遇害者中包括美国、澳大利亚、加拿大、中国、英国、法国、加纳、荷兰、印度、韩国、新西兰、南非等国公民。

[18] **the Horn of Africa:** 非洲之角位于非洲东北部，亚丁湾南岸，向东伸入阿拉伯海（Arabian Sea）数百公里，是非洲大陆上最东边的地区。包括吉布提（Djibouti）、埃塞俄比亚（Ethiopia）、厄立特里亚（Eritrea）和索马里（Somalia）四国，面积约为200万平方公里，人口约1.15亿。

[19] **Only five African writers have been awarded the prize since its inception: Wole Soyinka (1986), Naguib Mahfouz (1988), Nadine Gordimer (1991), J. M. Coetzee (2003) and Doris Lessing (2007):** 从诺贝尔奖诞生之日起，只有五位非洲作家摘取了诺贝尔文学奖的桂冠，他们是沃莱·索因卡（1986）、纳吉布·马哈富兹（1988）、纳丁·戈迪默（1991）、约翰·马克斯韦尔·库切（2003）以及多丽丝·莱辛（2007）。

①**Naguib Mahfouz:** 埃及作家纳吉布·马哈富兹（1911—2006）是阿拉伯世界最重要的知识分子之一。纳吉布四岁时就被送到私塾学习《古兰经》，接受宗教启蒙教育。1988年他被授予诺贝尔文学奖，是第一名荣获该奖项的阿拉伯语作家，被西方学者推崇为"埃及的歌德"。"开罗三部曲"（*Cairo Trilogy*）（包括《宫间街》（*Palace Walk*）、《思宫街》（*Palace of Desire*）和《甘露街》（*Sugar Street*））使他享誉世界。小说通过一家三代不同的命运，描绘了1917年至1944年间埃及社会的种种变迁，每一部侧重描写一代人的生活，并以他们居住的地区作为书名。

② **Nadine Gordimer:** 南非白人作家纳丁·戈迪默（1923—2014）出生在南非约翰内斯堡附近的矿业小城斯普林斯。戈迪默的作品以种族隔

离政策下的南非白人和黑人社会为背景,描绘了南非的政治格局、动荡的社会、以及白人和黑人觉醒后的革命运动。她的代表作有《七月的人民》(*July's People*, 1981) 以及《无人伴随我》(*None to Accompany Me*, 1994) 等等。1991年,戈迪默获得诺贝尔文学奖。

③ **J. M. Coetzee:** 约翰·马克斯韦尔·库切(1840—)是南非白人小说家、文学评论家、翻译家、大学教授。库切是第一位两度荣获布克奖的作家。他于2003年获得诺贝尔文学奖。他的代表作品包括《耻》(*Disgrace*)和《迈克尔·K的生活和时代》(*Life and Times of Michael K*)等。2002年,库切移居澳大利亚阿德莱德,2006年入澳洲籍。

④ **Doris Lessing:** 多丽丝·莱辛(1919—2013)是英国女作家,被誉为继伍尔芙(Virginia Woolf)之后最伟大的女性作家。2007年荣获诺贝尔文学奖的时候,她已经88岁高龄,是获奖时最年长的女性诺贝尔奖得主。1919年10月22日,多丽丝·莱辛出生于伊朗。父母是英国人。莱辛5岁时,父亲举家移居到南罗德西亚(今津巴布韦),在一个农场工作。1949年,她移居英国。在非洲早年的艰苦生活中,狄更斯、吉卜林、司汤达、托尔斯泰、陀思妥耶夫斯基等19世纪的小说大师是莱辛最重要的精神伴侣,也为她的文学生涯奠定了坚实的基础。她的代表作有《野草在歌唱》(*The Grass Is Singing*, 1950)和《金色笔记》(*The Golden Notebook*, 1962)等。

[20] **He lays bare the fabric of the Nigerian society and warns people as they are on the brink of a new stage in their history; independence**:他一语道破了尼日利亚的社会结构,并且在独立自主的历史新时期即将来临之际告诫民众。

Exercises

I. Read the following statements and decide whether they are true (T) or false (F).

_____ 1. In north Africa, the horrors of apartheid have, until the present, dominated

Unit XII   African Literature II

the literature.

_____ 2. More than half of Africa's population is illiterate, and hence many Africans cannot access written literatures.

_____ 3. In west Africa, manuscripts in Arabic verse have been dated to the fifteenth century.

_____ 4. Négritude emerged out of a sudden grasp of cultural values and racial identity and an awareness of the wide difference which existed between the promise of the British system of assimilation and the reality.

_____ 5. In the 1950s, a large readership made up of clerks and small traders and a steadily increasing number of high school students developed in Nigeria, and this readership enabled the emergence of Onitsha market literatures.

_____ 6. Among the first pieces of African literature to receive significant worldwide critical acclaim was *The Interesting Narrative of the Life of Olaudah Equiano or Gustavus Vassa, the African, Written by Himself* (1789).

_____ 7. Malawi's Jack Mapanje was incarcerated with charge with treason without trial because of an off-hand remark at a university pub; and, in 1995, Ken Saro-Wiwa.

_____ 8. Postcolonial studies were popular in England during the 1960s with the establishment of Commonwealth literature.

_____ 9. Much of Soyinka's writing has been concerned with "the oppressive boot and the irrelevance of the colour of the foot that wears it".

_____ 10. When *A Dance of the Forests* was released, it was an iconoclastic work that angered many of the elite in Soyinka's native Nigeria.

II. Fill in the following blanks with words that best complete the sentences.

1. As Africans became literate in their own languages, they often reacted against _____ in their writings. Others looked to their own past for _____.

2. The _____ of books available, the cost of those books, and the scarcity of _____ in Africa exacerbate this already critical situation.

3. The founders of Négritude looked to Africa to rediscover and rehabilitate the _____ that had been erased by French cultural _____.

4. In the _____ period, Africans exposed to Western languages began to write in those tongues. In 1911, Joseph Ephraim Casely Hayford of the Gold Coast published what is probably the first African novel written in English, _____ Unbound: Studies in Race _____.

5. Postcolonialism in Africa refers in general to the era between 1960 and 1970, during which period many African nations gained political _____ from their _____.

6. As nation after nation gained independence from their colonial rulers, beginning in the mid-twentieth century, a sense of _____ swept through Africa as each country celebrated its independence from years of political and cultural _____.

7. Postcolonial studies gained popularity in England during the 1960s with the establishment of Commonwealth literature–in the United States, this phenomenon did not reach its _____ until _____.

8. Breaking unrealistic _____ and existing _____ of African literary way of writing, while at the same time, borrowing-a-page from the old stock of African writers, is _____ of the new direction adopted by African literature.

9. Work by Assia Djebar _____ singular geographic, political, and formal borders as it can be read as Islamic, _____, _____, anti-colonial, Arab, French, (north) African and covers multiple forms including poetry, fiction, drama, essay, as well as, film screen plays.

10. In *A Dance of the Forests*, Soyinka espouses a unique vision for a new Africa, one that is able to forge a _____ free from the influence of _____.

Review and Reflect

- What are the common themes in African literature?
- What are the characteristics of contemporary poetry in Africa?
- Why do you think the African writers were able to win the Nobel Prize in Literature?

Key to Questions

Unit VII

I. Read the following statements and decide whether they are true (T) or false (F).

T. F. F. F. F. F. T. T. F. F

_____ 1. During colonial times in Africa, more educational and research films were produced than movies of dramas and documentaries.

_____ 2. **Senegalese** director Ousmane Sembène is considered by some to be the founder of African film making.

_____ 3. **Nigeria**, with its population of 125,000,000, is the largest market in Africa, and the **Nigerian** diaspora is important as well.

_____ 4. However, the films that reach African viewers are **Americans**. Bollywood musicals from India and kung fu films from Hong Kong are also very popular.

_____ 5. "New Nollywood" is a phrase used to describe a recent strategy by some Nigerian filmmakers to make films with **higher** budgets.

_____ 6. Nollywood is the world's second-biggest movie industry in terms of production, second only to **Bollywood**.

_____ 7. *Out of Africa* was nominated for 11 Academy Awards and won 7.

_____ 8. *Moolaadé* deals with rebellion by African women against female circumcision, a tradition upheld by elders, Muslims and animists.

_____ 9. *Virunga* was nominated for **an Oscar Award** in the Best Feature-length Documentary category in 2015.

_____ 10. Virunga National Park is situated in **the Democratic Republic of the**

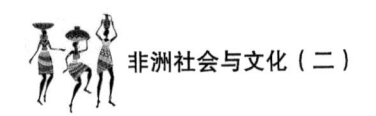

Congo, where dedicated park rangers struggle to protect the last of the mountain gorillas and preserve the park and its residents.

II. Fill in the following blanks with words that best complete the sentences.

1. **adventure, colonial conquest**
2. **outdated, racist**
3. **wild animals, scenery**
4. **commercial, documentary, festivals**
5. **2,000 low-budget, two-thirds**
6. **artistic, stereotypes**
7. **crackdown, regularize**
8. **video, subtitles**
9. **adherence, materialism**
10. **life-threatening, gorillas**

1. Many American and British moviemakers came to Africa to film stories of **adventure** and **colonial conquest**.
2. The viewpoints expressed in works by colonial officials and missionaries are now considered **outdated** and even **racist**.
3. Blessed with **wild animals** and **scenery**, in addition to film crews, Kenya became a favored location for Hollywood.
4. The history of African cinema is composed of three strands. First and best known is the **commercial** cinema: feature films made in Africa for the entertainment market. Second are the **documentary** films made in Africa by scientists, educators, political activists, and the like. Finally, since independence, a self-consciously African cinema has come into being, created by African directors and shown primarily at film **festivals**, but also available on DVD.
5. Nollywood generates an estimated **2,000 low-budget** films per year, with **two-thirds** of them in English, which exceeds India's Bollywood.
6. Some viewers are concerned that these films present Nigeria poorly to the rest of the world, and critics claim that they lack **artistic** content and encourage ethnic and religious **stereotypes**.
7. Nigeria's President Muhammadu Buhari earlier in 2015 ordered a **crackdown** on bootleg copies, to **regularize** sales and give actors and producers a fairer deal of revenues.

8. In the early 1990s, the resourceful Nigerian entrepreneur Ken Nnebue sponsored the production of *Living in Bondage,* a **video** movie in Igbo, a major Nigerian language with English **subtitles**.

9. *Moolaadé* comments on the **adherence** to traditional values that are good and **materialism** that pervades pristine African villages.

10. The filmmakers face many **life-threatening** situations as they go with park rangers through the park to check on the **gorillas** and other animals.

Unit VIII

I. Read the following statements and decide whether they are true (T) or false (F).

F. T. F. F. T. F. T. F. F. F.

____ 1. With more than **1 500** different languages, Africa boasts greater linguistic variety than any other continent.

____ 2. The Semitic language group, which includes Arabic, boasts the greatest number of speakers.

____ 3. Hausa, with about 40 million speakers throughout **western** Africa, is the most widespread language in the Semitic language group.

____ 4. Fulani, the language ranging over the widest area, is found throughout **western, central, and eastern Africa**.

____ 5. The Bantu languages are the most widespread of any linguistic group in Africa.

____ 6. A much smaller percentage of the indigenous population in French colonies was **literate** than in British colonies.

____ 7. Although there are thousands of African languages, most of the systems used to record them originated outside the continent.

____ 8. Swahili is the official language of Tanzania and Kenya and is spoken as a lingua franca throughout most of **east Africa, as well as parts of central Africa**.

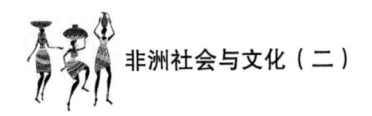

____ 9. A century of Anglicization in South Africa was specifically aimed at **the Dutch/Afrikaans-speaking population**.

____ 10. The Treaty of Vereeniging in 1902 marked the **British** military victory of the Anglo-Boer War.

II. Fill in the following blanks with words that best complete the sentences.

1. **Swahili, Hausa**
2. **Africa, Asia**
3. **Namibia, Botswana**
4. **dominant, subordinate**
5. **native, limited**
6. **Kenya, Tanzania**
7. **Afrikaans, English**
8. **tonal, pitches**
9. **Bantu, south**
10. **diamond, gold**

1. The tremendous linguistic range in Africa includes major languages such as **Swahili** and **Hausa**, spoken by millions of people, and minor languages such as Hazda, which have fewer than a thousand speakers.

2. The Afroasiatic languages consist of about 230 modern and a dozen dead (no longer spoken) languages that originated in northern and eastern **Africa** and in western **Asia**.

3. Khoisan languages are restricted to southern Africa, particular in present-day **Namibia** and **Botswana**.

4. Creole languages are usually based on the vocabulary and grammar of the **dominant** language, but they include many features of the **subordinate** language.

5. Pidgin languages differ from creoles in that they generally have no **native** speakers, are used for **limited** purposes such as trade, and have less complex grammatical structures.

6. Some countries use African language for government business. In **Kenya** and **Tanzania**, Swahili has become the official language because it is widely spoken.

7. The 11 official languages of South Africa are: **Afrikaans**, Ndebele, (isi)Xhosa,

(isi)Zulu, (se)Pedi, (se)Sotho, (se)Tswana, (si)Swazi, (Tshi)Venda, and (xi)Tsonga in addition to **English**.

8. Many African languages are **tonal**, meaning that the words must be pronounced at specific **pitches** to make sense.
9. The **Bantu** languages encompass most of the languages spoken in Africa **south** of the Sahara.
10. Resistance to British imperialist strategy in southern Africa was initiated from the independent Boer Republics of the Transvaal and the Orange Free State as the direct result of the discovery of **diamond** and **gold** in the territories of those republics.

Unit IX

I. Read the following statements and decide whether they are true (T) or false (F).

T. F. T. T. F. T. F. F. T. T.

_____ 1. Religion and custom play a crucial role in determining dietary patterns.
_____ 2. Africa is rich in food resources **and in diversity.**
_____ 3. African food culture is dynamic, which has constantly incorporated new foods into the farming system and diet.
_____ 4. African cuisine is basically a rural one, derived from a rural way of life.
_____ 5. Most African diets are based on **cereals (or grains) or tubers**.
_____ 6. The core of most meals in Sub-Saharan Africa is a starchy porridge made from cereals or tubers, accompanied by a soup or stew of cooked vegetables or crushed peanuts.
_____ 7. Maize is now cultivated in **most** parts of Africa.
_____ 8. African vegetables and fruits are eaten fresh **or** used as an ingredient in cooking.

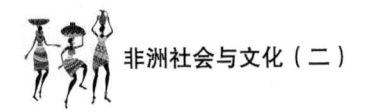

____ 9. Sub-Saharan Africa has an age-old beer tradition, and beer plays an indispensable role in ceremonies and certain social gatherings.

____ 10. Colonization led to significant changes both in what foods Africans produced and what foods were available to purchase.

II. Fill in the following blanks with words that best complete the sentences.

1. **the Portuguese**
2. **maize, flour**
3. **Ethiopian Highlands, teff**
4. **firmer, less sweet**
5. **perishable**
6. **fufu**
7. **rainbow, blend**
8. **stew, pot**
9. **taboos**
10. **colonial**

1. Tomato was brought from the New World by **the Portuguese** in the 16th century, and is now cultivated and consumed throughout much of Africa.

2. Common grains in Africa include **maize** (or corn), millet, sorghum, barley, and wheat, which are usually ground into **flour**.

3. In Ethiopia a staple pancake-like bread "injera" is made from a kind of grain in **Ethiopian Highlands** with limited production called "**teff**".

4. Plantains, which are similar to bananas, but **firmer** and **less sweet**, can also be easily processed into flour, which are often boiled or fried.

5. African traditional alcoholic beverages are **perishable** and have to be consumed soon after being made, which shapes its drinking customs.

6. "Ugali" is the east Africa's version of west Africa's "**fufu**".

7. The cooking of southern Africa is sometimes called "**rainbow** cuisine", as the food in this region is a **blend** of many cultures–the indigenous African tribal societies, Europe, Asia and America.

8. In South Africa, "potjiekos", literally translated into "small pot food", is a **stew** prepared outdoors. It is traditionally cooked in a round, three-legged iron **pot**, so "potjiekos" refers to the food cooked in it.

Key to Questions

9. Food avoidance or food **taboos** do exist, permanent or temporary.
10. Regional variations in some popular European food stuffs reflect the influence of the **colonial** power.

Unit X

I. Read the following statements and decide whether they are true (T) or false (F).

F. F. T. F. F. T. T. F. F. F.

____ 1. Objects that represent spirits or spiritual powers are often **abstract because the things they represent are abstract**.

____ 2. The first African pieces brought to Europe were regarded as **curiosities rather than works of art**.

____ 3. Wood decomposes and is easily destroyed, so few pieces of early wooden sculpture have survived.

____ 4. Among the earliest sculptures from northern Nigeria are realistic clay figures of animals made by the **Nok** culture as early as the 400s B.C.

____ 5. The human figures produced by the Nok, with their tube-shaped heads, bodies, arms, and legs, are **less realistic than the clay figures of animals**.

____ 6. Masks are one of the most important and widespread art forms in Sub-Saharan Africa.

____ 7. The Igbo people of Nigeria have two types of masks to mark the transition from childhood to adulthood–dark masks and delicate white masks.

____ 8. The earliest known African paintings are on rocks in **southern** Africa.

____ 9. The country that is now Ghana was formerly named **Gold Coast**.

____ 10. The multiple roles that art plays in African communities are as diverse as the forms of patronage. These include social, political, economic, historical, and **therapeutic** functions.

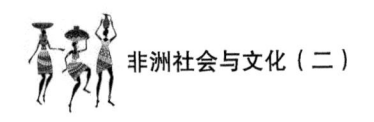

II. Fill in the following blanks with words that best complete the sentences.

1. **feminine**
2. **deceased**
3. **disguises, costume**
4. **helmet, crest**
5. **identity**
6. **hunting**
7. **naïve, surrealistic**
8. **integral**
9. **concentration, trance**
10. **icon**

1. The Asante carve dolls that represent their idea of **feminine** beauty.
2. Among the Konso of Ethiopia, the grave of a wealthy, important man may be marked by a group of carved wooden figures representing the **deceased**, his wives, and the people or animals he killed during his lifetime.
3. Masks are usually worn as **disguises** in ceremonies and rituals, along with a **costume** of leaves, cloth, feathers, and other materials.
4. In addition to face masks, there are **helmet** masks and **crest** masks.
5. Some central African masks function as symbols of **identity** for specific groups.
6. Rock paintings by the Khoisan people about 20,000 years ago portray human and animal figures, often in **hunting** scenes.
7. Tinga tinga paintings have attracted the attention of tourists for their colorful, both **naïve,** and **surrealistic** style.
8. Of the diverse art forms of the Yoruba, beads are an **integral** part of everyday lives.
9. The simple act of creating beadwork in a step-by-step or one-by-one manner is considered sacred because **concentration** is required and repetition places the artist in a **trance** like state that further heightens the spiritual value of the beadwork.
10. The **icon** of African cultural heritage around the world, Asante Kente is identified by its dazzling, multicolored patterns of bright colors, geometric shapes and bold designs.

Key to Questions

Unit XI

I. Read the following statements and decide whether they are true (T) or false (F).

F. T. F. T. T. T. T. F. T. T

_____ 1. Oral literature, including stories, dramas, riddles, histories, myths, songs, proverbs, and other expressions, is frequently employed to educate and entertain **children**.

_____ 2. Traditional written literature is limited to a smaller geographic area than oral literature, which is most characteristic of those Sub-Saharan cultures that have participated in the cultures of the Mediterranean.

_____ 3. The relationship between oral and written traditions and in particular between **oral** and modern written literature is one of great complexity and not a matter of simple evolution.

_____ 4. On the surface, it appears that the riddle is largely an intellectual rather than a poetic activity.

_____ 5. When one experiences proverbs in appropriate contexts, rather than in isolation, they come to life.

_____ 6. The proverb establishes ties with its metaphorical equivalent in the real life of the members of the audience or with the wisdom of the past.

_____ 7. By means of that lyrical pulse, the rhythmical ordering of those worlds brings them into such alignment that the members of the audience experience them as the same.

_____ 8. *The Epic of Sundiata* is about **west** African history.

_____ 9. In heroic poetry, history is fragmented, made discontinuous.

_____ 10. Stories deal with change: mythic transformations of the cosmos, heroic transformations of the culture, transformations of the lives of every man.

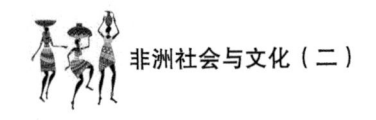

II. Fill in the following blanks with words that best complete the sentences.

1. **Ethiopia, Christianity**	2. **vigorous, creative**
3. **hackneyed, force**	4. **proximity, dupe**
5. **lyric, image**	6. **reality, fantasy**
7. **mesmerizing, relationship**	8. **temporally, timeless**
9. **context, existence**	10. **oral traditions, counterparts**

1. There are also works written in Ge'ez (Ethiopic) and Amharic, two of the languages of **Ethiopia**, which is the one part of Africa where **Christianity** has been practiced long enough to be considered traditional.

2. During the process of riddling, the literal mode interacts with the figurative in a **vigorous** and **creative** way.

3. The African proverb seems initially to be a **hackneyed** expression, a trite leftover repeated until it loses all **force**.

4. Masks are the weapons of the trickster: he creates illusions, bringing the real world and the world of illusion into temporary and shimmering **proximity**, convincing his **dupe** of the reality of metaphor.

5. It is in heroic poetry, or panegyric, that **lyric** and **image** come into their most obvious union.

6. The essential characteristic of epic is not that it is history but that it combines history and tale, fact and fancy, and worlds of **reality** and **fantasy**.

7. Story occurs under the **mesmerizing** influence of performance—the body of the performer, the music of her voice, the complex **relationship** between her and her audience.

8. Stories are not meant to be **temporally** frozen; they are always responding to contemporary realities, but in a **timeless** fashion.

9. The interpreative effects of the storytelling experience give the members of the audience a refreshed sense of reality, a **context** for their experiences that has no

existence in reality.

10. Of equal significance is the fact that the **oral traditions** of Africa find their **counterparts** in cultures around the world.

Unit XII

I. Read the following statements and decide whether they are true (T) or false (F).

F. T. F. F. T. F. F. T. T. T.

____ 1. In **South Africa**, the horrors of apartheid have, until the present, dominated the literature.

____ 2. More than half of Africa's population is illiterate, and hence many Africans cannot access written literatures.

____ 3. In west Africa, manuscripts in Arabic verse have been dated to the **fourteenth** century.

____ 4. Négritude emerged out of a sudden grasp of cultural values and racial identity and an awareness of the wide difference which existed between the promise of the **French** system of assimilation and the reality.

____ 5. In the 1950s, a large readership made up of clerks and small traders and a steadily increasing number of high school students developed in Nigeria, and this readership enabled the emergence of Onitsha market literatures.

____ 6. Among the first pieces of African literature to receive significant worldwide critical acclaim was *Things Fall Apart*.

____ 7. Malawi's Jack Mapanje was incarcerated with **neither** charge **nor** trial because of an off-hand remark at a university pub; and, in 1995, Ken Saro-Wiwa.

____ 8. Postcolonial studies were popular in England during the 1960s with the establishment of Commonwealth literature.

____ 9. Much of Soyinka's writing has been concerned with "the oppressive boot and the irrelevance of the colour of the foot that wears it".

____ 10. When *A Dance of the Forests* was released, it was an iconoclastic work that angered many of the elite in Soyinka's native Nigeria.

II. Fill in the following blanks with words that best complete the sentences.

1. **colonial repression, subjects**
2. **scarcity, publishing houses**
3. **African values, superiority**
4. **colonial, Ethiopia,** *Emancipation*
5. **independence, colonial rulers**
6. **euphoria, domination**
7. **zenith, the 1990s**
8. **conventions, paradigms, characteristic**
9. **topples, secular, feminist**
10. **new identity, European imperialism**

1. As Africans became literate in their own languages, they often reacted against **colonial repression** in their writings. Others looked to their own past for **subjects**.

2. The **scarcity** of books available, the cost of those books, and the scarcity of **publishing houses** in Africa exacerbate this already critical situation.

3. The founders of Négritude looked to Africa to rediscover and rehabilitate the **African values** that had been erased by French cultural **superiority**.

4. In the **colonial** period, Africans exposed to Western languages began to write in those tongues. In 1911, Joseph Ephraim Casely Hayford of the Gold Coast published what is probably the first African novel written in English, *Ethiopia Unbound: Studies in Race* **Emancipation**.

5. Postcolonialism in Africa refers in general to the era between 1960 and 1970, during which period many African nations gained political **independence** from their **colonial rulers**.

6. As nation after nation gained independence from their colonial rulers, beginning in the mid-twentieth century, a sense of **euphoria** swept through Africa as each country celebrated its independence from years of political and cultural **domination**.

Key to Questions

7. Postcolonial studies gained popularity in England during the 1960s with the establishment of Commonwealth literature–in the United States, this phenomenon did not reach its **zenith** until **the 1990s**.

8. Breaking unrealistic **conventions** and existing **paradigms** of African literary way of writing, while at the same time, borrowing-a-page from the old stock of African writers, is **characteristic** of the new direction adopted by African literature.

9. Work by Assia Djebar **topples** singular geographic, political, and formal borders as it can be read as Islamic, **secular**, **feminist**, anti-colonial, Arab, French, (north) African and covers multiple forms including poetry, fiction, drama, essay, as well as, film screen plays.

10. In *A Dance of the Forests*, Soyinka espouses a unique vision for a new Africa, one that is able to forge a **new identity** free from the influence of **European imperialism**.

Reference

[1] Abiodun, R. Yoruba Art and Language: Seeking the African in African Art [M]. New York: Cambridge University Press, 2014.

[2] Adekunle, J. O. & Williams, H. V. (eds). Color Struck: Essays on Race and Ethnicity in Global Perspective [M]. Lanham: University Press of America, 2010.

[3] Adogame, A., Chitando, E. & Bateye, B (eds.). African Traditions in the Study of Religion in Africa: Emerging Trends, Indigenous Spirituality and the Interface with Other World Religions: Essays in Honour of Jacob Kehinde Olupuna [M]. Famham, Surrey, Burlinton, Vt.: Ashgate, 2012.

[4] African Development Bank. African Statistical Yearbook 2013 [R]. Herndon: African Development Bank, 2015.

[5] African Developmnet Bank. Africa in 50 Years' Time-The Road towards Inclusive Growth [R]. Tunis: African Development Bank, 2011.

[6] African Union Development Agency. Agriculture in Africa-Transformation and Outlook [R]. Johannesburg: African Union Development Agency, 2013.

[7] Akande, A. T & Taiwo, P. Contact Linguistics in Africa and Beyond [M]. New York: Nova Publishers, 2013.

[8] Appiah, K. A. & Gates, Jr. H. L (eds.). Encyclopedia of Africa, Vol. 1-4 [M]. Oxford: Oxford University Press, 2010.

[9] Bale, R. Netflix's 'The Ivory Game' Goes Undercover Into Poaching Crisis [J]. National Geographic, 2016.

[10] Bausi, A (ed.). Languages and Cultures of Eastern Christianity: Ethiopian [M]. Famham, Surrey, Burlinton, VT: Ashgate, 2012.

[11] Beegle, K., Christiaensen L., Dabalen A. & Isis Gaddis. Poverty in a Rising Africa [R]. Washington B.C.: World Bank Group, 2016.

[12] Boff, C. & C, J, Radcliff. Encyclopedia of African Literature [M]. Reference & User Services Quarterly, 2003.

[13] Bosman, M. History of Christianity in Africa [M]. Philadelphia Project.

[14] Brautigam, D. The Dragon's Gift: The Real Story of China in Africa [M].Oxford: Oxford University Press, 2009.

[15] David Pilling. Chinese Investment in Africa: Beijing's Testing Ground [N]. Financial Times. 2017-6-13.

[16] Ekwe, H. A Required Reference for Understanding Contemporary Africa [J]. Journal of West African History, 2015.

[17] Entman, R. M. & Rojecki, A. The Black Image in the White Mind: Media and Race in America [M]. Chicago: University of Chicago Press, 2000.

[18] Erlich, H. Islam and Christianity in the Horn of Africa: Somalia, Ethiopia, Sudan [M]. Boulder, Colo.: Lynne Pienner Publishers, 2010.

[19] Fage, J. D. The Cambridge History of Africa, Volume 2: From c.500 B.C.to A.D. 1050 [M]. Cambridge: Cambridge University Press, 1979.

[20] Fetner, P. J. The African Safari: The Ultimate Wildlife and Photographic Adventure [M]. New York: St. Martin's Press, 1987.

[21] Gates, H. L. & Appiah K. A. (eds). Encyclopedia of Africa [M]. Oxford: Oxford University Press, 2010.

[22] Gulliver, P. H (ed.). Tradition and Transition in East Africa: Studies of the Tribal Element in the Modern Era [M]. London: Routledge, 2004.

[23] Harrison, D. Encyclopedia of African Literature [M]. New York: Routledge Press, 2003.

[24] Harry, N. U. African Youth, Innovation and the Changing Society [N]. The Huffington Post, 2013-11-9.

[25] Holmes, T. Journey to Livingstone: Exploration of an Imperial Myth [M]. Edinburgh: Canongate Press, 1993.

[26] Honey, M. Ecotourism and Sustainable Development: Who Owns Paradise? [M]. Washington, D.C.: Island Press, 1999.

[27] Horton, R. Patterns of Thought in Africa and the West [M]. Cambridge:

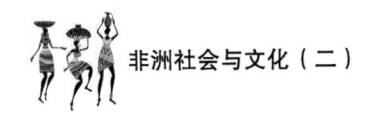

Cambridge University Press, 1993.

[28] Hudson, G (ed.). Essays on Gurage Language and Culture: Dedicated to Wolf Leslau on the Occasion of his 90th Birthday [M]. Wiesbade: Harrassowitz, 1996.

[29] Imperato, P. J. & Imperato, G. H. Historical Dictionary of Mali [M]. Lanham: Scarecrow Press, 2008.

[30] Irele, A. The African Experience in Literature and Ideology [M]. Bloomington: Indiana University Press, 1990.

[31] Irele, A. The Cambridge History of African and Caribbean Literature [M]. Cambridge: Cambridge University Press, 2004..

[32] Irele, F. Abiola (eds.). The Oxford Encyclopedia of African Thought, Vol. 1 & 2 [M]. Oxford: Oxford University Press, 2010.

[33] Iverem, E. We Gotta Have it: Twenty Years of Seeing Black at the Movies, 1986—2006 [M]. New York: Thunder's Mouth Press, 2007.

[34] Johnson K. & Jacobs S. (eds.). Encyclopedia of South Africa [M]. Boulder, Colorado: Lynne Rienner Publishers, 2011.

[35] July, Robert. A History of the African People [M]. Longrove: Waveland Press, 1998.

[36] Kalu, W. J., Wariboko, N. & Falola, T (eds.). Religions in Africa: Conflicts, Politics, and Social Ethics [M]. Trenton, New Jersey: Africa World Press, 2010.

[37] Kasomo, D. W. African Traditional Culture and Religion is Alive and Dynamic [M]. Saarbrucken: LAP Lambert Academic Publishing AG & Co KG, 2010.

[38] Kasomo, D. W. African Traditional Religion: Meaning, Significance and Relevance [M]. Saabrucken, LAP Lambert Academic Publishing, 2010.

[39] Kerr, D. African Popular Theatre: From Pre-colonial Times to the Present Day [M]. London: Heinemann Educational Publishers, 1995.

[40] Klaus K, Frieder, L, & Marian, D (eds.). History of Christianity in Asia, Africa, and Latin America, 1450—1990 [M]. Grand Rapids: Wm. B.

Eerdmans Publishing Company, 2007.

[41] Kretzmann, Paul E. John Ludwig Krapf: The Explorer-Missionary of Northeastern Africa. [M]. London: Forgotten Books, 2012.

[42] Kuo F. What China Knows about Africa That the West Doesn't [N]. The National Interest, 2016-5-22.

[43] Lewis, P. M. Growing Apart: Oil, Politics, and Economic Change in Indonesia and Nigeria [J] African Studies Review, 2009.Vol. 52.

[44] Li, Anshan. 2011. Chinese Medical Cooperation in Africa, with Special Emphasis on the Medical Teams and Anti-Malaria Campaign [M]. Uppsala: Nordic Africa Institute.

[45] Li,Anshan. 2014. Understanding Modern China Sino-African Relations: a Lifetime from Historical Cooperation to Today's Co-dependence. Retrieved August, 11, 2017 from https://uosm2018.wordpress.com/2014/03/27/sino-african-relations-a-timeline-from-historical-cooperation-to-todays-co-dependence/.

[46] Martelli, G. 1970. Livingstone's River: A History of the Zambezi Expedition, 1858—1864 [M]. London: Chatto & Windus.

[47] Mazonde, Issac Ncube. Culture and Education in the Development of Africa [P// C]. Paper Presented at the International Conference on the Cultural Approach to Development in Africa. Dakar: Senegal, 2001.

[48] Mbiti, J. S. Christian Spirituality in Africa: Biblical, Historical, and Cultural Perspectives from Kenya [M]. Eugene, Oregon: Pickwick Publications, 2013.

[49] McGrail, S. Boats of the World [M]. Oxfordshire: Oxford University Press, 2004.

[50] Meredith, Martin. The State of Africa, A History of Fifty Years of Independence [M]. London: The Free Press, 2006.

[51] Middleton, J. Africa: an Encyclopedia for Students, vol. 1-4 [M]. Detroit: Gale, 2001.

[52] Middleton, J. & Miller, J. C (eds.). New Encyclopedia of Africa, vol.1-4

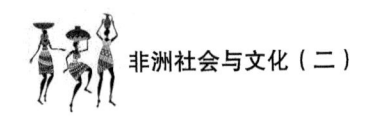

[M]. Detroit: Thomson/Gale, 2008.

[53] Middleton, John (eds.). Africa, an Encyclopedia for Students, Vol. 2 [M]. New York: The Gale Group, 2002.

[54] Middleton, John (eds.). Encyclopedia of Africa: South of the Sahara, Vol. 2, Vol. 3 [M]. New York: C. Scribners Sons, 1997.

[55] Mitchell, P. & Lane, P. (eds). The Oxford Handbook of African Archaeology [M]. Oxford: Oxford University Press, 2013.

[56] Mokhtar, G. Ancient Africa [M]. California: University of California Press, 1990.

[57] Moran, S. Representing Bushmen: South Africa and the Origin of Language [M]. Rochester, New York: University of Rochester Press, 2009.

[58] Morrill, L. & Haines M. Livingstone, Trail Blazer for God [M]. Mountain View: Pacific Press Publication Association, 1959.

[59] Muthwii, M. J. & Kioko, A. N. New Language Bearings in Africa: a Fresh Quest [M]. Buffalo, New York: Multilingual Matters, 2004.

[60] Nelson, F (ed.). Community Rights, Conservation and Contested Land: the Politics of Natural Resource Governance in Africa [M]. London: Earthscan, 2010.

[61] NourbeSe, P. M. Looking for Liviparingstone: An Odyssey of Silence [M]. Stratford: The Mercury Press, 1991.

[62] Oliver, R & A. Atmore. Africa since 1800 [M]. Cambridge: Cambridge University Press, 1994.

[63] Olney, J. Tell Me Africa: An Approach to African Literature [M]. Princeton: Princeton University Press, 1973.

[64] Owusu-Ansah, D. Historical Dictionary of Ghana [M]. Lanham: Littlefield Publishers, 2014.

[65] Page, Willie F. (eds.). Encyclopedia of African History and Culture: from conquest to colonization (1500—1850) [M]. New York: Learning Source Books, 2001.

[66] Paris, P. J (ed.). Religion and Poverty: Pan-African Perspectives [M]. Durham: Duke University Press, 2009.

[67] Rodney, W. How Europe Underdeveloped Africa [M]. London and Dar Es Salaam: Bogle-L'Ouverture Publications, 1973.

[68] Ross, A. C. David Livingstone: Mission and Empire [M]. London and New York: Hambledon and London, 2002.

[69] Saul, M. & Austen, R. A (eds.). Viewing African Cinema in the Twenty-first Century: Art Films and the Hollywood Video Revolution [M]. Athens: Ohio University Press, 2010.

[70] Seaver, G. David Livingston: His Life and Letters [M]. London: Lutterworth Press, 1957.

[71] Shavit, J. & Yaacov. History in Black: African-Americans in Search of an Ancient Past [M]. Abingdon: Taylor & Francis, 2001.

[72] Shinn, D. H. & Ofcansky, T. P. Historical Dictionary of Ethiopia [M]. Lanham, Maryland: Scarecrow Press, 2013.

[73] Soares, B. F (ed.). Muslim-Christian Encounters in Africa [M]. Leiden, Boston: Brill, 2006.

[74] Stewart, J. N. Migrating to the Movies: Cinema and Black Urban Modernity [M]. Berkeley: University of California Press, 2005.

[75] Suberu, R. T. Federalism and Ethnic Conflict in Nigeria [M]. Washington: US Institute of Peace Press, 2001.

[76] Taye, B. A. Islamic Fundamentalism in East Africa: Ethiopia in Focus [M]. Saarbrucken: Scholar's Press, 2013.

[77] Toyin, F & Ann, G. Historical Dictionary of Nigeria [M] Lanham: Scarecrow Press, 2009.

Trimingham, J. S. Islam in Ethiopia [M]. London, New York: Routledge, 2008.

[78] Tudge, C. The Variety of Life [M]. Oxfordshire: Oxford University Press, 2002.

[79] UNDP. If Africa builds nests, will the birds come? Comparative Study on

Special Economic Zones in Africa and China [R]. Beijing: International Poverty Reduction Center in China & UNDP China, July 2015.

[80] UNESCO. EFA Global Monitoring Report, 2015-Education for All 2000—2015 Achievements and Challenges [R]. Paris: UNESCO, 2015.

[81] UNESCO. Global Education Monitoring Report 2016-Education for People and Planet: Creating Sustainable Futures for all [R]. Paris: UNESCO, 2016.

[82] United Nations Economic Commission for Africa. Economic Report on Africa: Industrializing Through Trade [R]. Addis Ababa: United Nations Economic Commission for Africa, 2015.

[83] Wei Jianguo. Africa: A Lifetime of Memories [R]. Beijing: Foreign Languages Press, 2012.

[84] Williams, D. L. & Challis, S. Deciphering Ancient Minds: The Mystery of San Bushman Rock Art [M]. New York: Thames & Hudson, 2011.

[85] Winkler, A. M. Uncertain Safari: Kenyan Encounters and African Dreams [M]. Dallas: Hamilton Books, 2004.

[86] World Bank. Africa Can Help Feed Africa-Removing Barriers to Regional Trade in Food Staples [R]. Washington D.C.: World Bank, 2012.

[87] World Economic Forum. The Travel & Tourism Competitiveness Report 2017 [R]. Geneva: World Economic Forum, 2017.

[88] 艾周昌，舒运国.非洲黑人文明 [M].福州：福建教育出版社，2008.

[89] 李安山. 非洲古代王国 [M].北京：北京大学出版社，2011.

[90] 贺文萍. 中国在非洲的软实力建设：问题与出路 [C].北京：社会科学文献出版社，2015.

[91] 孙丽华，穆育枫，韩红，蒋春生. 非洲部族文化纵览（第二辑）[M].北京：知识产权出版社，2016.

[92] 孙丽华，穆育枫，蒋春生，韩红. 非洲部族文化纵览（第一辑）[M].北京：知识产权出版社，2015.

[93] 王飞鸿.非洲简史 [M]. 长春：吉林大学出版社，2010.

[94] http://africanhistory.about.com. Retrieved on July, 7, 2016.

[95] http://africanhistory.about.com/library/timelines/blIndependenceTime.htm.

Retrieved on Sept. 5, 2016.

[96] http://exhibitions.nypl.org/africanaage/essay-colonization-of-africa.html. Retrieved on August, 5, 2016.

[97] http://muse.jhu.edu/article/543062. Retrieved on August, 5, 2016.

[98] http://plato.stanford.edu/entries/colonialism/ Stanford Encyclopedia of Philosophy. Retrieved on August, 5, 2016.

[99] http://www.ascleiden.nl/content/webdossiers/african-cinema. Retrieved on August, 25, 2016.

[100] http://www.focusfeatures.com/article/hooray_for_nollywood_/print. Retrieved on August, 17, 2016.

[101] http://www.imdb.com/title/tt0416991/. Retrieved on August, 9, 2016.

[102] http://www.jrmartinmedia.com/documentary/virunga/. Retrieved on August, 2, 2016.

[103] http://www.modernghana.com/movie/211/3/the-birth-of-nigerian-films-and-movies.html. Retrieved on August, 19, 2016.

[104] https://africa.si.edu/exhibits/kente/strips. htm.

[105] https://nationalinterest.org/feature/what-china-knows-about-africa-the-west-doesnt-16295?page=0%2C1, Retrieved on August, 14, 2017.

[106] https://www.enca.com/africa/nigerias-nollywood-seeks-worldwide-audience. Retrieved on August, 11, 2016.

[107] https://www.ft.com/content/0f534aa4-4549-11e7-8519-9f94ee97d996, Retrieved on August, 14, 2017.

Vocabulary List

A

abstract *adj.* 抽象的
abusive *adj.* 使用暴力的
Académie Française 法兰西学术院
Academy Award 奥斯卡金像奖
acclaim *n.* 喝彩
acre *n.* 英亩
activate *v.* 激活
activist *n.* 活动家
additive *n.* 添加物
adorn *v.* 装饰
adulterer *n.* 通奸者
advocacy *n.* 倡导
aesthetic *adj.* 审美的，美学的
a far cry from 与……大相径庭
AFP 法新社
Afrikaans 阿非利堪斯语
Afrikaner 阿非利卡人
Afroasiatic 亚非语系
Afro-Asiatic 亚非语系的
aftermath *n.* 创伤
Air France 法国航空公司
ajami （用阿拉伯语创造的非洲文学作品）阿贾米

Akira Kurosawa（日本知名导演）黑泽明
alienate *v.* 使疏远
alignment *n.* 排成直线
a lion's share 最大的部分
Alioune Diop （塞内加尔作家）阿利翁·迪奥普
allegedly *adv.* 据称
allocation *n.* 分配
aloof *adj.* 冷漠的
aluminum *n.* 铝
ambassador *n.* 大使
Amharic 阿姆哈拉语
amulet *n.* 护身符
ancestor *n.* 祖先
ancestral *adj.* 祖先的
ANC 非洲人国民大会
Angelique Kidjo（歌手）安洁莉克·琪蒂欧
anglicization *n.* （其他语言的）英语化
Anglophile *adj.* 亲英的
angular *adj.* 有尖角的
Angus Wilson （英国讽刺小说家）安格斯·威尔逊
animist *n.* 万物有灵论者
anklet *n.* 脚镯
annex *v.* 并吞

Vocabulary List

annihilate *v.* 歼灭

anonymity *n.* 匿名

antagonistic *adj.* 敌对的

antelope *n.* 羚羊

anthology *n.* 诗集

anthropological *adj.* 人类学的

anthropologist *n.* 人类学家

anthropology *n.* 人类学

antic *adj.* 滑稽的

antiquity *n.* 古物

antithetical *adj.* 对立的

apartheid *n.*（南非前政府推行的）种族隔离政策

apparatus *n.* 装置

appeal *n.* 吸引力

apricot *n.* 杏

Arabic 阿拉伯语

archaeologist *n.* 考古学家

arid *adj.* 干旱的

aromatic *adj.* 有香味的

aromatize *v.* 加香味

arranged marriage 包办婚姻

artisan *n.* 工匠

Ashanti 阿散蒂族

aspirant *n.* 有抱负的人

aspiration *n.* 抱负

assert *v.* 坚持主张

Assia Djebar（阿尔及利亚小说家）阿西娅·吉巴尔

assimilation *n.* 同化

assistant director 助理导演

assortment *n.* 各种各样

astronomy *n.* 天文学

asymmetry *n.* 不对称现象

Athol Fugard（南非剧作家）阿索尔·富加德

at odds with 与……不和

atrocity *n.*（战争中的）残暴行为

authenticity *n.* 真实性

autobiographical *adj.* 自传体的

aversion *n.* 厌恶

avocado *n.* 牛油果

awardee *n.* 获奖者

Axumite Empire 阿克苏姆王国

B

baguette *n.*（法国）长面包

ballad *n.* 民谣

Bambara 班巴拉族

Bamiléké 巴米来科族

Bamum 巴蒙语

Bantu-speaking 讲班图语的

Bantu 班图语支

baobab *n.* 猴面包树

baptismal *adj.* 浸礼的

barbarian *n.* 野蛮人

barbecue *n.* 户外烧烤

bard *n.* 吟游诗人

bark *n.* 树皮

barley *n.* 大麦

baron *n.* 男爵

basketry *n.* 筐

Baule 鲍勒族

bead *n.* 有孔的小珠子

beehive *n.* 蜂巢

bell pepper 柿子椒

Berber 柏柏尔人，柏柏尔语族

beset *v.* 困扰

be subject to 易受……影响

beverage *n.* 饮料

Biafra（尼日利亚东南部地区）比夫拉

billboard *n.* 大幅广告牌

black-eyed bean 眉豆

black magic 巫术

black pepper 黑胡椒粉

blade *n.* 刀刃

bland *adj.* 没滋味的

blend *n.* 混合物　*v.* 融合

blight *n.* 荒芜

boast *v.* 有（值得自豪的东西）

Boer 布尔人

Bollywood（印度电影中心）宝莱坞

bondage *n.* 奴役

bonfire *n.* 火堆

boom *n.* 繁荣昌盛

bootleg *adj.* 非法制造贩卖的

Botswana 博茨瓦纳

bound *n.* 限制

bounty *n.* 恩惠

bracelet *n.* 手镯

bracket *n.* 等级

braizer *n.* 烤炉

brass *n.* 黄铜

brewery *n.* 酿酒厂

brew *v.*（酿造）啤酒

bronze *n.* 青铜

buffalo *n.* 野牛

bulk *n.* 主体

burgeoning *adj.* 迅速发展的

Bushman 布须曼人

bushpig *n.* 薮猪

C

cabbage *n.* 卷心菜

cadre *n.* 骨干

caesarean section 剖腹产

calamari *n.* 鱿鱼

canon *n.*（某作家的）精品

Canton 广州

canvas *n.* 油画布

can *v.* 把……装罐保存

cardamom *n.* 豆蔻干籽

caricatural *adj.* 讽刺的

cast *n.* 全体演员

catalytic *adj.* 催化的

caterpillar *n.* 毛毛虫

cathedral *n.* 天主教大教堂

cauliflower *n.* 菜花

cautionary *adj.* 警示的

Celtic 凯尔特语的

Vocabulary List

cement *n.* 水泥

censor *n.* 审查员

censure *v.* 谴责

cereal *n.* 谷物

Chadic 乍得语族

Chad 乍得

chaos *n.* 混乱

charcoal *n.* 木炭

Charles De Gaulle（法国巴黎）戴高乐国际机场

checkerboard *n.* 国际跳棋棋盘

chef *n.* 主厨

Chichewa 奇契瓦语

chief *n.* 酋长

chili pepper 辣椒

Chinua Achebe（尼日利亚作家）钦努阿·阿契贝

Chokwe 乔克维族

Christianity *n.* 基督教

Christopher Okigb（尼日利亚诗人）克里斯托弗·奥基博

chronicle *n.* 编年史

churn out 粗制滥造

cinematography *n.* 摄影

cinnamon *n.* 桂皮

circumcise *v.* 行割礼

clan *n.* 氏族

classification *n.* 分类

clay *n.* 陶土

cleanse *v.* 使（免除）罪过

cliché *n.* 陈词滥调

click *n.*（尤见于非洲南部某些语言的）吸气音

clove *n.* 丁香

cluster *n.* 集群

coarse *adj.* 大颗粒的

cocoyam *n.* 芋头

coffee ceremony 咖啡道

coffee grounds 咖啡渣

coffin *n.* 棺材

coil *n.* 一卷

colonel *n.* 陆军上校

colonial *n.* 生活在殖民地的宗主国居民

colonist *n.* 殖民者

colossus *n.* 巨人

comedy *n.* 喜剧

come of age 成年

coming-of-age 成年

commentary *n.* 评论

commercial *n.* 商业广告

commission *v.* 正式委托

commoner *n.* 平民

Comoros 科摩罗

compelling *adj.* 引人入胜的

complement *v.* 使完美

component *n.* 成分

composite *adj.* 合成的

composition *n.* 构成

compound *v.* 使……复杂化

concentration *n.* 专心

condemnation *n.* 谴责

condensed milk 炼乳

condiment *n.* 调料

confection *n.* 甜食

conflictual *adj.* 冲突的

conscience *n.* 良心

consonant *n.* 辅音字母

consortium *n.* （合作进行某项工程的）联盟

Constitution *n.* 宪法

constraint *n.* 约束

contemporary *adj.* 当代的

contempt *n.* 蔑视

contender *n.* 角逐者

contend *v.* 争夺

contradiction *n.* 矛盾

contradict *v.* 与……矛盾

convention *n.* 惯例

converge *v.* 汇合

copious *adj.* 大量的

coral *n.* 珊瑚

coriander *n.* 香菜

Cornell University 康奈尔大学

corpus *n.* 语料库

cosmos *n.* 宇宙

counterpart *n.* 对应的事物

countryman *n.* 同胞

coup *n.* 政变

cowry *n.* （旧时亚非部分地区用作货币的）小贝壳

coyly *adv.* 含蓄地

crab *n.* 螃蟹

crackdown *n.* 镇压

craft *n.* 手工艺品；*v.* 精心制作

creole *n.* 克里奥语

crest *n.* 顶部

critique *n.* 批判

crown *n.* 王冠

cuisine *n.* 烹饪

culinary *adj.* 烹饪的

culminate *v.* 达到顶点

cult *n.* 偶像

cult *n.* 异教团体

cumin *n.* 孜然

curiosity *n.* 珍稀的物品

currency *n.* 货币

curriculum *n.* 课程

curry *n.* 咖喱

cushion *n.* 靠垫

Cushitic 库希特语族

cyclical *adj.* 周期的

cylinder *n.* 圆柱体

cylindrical *adj.* 圆柱形的

D

Dagon 多贡族

dairy product 乳制品

dangle *n.* 悬垂物

Danish 丹麦的

Dan 丹族

Dar es Salaam （坦桑尼亚）达累斯萨拉姆

Vocabulary List

dazzling *adj.* 耀眼的

debut *n.* 首部作品

deceased *adj.* 死去的

deceptively *adv.* 欺骗地

decolonization *n.* 去殖民化

decompose *v.* 分解

de facto *adj.* 实际上存在（但是不一定合法的）

dehydration *n.* 脱水

delicacy *n.* 美食

deluge *n.* 蜂拥而至的事物

demographics *n.* 人口统计数据

demon *n.* 恶魔

denigrate *v.* 贬低

denounce *v.* 谴责

deposit *n.* 沉积物

descendant *n.* 后代

descend from *v.* 起源于

descent *n.* 血统

dessert *n.* 甜食

detain *v.* 扣押

detrimental *adj.* 有害的

diabolical *adj.* 道德败坏的

dialect *n.* 方言

diaspora *n.* （民族或群体的）大移居

dictator *n.* 独裁者

didactic *adj.* 道德说教的

dietary *adj.* 饮食的

dignitary *n.* 要人

dilemma *n.* 进退两难的局面

diminish *v.* 减少

Dinka 丁卡族；丁卡语

dip *v.* 蘸

discernment *n..* 识别能力

discrepancy *n.* 差异

disguise *n.* 伪装

disillusionment *n.* 幻灭

disjointed *adj.* 不连贯的

disjunction *n.* 脱节

disparate *adj.* 迥然不同的

dispatch *v.* 派遣

dispensation *n.* （政治、宗教）制度

displace *v.* 取代，替代

disposition *n.* 布置

dispossession *n.* 剥夺原住民的土地和水源

disregard *v.* 漠视

dissent *n.* 异议

disservice *n.* 伤害

distill *v.* 提取……精华，蒸馏

distinction *n.* 卓越

distort *v.* 扭曲

distribute *v.* 分配

distribution *n.* 发行

divination *n.* 占卜

divine *adj.* 神圣的

diviner *n.* 占卜师

Djibouti 吉布提

documentary *n.* 纪录片

Dogon 多贡族

dominant *adj.* 占优势的

dough *n.* 生面团

draft beer 生啤

drama *n.* 戏剧性事件

dramatic *adj.* 引人注目的

drill *v.* 钻孔

dual *adj.* 双重的

Dumisani Phakathi（南非导演）杜米萨尼·帕卡斯

dung *n.*（大型动物的）粪便

dupe *n.* 被愚弄的人

Dutch East India Company 荷属东印度公司

dweller *n.* 居住者

dynamic *n.* 动态

dynamism *n.* 活力

E

ebony *n.* 乌木

ecclesiastical *adj.* 基督教会的

eclipse *n.* 消失

economize on 节省

edible *adj.* 可食用的

Efik 埃菲克族

Efuru《埃福汝》

eggplant *n.* 茄子

Egungun 约鲁巴族的面具舞会

Eid 开斋节

elaborate *v.* 详细阐述

elevate *v.* 提高

elicit *v.* 诱发

elite *n.* 精英

emanate *v.* 产生

emancipation *n.* 解放

embellish *v.* 对……加以渲染

embroidery *n.* 刺绣

Emory University 艾默里大学

emulate *v.* 模仿

enchant *v.* 使……着迷

enclave *n.*（隶属外国或外市，具有不同宗教、文化或民族的）领土

encompass *v.* 包含

encroach *v.* 侵占

encrust *v.* 使在表面形成硬壳

engender *v.* 造成

engulf *v.* 吞没

ensue *v.* 接踵而来

entrenched *adj.* 根深蒂固的

entrench *v.* 确立

entrepreneur *n.* 企业家

envelop *v.* 笼罩

envision *v.* 预想

ephemeral *adj.* 短暂的

epic *adj.* 史诗般的

epic *n.* 史诗

Epic of Sundiate（马里帝国史诗）《松迪亚塔》

epidemic *n.* 传染病

episodic *adj.* 由松散片段组成的

erect *v.* 站直

Eritrea 厄立特里亚

escalate *v.* 逐步升级

espouse *v.* 支持

Vocabulary List

eternity *n.* 永恒

Ethiopian Highlands 埃塞俄比亚高原

Ethiopian Orthodox Christian 埃塞东正教

Ethiopian Orthodox Church 埃塞俄比亚正教

Ethiopic 埃塞俄比亚语的

ethnic *adj.* 民族的

ethnic group 部族

etiological *adj.* 病因学的

etiology *n.* 病因学

euphoria *n.* 极度愉悦的心情

evangelical *adj.* 福音派教会的

evoke *v.* 唤起（感情）

exacerbate *v.* 使……加剧

exclusively *adv.* 仅仅

exemplify *v.* 是……的典范

exile *n.* 流亡

existentialist *n.* 存在主义者

exorcise *v.* 驱除

exotic *n.* 外来物

expendable *adj.* 可以牺牲的

exploit *n.* 壮举

extant *adj.* 尚存的

exterminate *v.* 斩尽杀绝

extermination *n.* 灭绝

extinct *adj.* 灭绝的

extra *n.* 群众演员

extremist *n.* 极端分子

eyelid *n.* 眼皮

F

fable *n.* 寓言

fabric *n.* 织物，布料

fair game 可以捉弄的对象

fake *n.* 赝品

fakery *n.* 伪造

fanciful *adj.* 想象的

Fang 芳族

fantasy *n.* 幻想

fauna *n.* 动物群

fearsome *adj.* 令人生畏的

feature film 故事片

feature-length *adj.*（电影）达到正片（应有）长度的

fellow *n.* 伙伴

female genital mutilation 女性割礼

feminine *adj.* 女性的

feminist *n.* 女权主义者

ferment *v.* 发酵

festivity *n.* 庆祝活动

Fes（摩洛哥历史名城）菲斯

fetish *n.* 物神

fictional *adj.* 虚构的

fiction *n.* 小说

fig *n.* 无花果（树）

figurative *adj.* 比喻的

figurine *n.* 小雕像

film *n.* 胶片

filter *n.* 过滤器

fixation *n.* 定位

fixture *n.*（定期定点举行的）活动

flake *v.* 加工成薄片

flavorful *adj.* 可口的

flavoring *n.* 调味品

flavor *v.* 给……调味；*n.* 香料

Flora Nwapa 弗洛拉·恩瓦帕

flux *n.* 变迁

foil *n.* 箔

font *n.* 教堂的圣洗池

Fon 丰族

food taboo 食物禁忌

footage *n.* 电影胶片

footrest *n.* 搁脚板

forebear *n.* 祖先

forge *v.* 打造

formulaic *adj.* 用套话堆砌的

forsake *v.* 舍弃

fowl *n.* 家禽

fraction *n.* 小部分

fragility *n.* 脆弱

fragmented *adj.* 支离破碎的

frailty *n.* 脆弱

Francophone *adj.* 说法语的

frankincense *n.* 乳香

fufu 富富

Fulani 富拉尼人，富拉尼语

Fulani 富拉尼语

fully-fledged *adj.* 全面发展的

furnishing *n.* 陈设

fuse *v.* 熔解

G

game *n.* 野味

gang *n.* 一帮

garner *v.* 获得

Ge'ez 吉兹语

genealogical *adj.* 家谱的

genocide *n.* 种族灭绝

genre *n.* 体裁，类型

geometric *adj.* 几何的

Germanic 日耳曼语（族）的

Ghanaian 加纳人（的）

Ghana 加纳

ghee *n.* 酥油

Gikuyu 基库尤语

ginger *n.* 生姜

gin *n.* 杜松子酒

given *prep.* 考虑到

glutton *n.* 贪吃的人

Golden Globe 金球奖

gorilla *n.* 大猩猩

gourd *n.* 葫芦属植物

Grammy 格莱美奖

granary *n.* 粮仓

grapefruit *n.* 柚子

graphic *adj.* 图案的

grassroots *adj.* 基层的

grease the wheels 贿赂

grid *n.* 网格

grill *v.* （用烤架）烧烤

grimy *n.* 肮脏的

griot *n.* （西非传统的）说唱艺人

grocery store 杂货店

groundnut *n.* 花生

guerrilla *n.* 游击队员

Guinea-Bissau 几内亚比绍

guinea fowl 珍珠鸡

Guinea pepper 几内亚胡椒

Guinness 健力士啤酒

gum arabic 阿拉伯树胶

H

hackneyed *adj.* 陈腐的

hairdo *n.* 发型

Haiti 海地

halva 哈发糕

handiwork *n.* 手工制品

harass *v.* 折磨

hardcore hip-hop 硬核说唱

hardcover *adj.* （书籍）精装的

hardship *n.* 困境

hare *n.* 野兔

haul *v.* 拖曳

Hausa 豪萨族

hawker *n.* 沿街叫卖的小贩

Hazda 哈扎语

headdress *n.* 头饰

headrest *n.* 头枕

Heart of Darkness 《黑暗之心》

heft *n.* 重量

hegemonic *adj.* 支配的

hegemony *n.* 霸权

Heinemann （英国）海尼曼出版社

helmet *n.* 头盔

henceforth *adv.* 从此以后

Henri Storck （比利时纪录片大师）亨利·斯托克

herald *v.* 预示……的来临

herder *n.* 牧民

high commissioner 高级专员

highly-acclaimed *adj.* 倍受赞誉的

Hindi 印地语

holiness *n.* 圣洁

Hollywood 好莱坞

homily *n.* 说教

homologous *adj.* 类似的

hone one's skills 提高技能

horrifically *adv.* 令人震惊地

horsehair *n.* 马鬃

Hotel Des Milles Collines 千丘饭店

Hotel Rwanda （电影）《卢旺达饭店》

humane *adj.* 人道的

humanity *n.* 人性

Hutu 胡图族

hymnal *n.* 赞美诗集

hymn *n.* 赞美诗

hypocrisy *n.* 虚伪，伪善

hypocritical *adj.* 伪善的

I

Ibadan（尼日利亚）伊巴丹

Ibibio 伊比比奥族

Ibn Khaldun（历史学家）伊本·赫尔敦

icon *n.* 偶像，标志

iconoclastic *adj.* 批评传统信仰/习俗思想的

idealize *v.* 把……理想化

identical *adj.* 相同的

Idi Amin（乌干达军事独裁者）伊迪·阿明

Ife（尼日利亚）伊费城

Igbo 伊博族，伊博语

Ijaw 伊贾族

illusion *n.* 假象

image *n.* 形象

imagery *n.* 肖像，意象

imaginary *adj.* 虚构的

imbue *v.* 使……充满

immortal *n.* 神

impala *n.* 黑斑羚

imperial *adj.* 帝国的

imperialist *adj.* 帝国主义的

imperil *v.* 使……处于危险当中

implement *n.* 工具

impracticable *adj.* 行不通的

in absentia 缺席审判

inaccessible *adj.* 难以接近的

inaugurate *v.* 开创

incarcerate *v.* 监禁

incense *n.* 熏香/ *v.* 使发怒

inception *n.* 开始

incidentally *adv.* 顺便提一句

incorporate *v.* 吸收

inculcation *n.* 谆谆教诲

indenture *v.* 用契约束缚

indeterminate *adj.* 模糊的

indigenous *adj.* 本土的

indispensable *adj.* 不可或缺的

Indo-Arabic system 印度–阿拉伯数字体系

induct *v.* 吸收为正式会员

inexorably *adv.* 不可抗拒地

infamously *v.* 声名狼藉地

infancy *n.* 幼儿期

inference *n.* 推断

inflect *v.* 转向

infusion *n.* 灌输

ingest *v.* 咽下

ingredient *n.* 食材

inherent *adj.* 内在的

inheritance *n.* 遗产

initiate *v.* 介绍或准许某人加入

initiation *n.*（常指通过特别仪式）入会

initiative *n.* 倡议

insofar as 在……范围内

institutionalization *n.* 体制化

integral *adj.* 不可或缺的

intellect *n.* 逻辑思维能力

intellectual *n.* 知识分子

intelligible *adj.* 可以理解的

intercom *n.* 对讲机

interdependence *n.* 相互依存

interpretive *adj.* 说明的

interviewee *n.* 被采访者

interweave *v.* 交织

in thrall to 受控制

intransigence *n.* 不妥协态度

invoke *v.* 引起

Irish 爱尔兰的

iROKOtv 尼莱坞电影网络平台

iron-rich *adj.* 含铁量高的

Isak Dinesen（丹麦女作家）伊萨克·迪内森

(isi)Xhosa 科萨语

(isi)Zulu 祖鲁语

Islamic 伊斯兰教的

Islam 伊斯兰教

Island of Pate 帕泰岛

J

Jack Mapanje（马拉维作家、诗人）杰克·马帕涅

Jamaica 牙买加

Jamie Uys（南非导演）加美·尤伊斯

Jean-Paul Sartre（法国哲学家）让·保罗·萨特

jebena *n.* 咖啡壶

jerky *n.* 干肉条

jihad *n.* 圣战

John Bunyan（英国基督教作家）约翰·班扬

Jollof rice 辣椒炖鱼/肉饭

Joseph Conrad（英国作家）约瑟夫·康拉德

Julius Nyerere（坦桑尼亚国父）朱利叶斯·尼雷尔

juxtapose *v.* 把……并列

K

kaasa *n.* 毛毯，毛毡

Kabul（阿富汗首都）喀布尔

Kalahari Desert 卡拉哈里沙漠

Kamba 康巴族

Kanuri 卡努里语

Karen Blixen 凯伦·布里克森

Ken Saro-Wiwa（尼日利亚作家、环保人士）卡山伟华

Kente（加纳）肯特布

Khoi-Khoi 科伊科伊人

Khoikhoi 科伊科伊语

Khoisan 科伊桑人，科伊桑语，科伊桑语系

Kigali（卢旺达首都）基加利

Kikuyu 基库尤语

kiln *n.* 窑炉

Kinyarwanda 卢旺达语

Kirundi 基隆迪语

Kiswahili 斯瓦希里语

Kongo 刚果族

Konso 孔索族

Kordofanian 科尔多凡语族

Kota 科塔族

Kpelle 格贝列语

Kuba 库巴族

kwaito（南非）库威多舞曲

Kwame Nkrumah（加纳国父）克瓦米·恩克鲁玛

L

lactation *n*. 哺乳期

ladle *n*. 长柄勺

Lagos（尼日利亚最大城市）拉各斯

laissez-faire *adj*. 自由放纵的

Land Rover 路虎车

Latin 拉丁语

laureate *n*. 获奖者

leftover *n*. 剩余物

legible *adj*. 清晰可读的

legume *n*. 豆类蔬菜

lentil *n*. 小扁豆

leopard *n*. 花豹

Lesotho 莱索托

lethal *adj*. 致命的

lexical *adj*. 词汇的

lexicographic *adj*. 按字母顺序排列的

liberal *adj*. 开明的

Libya 利比亚

light bulb 灯泡

lime *n*. 酸橙

linear *adj*. 直线的

Lingala 林格拉语

lingua franca 通用语言

linguistic *adj*. 语言的

linguist *n*. 语言学家

liquor *n*. 烈性酒

literacy *n*. 读写能力

literal *adj*. 字面意思的

literate *adj*. 有文化的

livelihood *n*. 赚钱谋生的手段

livestock *n*. 家畜

Living in Bondage（尼日利亚电影）《生存枷锁》

loaf *n*. 一条面包

lobster *n*. 龙虾

logographic *adj*. 词符性的

loom *n*. 织布机

Lord Charles Somerset 查尔斯·萨默赛特伯爵

Lovedale Press（南非）拉乌德勒出版社

Loyola Marymount University 洛约拉·马利蒙特大学

Luo 卢奥族，卢奥语

lurid *adj*.（故意）骇人听闻的

Luvale 卢瓦勒族

lychee *n*. 荔枝

lyric *adj*. 抒情的；*n*. 抒情诗

M

Maasai 马赛族，马赛族的

magnum opus 代表作

Mahafaly 马哈法利族

maize *n*. 玉米

Makerere College（乌干达）马凯雷雷大学

Makonde 马孔德族

Malagasy 马尔加什语

Malawi 马拉维

Mamprusi 曼普鲁西族

Mandé-speaking 说曼德语的

Mande 曼德语

maneuver *n.* 策略

manifestation *n.* 表现

manipulation *n.*（熟练的）控制

manuscript *n.* 原稿，手稿

margarine *n.* 人造黄油

marginalization *n.* 边缘性

Mariama Bâ（塞内加尔女作家）玛丽亚玛·巴

marinate *v.* 腌制

martinet *n.* 严格执行纪律的人

masculinist *n.* 大男子主义者

masonite *n.* 硬质纤维板

masquerade *n.* 面具舞会

massacre *v.* 屠杀

materialism *n.* 拜金主义

Mau Mau Struggle（肯尼亚1952—1960）茂茂起义

Mauritania 毛里塔尼亚

Mbundu 姆邦杜族

meat pie 肉馅饼

mediate *v.* 调解

mediation *n.* 斡旋

medieval *adj.* 中世纪的

melodrama *n.* 情节剧

melodramatic *adj.* 夸张的

menace *n.* 威胁

Mende 塞拉利昂的曼迪族，曼迪语

mesmerizing *adj.* 令人着迷的

metamorphosis *n.* 蜕变

metaphorical *adj.* 暗喻的

metaphor *n.* 暗喻

meticulously *adv.* 精心地

metrical *adj.* 韵律的

Metro-Goldwyn-Mayer（美国）米高梅电影公司

migrate *v.* 移居

militant *adj.* 富有战斗性的

militia *n.* 民兵组织

millennium *n.* 一千年

millet *n.* 小米

mine *n.* 矿井

mint *n.* 薄荷

miser *n.* 守财奴

misery *n.* 悲惨

missionary *adj.* 传教士的；*n.* 传教士

mobilization *n.* 动员

Mohammed（伊斯兰教创始人）穆罕默德

mold *n.* 模子

monastery *n.* 修道院

monolingual *adj.* 单语的

Moolaadé（电影）《割礼龙凤斗》

morality *n.* 道德

morpheme *n.* 语素

morphological *adj.* 形态的

mortal *adj.* 不能永生的

mortar *n.* 研钵

mosque *n.* 清真寺

motif *n.* 装饰图案，主题

mountain gorilla 山地大猩猩

mug *v.* 抢劫

Muhammadu Buhari （尼日利亚总统）穆罕马杜·布哈里

multilingual *adj.* 多语言的

multilingualism *n.* 多语制

musical *n.* 音乐剧

mussel *n.* 贻贝

mythical *adj.* 神话的

mythological *adj.* 虚构的

mythology *n.* 神话传说

N

NADECO 尼日利亚民主联盟

Nairobi 内罗毕

naïve *adj.* 朴素的

narrative *n.* 故事，叙述；*adj.* 叙事的

nascent *adj.* 初期的

Natal （南非）纳塔尔省

nationalist *n.* 民族主义者

National Party 南非国民党

naturalistic *adj.* 写实的

Ndebele 恩德贝勒族，恩德贝勒语

Neustadt International Prize for Literature （美国）纽斯塔特国际文学奖

Nguni 恩古尼语

Niger-Congo 尼日尔–刚果语系

Nigeria 尼日利亚

Nilo-Sarahan 尼罗–撒哈拉语系

Nollywood 尼莱坞

nomadic *adj.* 游牧的

nomad *n.* 游牧民

nominate *v.* 提名

no-strings *adj.* 无附带条件的

noteworthy *adj.* 值得注意的

novel *adj.* 新颖的

novelty *n.* 新奇的事物

NoViolet Bulawayo 诺维奥莉特·布拉瓦约

Nuer 努尔族

Nurrudin Farah 努鲁丁·法拉赫

nurture *v.* 培养

nutmeg *n.* 肉豆蔻

O

Obafemi Awolowo University 奥巴费米·亚沃洛沃大学

obligation *n.* 义务

obscene *adj.* 下流的

obscure *adj.* 难以理解的

off-hand *adj.* 漫不经心的

offspring *n.* 后代

ogre *n.* （传说中的）食人恶魔

Ogun 奥贡

oil reserve 石油储备

okra *n.* 秋葵

Ola Balogun （尼日利亚约鲁巴族导演）奥拉·巴洛贡

Omotic 奥默语族

Onitsha 奥尼查

opposition *n.* 反对

oppressive *adj.* 压制的，高压的

oppressor *n.* 压迫者

oral literature 口述文学

oratory *n.* 演讲术

originality *n.* 独创性

originate *v.* 发明

Oromo 奥罗莫语

orphan *v.* 使……成孤儿

ostrich *n.* 鸵鸟

Out of Africa（电影）《走出非洲》

outsell *v.* 卖得比……多

oval *adj.* 椭圆形的

overlord *n.* 领主

oversee *v.* 监督，监管

overwhelmingly *adv.* 压倒性地

oyster *n.* 牡蛎

P

pageant *n.* 庆典

palm *n.* 棕榈（树）

pan-African *adj.* 泛非的

pancake *n.* 薄饼

panegyric *n.* 颂词

panel *n.* 木板

papaya *n.* 木瓜

paradigm *n.* 范例，范式

paradoxical *adj.* 矛盾的

paradox *n.* 矛盾的情况（自相矛盾的话）

parastatal *adj.* 半国营的

parchment *n.* 羊皮纸

parsley *n.* 西芹

passionate *adj.* 充满热情的

pasta *n.* 意大利面

paste *n.* 糊状食物

pastry *n.* 油酥糕点

patronage *n.* 赞助

pedagogical *adj.* 教学法的

peek *n.* 一瞥

peel *v.* 去皮

Pende 彭代族

pepper *n.* 辣椒；*vt.* 使……布满

perishable *adj.* 易变质的

Persian *n.* 波斯人，波斯语

adj. 波斯的

personage *n.* 名人

personification *n.* 化身

pervade *v.* 遍布

pervasive *adj.* 普遍的

pestle *n.* 捣锤

Petina Gappah 佩蒂纳·加帕

phenomenally *adv.* 极其

philanthropic *adj.* 与慈善事业有关的

phonetic *adj.* 表示语音的

pickle *n.* 腌菜

pidgin *n.* 洋泾浜语

pigment *n.* 色素

pinch off 掐掉

piracy *n.* 海盗行为

pitcher *n.* 带柄的陶罐

pitch *n.* 音高

plaited *adj.* 打褶的

plantain *n.* 大蕉

plantation *n.* 种植园

plaque *n.* 匾额

playwright *n.* 剧作家，编剧

pluck *v.* 摘取

poacher *n.* 偷猎者

poetry *n.* 诗歌

poignant *adj.* 心酸的，深刻的

pole *n.* 杆子

poll *n.* 选举投票

polygamous *adj.* 多配偶的

polygamy *n.* 一夫多妻制

pomegranate *n.* 石榴

porcupine *n.* 豪猪

porous *adj.* 多孔的

porridge *n.* 粥

Portuguese 葡萄牙语

posh *adj.* 时髦的

posthumously *adv.* 在死后

potent *adj.* 影响身心的

Potjiekos 三脚铁锅炖菜

potjie *n.* 三足的铸铁圆形焖烧锅

pottery *n.* 陶器

poultry *n.* 禽类

pound *v.* 捣碎

powdered milk 奶粉

pragmatic *adj.* 讲求实效的

prairie *n.* 草原

prawn *n.* 大虾

preach *v.* 布道

precarious *adj.* 危险的

precedent *n.* 先例

precede *v.* 在……之前出现

predicament *n.* 困境

preeminent *adj.* 卓越的

preface *n.* 序言

prefigure *v.* 预示

preoccupation *n.* 焦点

prescient *adj.* 有先见之明的

prescription *n.* 规定

prevalence *n.* 普遍

prevalent *adj.* 普遍存在的

primeval *adj.* 原始的

primitive *adj.* 原始的

priority *n.* 优先权

pristine *adj.* 处于原始状态的

pro-English *adj.* 支持英语的

professor emeritus 荣誉退休教授

progeny *n.* 后代

progressive *adj.* 逐步发展的

prolific *adj.* 多产的

proofreader *n.* 校对员

propagate *v.* 传播

propel *v.* 推进

proselytize *v.* （使）改变宗教

prose *n.* 散文

Vocabulary List

prostitute *n.* 妓女
proverb *n.* 谚语
provision *n.* 条款
proximity *n.* 接近性
pseudonym *n.* 笔名
pudding *n.* 布丁蛋糕
pumpkin *n.* 南瓜

Q

quandary *n.* 左右为难的局面
quill *n.* 翎（鸟的翅膀或尾部的大羽毛）；（豪猪的）棘刺

R

racism *n.* 种族歧视
raffia *n.* 拉菲亚草
Ramayana（印度史诗）《罗摩衍那》
ranger *n.* 护林人
ransack *v.* 抢劫
rap *n.* 说唱音乐
rating *n.* 收视率
rayon *n.* 人造丝
reactionary *adj.* 保守的
realistic *adj.* 现实的；逼真的
realm *n.* 领域
rebel group M23 刚果（金）叛军M23
recipe *n.* 菜谱
recollection *n.* 回忆
reconciliation *n.* 和解
recruit *v.* 吸收（新成员）

rectangular *adj.* 长方形的
redemption *n.* 救赎
reed *n.* 芦苇
refrigeration *n.* 冷藏方法
regime *n.* 政权
rehabilitate *v.* 使……恢复原状
rehash *n.* 用旧材料改编的作品
reinvigorate *v.* 使……重新振作
rekindle *v.* 重新激起
relegation *n.* 降级
relic *n.* 文物
relief *n.* 浮雕
reliquary *n.* 盛放圣人遗物的容器
remnant *n.* 残余部分
rendering *n.* 翻译
rendition *n.* 表现
renowned *adj.* 有声望的
repertory *n.* 保留剧目
repression *n.* 镇压
requisite *adj.* 必需的
resemble *v.* 与……相似
residue *n.* 残余物
resolution *n.* 决心
resonance *n.* 反响
resonate *v.* 引起共鸣
resourceful *adj.* 足智多谋的
restraint *n.* 约束
resurrection *n.* 复活
retrieve *v.* 取回
revelation *n.* 揭示

reverence *n.* 崇敬

reverse *v.* 扭转

revoke *v.* 使……无效

Rhodesia（津巴布韦旧称）罗德西亚

rhythmical *adj.* 有节奏的

riddle *n.* 谜语；*v.* 充斥

riddling *adj.* 难以捉摸的

ritual *n.* 仪式

roast *v.* 烘烤

Robert Gabriel Mugabe（津巴布韦前总统）罗伯特·加布里埃尔·穆加贝

Robert W. Woodruff（可口可乐之父）罗伯特·伍德鲁夫

Royal Court Theatre（英国伦敦）皇家宫廷剧院

royalty *n.* 王室成员

rudimentary *adj.* 原始的

rum *n.* 朗姆酒

S

Sabaean 塞巴语

sacrifice *n.* 祭品

saffron *n.* 藏红花

sage *n.* 鼠尾草

Sahel 萨赫勒地带

Sambizanga 电影《桑比赞噶》

sanction *n.* 支持

Sango 桑戈语

Sani Abacha "尼日利亚独裁者"萨尼·阿巴察

San 桑人；桑人语言

sap *n.*（树的）汁液

sarcasm *n.* 讽刺，挖苦

satire *n.* 讽刺作品

saturate *v.* 使饱和

Satyajit Ray（印度电影大师）萨蒂亚吉特·雷伊

sauce *n.* 酱汁

savanna *n.* 热带稀树草原

savory *adj.* 可口的

Sayyid Aidarusi 赛义德·艾达鲁斯

scarcity *n.* 缺乏

scarlet *adj.* 鲜红的

scar *n.* 伤疤

scheme *n.* 体系

scheme *v.* 图谋

scoop up *v.* 舀出来

screen *v.* 上映

script *n.*（一种语言的）字母表；剧本；字母

seamy *adj.* 肮脏丑恶的

seasoned *adj.* 有经验的

seasoning *n.* 调料

secular *adj.* 非宗教的

see-saw *adj.* 上下摇摆的

segregation *n.* 种族隔离

self-conscious *adj.* 有自我意识的

semi-autobiographical *adj.* 半自传体的

semi-consciousness *n.* 半意识状态

seminal *adj.* 影响深远的

Vocabulary List

Semitic 闪米特语族

Senegalese 塞内加尔的

Senegal 塞内加尔

sensory *adj.* 感官的

Senufo 塞努福族

(se)Pedi 佩迪语

serial *n.* 连载小说

sesame *n.* 芝麻

(se)Sotho 索托语

(se)Tswana 茨瓦纳语

sexism *n.*（针对女性的）性别歧视

Seychellois 塞舌尔的

Shaaban Robert 夏巴尼·罗伯特

shack *n.* 窝棚

Shadows on the Grass《草地恋影》

Shaka（祖鲁王）夏卡

shantytown *n.* 贫民窟

shard *n.* 碎片

shea nut 乳木果

sheath *n.* 护套

shellfish *n.* 贝类海鲜

sherry *n.* 雪利酒

shield *n.* 盾牌

shimmer *v.* 闪闪发光

shoddy *adj.* 粗制滥造的

shoestring *adj.* 预算很少的

Shona 绍纳语

short *n.* 电影短片

shrimp *n.* 虾

shrine *n.* 圣地

Sidney Pollack（美国导演）西德尼·波拉克

sign language 手语

simmer *v.*（小火）炖

simultaneously *adv.* 同时

sinfulness *n.* 有罪

singular *adj.* 单一的

(si)Swazi 斯威士语

sizable *adj.* 相当大的

sketch *n.* 素描

skull *n.* 颅骨

slab *n.* 厚板

slaughter *v.* 屠杀

slum *n.* 贫民窟

slurry *n.* 浆状物

smack *n.* 一点儿

smuggle *v.* 偷偷运进

snake charmer 耍蛇人

snowboarder *n.* 滑雪运动员

sociohistorical *adj.* 社会历史的

sociolinguistic *adj.* 社会语言学的

soft drink 不含酒精的饮料

solidarity *n.* 团结

solitary confinement 单独禁闭

So Long a Letter《如此长信》

Somalia 索马里

Somali 索马里族的

Songhai 桑海人，桑海语

sorghum *n.* 高粱

Sotho 索托语

South Arabian 南部阿拉伯语

Soweto（南非黑人城镇）索韦托

spawn v. 孕育

specificity n. 独特性

spherical adj. 球形的

spice n. 调料

spoilage n. 食物变质

spongy adj. 海绵状的

sporadic adj. 间或出现的

spout n. 喷嘴

staff n. 权杖

stain v. 给……染色

stall n. 货摊

stance n. 立场

stand n. 摊位

staple n. 主食/主要成分

starch n. 淀粉

starchy adj. 富含淀粉的

starkly adv. 明显地

star v. 使……担任主角

steadfast adj. 坚定不移的

steam v. 蒸（食物）

steer away 驶离

stereotype n. 成见

stereotypical adj. 老套的

stew n. 炖肉

stir v. 搅拌

stitch v. 缝

strainer n. 滤网

strand n. 缕，线

strap v. 用带子捆好

strata n.（复数）阶层

stream v. 在互联网上播放视频或音频文件

streetwise adj. 适应都市生活的

strife n. 冲突

striking adj. 引人注目的

string n. 绳子；v. 把……连在一起

strip n. 条

sturdy adj. 坚固的

stylish adj. 时尚的

subject n. 表现对象

subjugation n. 镇压

submission n. 顺从

subordinate adj. 次要的

subordination n. 从属

Sub-Saharan Africa 撒哈拉以南非洲

Sub-Saharan 撒哈拉以南非洲的

subservient adj. 恭顺的

subtitles n.（影视作品的）字幕

subvert v. 破坏

successor n. 接替的事物

succinct adj. 言简意赅的

sugar cane 甘蔗

Sukuma 苏库马族

summation n. 概括

supervise v. 主管

supplement v. 补充

surrealistic adj. 超现实主义的

Swahili 斯瓦希里语，斯瓦希里人

swallow n. 燕子

swathe n. 一长条

Vocabulary List

Swaziland 斯威士兰

sweet potato 甘薯

swell *v.* 增大

syllable *n.* 音节

symmetrical *adj.* 对称的

T

tactic *n.* 策略

take up the slack 治理整顿

talking-to *n.* 训斥

tangerine *n.* 柑橘

tattoo *n.* 文身

tawdry *adj.* 粗俗的

teff *n.* 苔麸

telecoms *n.* 通信

tend *v.* 打理

tenet *n.* 宗旨

terminology *n.* 术语

tertiary *adj.* 第三级的

textile *n.* 纺织品

textured *adj.* 有纹理的，有织纹的

texture *n.* 纹理；质地

thatched *adj.* （用稻草等）盖屋顶的

the Cape Colony 开普殖民地

The Epic of Odysseus（希腊史诗）《奥德赛》

The Kebra Negast《列王荣耀记》

thematically *adv.* 从主题上说

the Mediterranean 地中海

the New World 美洲大陆

the Niger River 尼日尔河

The Observer（英国）《观察家报》

theology *n.* 神学

the Orange Free State 奥兰治自由邦

The Pilgrim's Progress from This World, to That Which Is to Come《天路历程》

therapeutic *adj.* 治疗的

therapy *n.* 治疗

The Second Coming《第二次降临》

the Swedish Academy（诺贝尔文学奖评选机构）瑞典学院

The Times Literary Supplement《泰晤士报文学增刊》

the Treaty of Vereeniging《弗里尼欣条约》

thorn *n.*（植物的）刺

thoroughgoing *adj.* 彻底的

thrive *v.* 蓬勃发展

thug *n.* 暴徒

Tigrinya 提格雷尼亚语

tile *n.* 地砖

tilt *v.* 倾斜

Timbuktu（马里）廷巴克图

timeless *adj.* 永不过时的

Tinga Tinga 挺噶挺噶画

toast *v.* 把……烤得焦黄

tonal *adj.* 音调的

top *n.* 上装

topple *v.* 推翻

totality *n.* 整体性

towering *adj.* 卓越的

traitor *n.* 叛徒

trance *n.* 催眠状态

transition *n.* 过渡

transmit *v.* 传播

Transvaal 德兰士瓦共和国

traumatize *v.* 使……受到精神创伤

trial off 逐渐减少

triangular *adj.* 三角形的

tribalism *n.* 部族主义

trickster *n.* 骗子

trilogy *n.* 三部曲

trite *adj.* 陈腐的

triumph *v.* 成功

tropic *n.* 热带

(Tshi)Venda 文达语

Tsotsi （电影）《黑帮暴徒》

Tuareg 图阿雷格族

tuber *n.* 块茎

tuck away 把……藏起来

tuft *n.* 一束，一簇

Tutsi 图西族

twine *v.* 缠绕

tyranny *n.* 暴君统治的国家

U

Ubangi 乌班吉语

ubiquitous *adj.* 十分普遍的

Uganda 乌干达

unabashed *adj.* 不害臊的

underbelly *n.* 薄弱环节

underlie *v.* 构成……基础

UNESCO 联合国教科文组织

unfavorable *adj.* 不利的

unfold *v.* 展开

unilingual *adj.* 统一语言的

Union of South Africa 南非联邦

unscrupulous *adj.* 不道德的

unsettle *v.* 扰乱

unveil *v.* 揭露

up-and-coming *adj.* 积极进取的

uprising *n.* 起义

Urdu 乌尔都语

utensil *n.* 器皿，餐具

V

Vai 瓦伊语

validity *n.* 合法性

vantage point （观察事物的）有利地点

variant *n.* 变种

veil *n.* 面罩

vendor *n.* 小摊贩

venison *n.* 鹿肉

vernacular *adj.* 本国的

versatile *adj.* 多用途的

verse *n.* （古兰经的）一节

vestige *n.* 遗迹

vibrant *adj.* 充满活力的

videocassette *n.* 录影带

vigorous *adj.* 充满活力的

viper *n.* 阴险小人

Virunga National Park 维龙加国家公园

Virunga（纪录片）《维龙加》

visualize *v.* 想象

vowel *n.* 元音字母

W

waft *v.* 吹拂

wagon *n.* 四轮马车

watershed *n.* 分水岭

wattle-and-daub *adj.* 夹条并涂泥的

wat 吃英吉拉专用的酱汁

weighty *adj.* 严重的

weld *v.* 使……紧密结合

well-appointed *adj.* 设备完善的

well *n.* 水井

wheelbarrow *n.* 独轮手推车

white potato 土豆

wicker *n.* 柳条

widow *n.* 寡妇

William Butler Yeats（爱尔兰诗人）威廉·巴特勒·叶芝

wire *n.* 金属线

witchcraft *n.* 巫术

witchdoctor *n.* 巫医

wobbly *adj.* 摇摇晃晃的

Wolof 沃洛夫族，沃洛夫语

womanize *v.* 追逐女色

X

Xhosa 科萨族

(xi)Tsonga 聪加语

Y

Yakubu Gowon（尼日利亚前军政府元首）雅库布·戈翁

yam *n.* 薯类

yearning *n.* 渴望

yeast *n.* 酵母

Yoruba 约鲁巴人；约鲁巴族；约鲁巴语

Yvonne Vera 伊冯娜·维拉

Z

Zara Yakob（埃塞俄比亚所罗门王朝国王）扎拉·雅克布

zenith *n.* 鼎盛时期

Zerma 杰尔马人

Zulu 祖鲁人；祖鲁族